Advance Praise for

The Sustainable Kitchen

My husband and I time our frequent drives from California to Eugene, Oregon
to visit family so that we can stop in Ashland and eat a meal at Stu and Mary's restaurant.
These two young chefs are national treasures. Their simple, yet inspired, food is a joy to behold.
This is a book for people who love to cook and repect the food that nourishes us.
The authors have woven a tapestry of words that captures the passion of these
bright young chefs and inspires us to enjoy the magic of the table and the miracle
of the earth that nourishes our food.

— MARIE SIMMONS, author of *The Good Egg* and *Fig Heaven*

Sustainable. Regional. Organic. Delicious. What more could you ask for!
The time is right to change our lifestyles, to make smart choices, to take a stand.

— TOM DOUGLAS, Seattle restauranteur and cookbook author,
and winner of the James Beard Association Award for Best Northwest Chef.

The Sustainable Kitchen makes the important connection between the food we eat,
our health, and the environment while providing us with a strong sense
of the sights, smells and taste of the Northwest.

— ROCHELLE DAVIS, Author of *Fresh Choices*
and Executive Director of Generation Green.

The Peerless serves up some dazzling dishes in an impressive environment — casually
elegant inside, a green courtyard outside to go with its natural-thinking kitchen.

— DAVID SARASOHN, Associate Editor, *The Oregonian*

The Sustainable Kitchen

The Sustainable Kitchen

Passionate Cooking Inspired by Farms, Forests and Oceans

STU STEIN *and* MARY HINDS

EXECUTIVE CHEFS / CO-OWNERS
THE PEERLESS RESTAURANT

with

Judith H. Dern

Photography by John A. Rizzo
Foreword by Caroline Bates

NEW SOCIETY PUBLISHERS

Cataloguing in Publication Data:
A catalog record for this publication is available from the National Library of Canada.

Cover design by Diane McIntosh. Cover images by John A. Rizzo.
Book design & layout by Greg Green.

Printed in Canada by Transcontinental Printing.

Inquiries regarding requests to reprint all or part of *The Sustainable Kitchen* should be addressed to New Society Publishers at the address below.

To order directly from the publishers, please add $4.50 shipping to the price of the first copy, and $1.00 for each additional copy (plus GST in Canada). Send check or money order to:

New Society Publishers
P.O. Box 189, Gabriola Island, BC V0R 1X0, Canada
1-800-567-6772

New Society Publishers' mission is to publish books that contribute in fundamental ways to building an ecologically sustainable and just society, and to do so with the least possible impact on the environment, in a manner that models this vision. We are committed to doing this not just through education, but through action. We are acting on our commitment to the world's remaining ancient forests by phasing out our paper supply from ancient forests worldwide. This book is one step towards ending global deforestation and climate change. It is printed on acid-free paper that is **100% old growth forest-free** (100% post-consumer recycled), processed chlorine free, and printed with vegetable-based, low VOC inks. For further information, or to browse our full list of books and purchase securely, visit our website at: www.newsociety.com

NEW SOCIETY PUBLISHERS   www.newsociety.com

To Henry Koerner for his classical palate
and his young mind and heart
and to Teri Koerner for being "Mom."

Contents

Foreword

EVERY YEAR when I drive from my southern California home to Seattle, about an hour into the trip I begin counting the miles to Ashland, Oregon. "Not too far now," I say to my husband, even though the worst of the mountain switchbacks still lies ahead. At last, after a white-knuckle descent into the Rogue River Valley, there it is, cupped in the green hills and gleaming like Shangri-la.

Ashland is, of course, world-renowned for its Shakespeare festival, but I confess I've never seen a performance. I haven't seen much of the town, either. Ashland, for me, means the cooking of Stu Stein and Mary Hinds at their Peerless Restaurant, a name that sounds a bit boastful until you understand that the dining room is attached to the historic Peerless Inn, circa 1900. Yet "peerless" isn't far off the mark. After three hundred miles of McDonald's, Wendy's and Burger King, I hunger for food expressive of the here and now, food that tells me I'm in southern Oregon and not just in Anyplace, USA, and Peerless never disappoints me. I find seafood from Northwestern waters — impeccable oysters (if I'm lucky, sweet and creamy Kumamotos from Netart's Bay, on the Oregon coast); sturgeon from the Quinalt River; superb Copper River sockeye salmon during the few late-spring weeks that it's available, and only then; and tiny Oregon Bay shrimp that Stu and Mary sometimes pair with a tarragon flan. In early fall, when tomatoes fairly burst from their skins, there is a gazpacho of yellow heirloom tomatoes that tastes like a bowl of sunshine. Every tomato as well as every snap bean, head of lettuce and bulb of fennel that comes through the kitchen door is grown by farmers the chefs know and trust, people who take care of their land. Their squabs, rabbits, suckling pigs, free-range lambs, and grass-fed beef are Oregon-bred on small family farms. Today, all across America, more and more chefs are doing as Stu and Mary do, forging mutually rewarding relationships with growers and purveyors in their communities to create food that is fresh, seasonal and full of vitality. In the process, they are preserving small-scale agriculture, local economies and healthy regional food supplies.

Anyone, anywhere, can do the same thing. We can't all be skilled professional chefs, but we can all be responsible and responsive cooks. *The Sustainable Kitchen* shows you how. If you don't already cook by the calendar, savoring all things in their season, and know the pleasures of shopping at farmers' markets, this book will open up a world of new ideas and flavors. If you haven't yet discovered that good farmers are the earth's best friends and yours, read about vegetable grower Steve Florin of Dancing Bear Farm or pig farmer Paul Atkinson of Laughing Stock Farm, two of the remarkable producers profiled in this book. You can find people in every corner of the country who farm with a sense of ethics and a passion for the land.

The Sustainable Kitchen is also, of course, a cookbook, and an eminently practical and useful one. Unlike many chefs whose vanity efforts are best left on the coffee table, Stu and Mary have written a book that you can take into the kitchen, full of recipes that you can actually cook. Among them are dishes I've loved over long, wine-filled dinners at Peerless and many more I'll try at home. They are, like the chefs who created them, a testament to the joys of cooking and eating well.

Caroline Bates
Contributing Editor, *Gourmet* magazine

Acknowledgments

"A good cookbook is not just a collection of recipes set down in formulaic prose. What makes a cookbook unique is how the writer makes a procedure his or her own and then translates it into terms the reader can understand. It is also the way the writer remembers certain tastes and textures and all that is associated with the savoring of a dish."

— JUDITH JONES, Senior Editor and VP at Alfred A. Knopf

Stu and Mary

First we would like to thank the people directly involved with this book: Judith Dern for her never ending enthusiasm and her skills as a writer; John Rizzo for his creativity, vision and his pure enjoyment of the moment; and Heather Wardle for her insightful and penetrating questions and critiques. She was part cheerleader, part coach, but mostly the best editor we could imagine. Thank you to Chris and Judith Plant for allowing us to be part of the New Society family and for giving us a mountain to preach from. Our thanks to Chris Molé for her design talent and inspiration. We also want to thank Lisa Ekus for her tenacity and support of both the restaurant and *The Sustainable Kitchen* project; and Michael Biggs, the Peerless's sommelier, front-of-the-house manager and all-round wine geek, for his sense of humor, zest for life and his palate. His wine knowledge was invaluable and his personality kept us going through the busiest time of our year. We are also grateful to Pete Lassen of Marinelli Shellfish for his in-depth seafood knowledge, his exacting customer service and his friendship; Christi Raymond and Kelli Schroeder for testing the recipes and putting up with the bipolar nature of the restaurant business; Jim and Beth Deland for their unwavering support of the restaurant and their willingness to be recipe guinea pigs; and to Jefferson Public Radio for giving Stu a weekly forum for expressing his culinary philosophy, and a podium to rally others behind the concepts of sustainability.

We would like to thank the entire Peerless staff: Tiffany Dodge, our oldest and most dedicated employee; Irene Cruz; Moises Cruz; Luisa Binzha; Esta Reyes; Ivan Piesh; John Mullowney; Kami Farmer; Angie Mitchell; Linda Zurich and the rest of the Peerless staff for their support, hard work and for striving to be the best. Our thanks to Billye Jo and Bill Johnson for being the restaurant parents — scolding and nurturing us as appropriate. We want to say a big thank you to our local clientele for their continued support of what we are trying to accomplish at The Peerless. We also want to thank Crissy Barnett, our business partner, for her spirit and her willingness to believe in us and our ideas, no matter how outrageous they may have seemed.

We want to acknowledge the supplier network that makes what we do possible: Vince and Mary Alionis from Whistling Duck Farm; Kris Hoien from Spirit Ranch; Steve Florin from Dancing Bear Farm; John Neumiester for his Cattail Creek Farm lamb; Paul Atkinson for his Laughing Stock Farm suckling pigs; Roy Jones, our favorite mushroom forager; and "our" fishermen, Jeff Werner, Scott Boley, David Young and everyone at Fishermen Direct Seafood for supplying us with the best the Oregon coast has to offer. We love our network of artisan cheese producers: Pierre Kolisch, Sally Jackson, Jeff Brown, David Gremmels and everyone at Cowgirl Creamery for supplying us with the "purest and most romantic link between humans and the earth."

Stu would like to thank his culinary mentors, upon whose shoulders he stands: Jean Claude Poliviey for taking a chance on a cocky kid with only a little culinary knowledge; Jean Banchet for allowing him to grab, steal and pry every ounce of culinary knowledge he could during their tenure together; Steve Cole for showing Stu how to run a successful restaurant and how to seek out the best in local products; and Richard Olney for allowing Stu to invade his peaceful retreat in the south of France, and for briefly sharing his lifetime of knowledge, experience and stories, before he was taken from us all.

Mary would like to thank her grandmother Franchere who gave her the first taste of a fresh pea just shucked from the pod, and for always having freshly baked cookies when she came over to swim at the lake; Grandmother Hinds whose bread-and-butter pickles and dinner rolls became legendary; her parents Hugh and Julie, who always have a garden full of vegetables and who never fail to make each meal from scratch; Star Gossard-Dirette, who first planted the idea of becoming a chef in her mind; and Mary's culinary mentors, specifically Kaspar Donier.

We would also like to thank Shamrock and Cori, two faithful companions who patiently wait for us to come home and want nothing in return for their unconditional love.

Judith

Several serendipitous paths converged and led me to write this book and I want to acknowledge several people along the way. My parents started the journey by taking me off to Stratford, Ontario, to the Stratford Festival, when I was a teenager. My dad especially adored the history plays and those summer station wagon trips initiated my love affair with the theater. Without this legacy, I might not have sought out the Oregon Shakespeare Festival when I moved to Seattle, or been so eager when my friend Helen Johnson asked if I'd join her one Labor Day weekend on her annual pilgrimage to Ashland.

Theater connected with cuisine when Lisa Ekus opened the door to meeting Stu and Mary. From my first article about The Peerless Restaurant in *Northwest Palate* (2002), my culinary-literary relationship with Stu and Mary has been one of shared philosophies about sustainability and seasonal cuisine. We are on the same wavelength. When Lisa asked if I'd be interested in working with them on their cookbook, I didn't hesitate.

Many thanks to each of them — to Lisa for her encouragement, enthusiasm and for opening the door; and to Stu and Mary for welcoming my suggestions and edits, and for making this a sincere collaboration. I also thank them for giving me the opportunity to contribute to a project that promotes the health of our planet and our souls. It begins in everyone's kitchen.

Introduction

Sustainable Cuisine "… celebrates the pleasures of food and the diversity of cultures, while recognizing the impact of food on our health and our environment. Sustainable Cuisine preserves culinary traditions and addresses the need to safely nourish a growing world population."

— *Sustainable Cuisine White Papers* by Earth Pledge Foundation

Overview & Philosophy of *The Sustainable Kitchen*

Every morning on the way to our restaurant we drive between the soft rounded hills of southern Oregon's Rogue Valley. Vibrant green shadowed with purple vetch in springtime, tawny gold in summer and autumn, and a soft gray in winter, the hills cradle the region's famed pear and apple orchards. Streams chase each other down their canyons. Numerous microclimates and areas rich with alluvial soil from the region's ancient collapsed volcanoes host small family farms and young wineries. Stately firs and pines stretch skyward along the higher crests. When we arrived here (Stu first, Mary to follow) as co-owners and executive chefs of The Peerless Restaurant in Ashland, we had no idea woodland foragers would regularly appear at the restaurant's kitchen door with baskets of Yellow Foot chanterelles or Oregon truffles, nor were we aware that a new generation of local farmers were growing English peas, sweet fennel, baby kale and a dozen varieties of heirloom tomatoes, along with raising suckling pigs, lamb and organic, grass-fed beef. But we soon learned that the area supported several thriving farms operating along Community Supported Agriculture, or CSA, principles.

Of course, we'd done our homework and knew there was an accessible network of wholesale purveyors and several farmers' markets to support a fine dining establishment of the type we envisioned. We also were convinced of a welcoming clientele in a town that's home to the acclaimed Oregon Shakespeare Festival nine months of every year, and a sophisticated community year-round. We had no doubt its residents were as attracted by the area's vibrant quality of life as we were. As different as Ashland was from the many cities we'd lived in — Chicago, Portland, Philadelphia, Washington, D.C., San Francisco, Kansas City and Atlanta — on our cross-country journey developing our culinary careers, in many ways, coming to Ashland and the Rogue Valley was like coming home. What made it so was that our cooking styles, our fierce commitment to quality and flavor, to seasonal ingredients with fresh tastes and bold flavors, to playful and innovative dishes grounded in classic techniques, came home to a place that offered abundant resources and enthusiastic collaborators in the area's farmers, in a community that values our culinary philosophy of responsible seasonal cooking and eating.

We've arrived at our culinary philosophy of responsible seasonal cooking from very different backgrounds. Stu grew up in the heart of Chicago and worked his way up in the Windy City's restaurants, understudying with two French chefs at a young age, and continuing on to lead the kitchens of star restaurants in Washington, D.C., Atlanta and Kansas City. Along the way, chef mentors taught him about local purveyors and how to seek them out, knocking on farmers' doors to find the best wild mushrooms or specialty game. Mary grew up in Oregon in a family that always planted a huge garden, picked blackberries every summer, fished for wild salmon, and foraged for mushrooms in the autumn. The indelible flavors of her childhood cooking and eating experiences were ones she always sought to duplicate in her positions as executive chef at restaurants on both coasts.

After more than a dozen years of building our culinary expertise, seeking out local food sources wherever we cooked, we've brought that knowledge full circle at The Peerless Restaurant. Here in the Rogue Valley we cook good food for our guests and revel in the splendid abundance from farms, fields, forests, streams and the nearby ocean as each season turns and different ingredients arrive in the kitchen. It's responsible seasonal eating, responsibility in this case meaning making food choices that promote the economic, environmental and social health of ourselves and our community. It's our contribution to creating a sustainable community that starts with farmers and paying attention to the land. The beauty of cooking this way is that it can be done anywhere. We know. We've done it and we want to share our passion for this style of cooking in the pages of *The Sustainable Kitchen* so that anyone cooking at home can discover the thrill and pleasure of tasting something made from the best seasonal ingredients grown in their own community.

Our goal with *The Sustainable Kitchen* is to take sustainable and seasonal cuisine out of the restaurant, out of vegetarian magazines and natural food stores, and into the home, where it can flourish on an everyday basis with readily available fruits, vegetables, fish and meats. We want to share our passion for the culinary arts and to inspire home cooks to connect with their own local farmers and purveyors. We believe these connections will encourage a regional food supply and a strong local economy, maintain a sense of community, encourage earth stewardship, and protect the future of small to medium-size family farms. We do this by talking about our own Oregon valley specifically, and regionalism generally, in the hope that we may encourage others to explore and take advantage of their own local culinary resources. Within the pages of *The Sustainable Kitchen*, we provide the connections for this celebration of local, seasonal, culinary resources, bringing together our chefs' knowledge of cuisine, a sommelier's understanding of flavor, and a home cook's willingness to experiment and learn, with farmers and the land. Farming is the first step of cooking; the raw ingredients are the stars of the show. The role of the cook is to coax and encourage the best out of his or her stars — and have fun while doing so.

To make the connections, our book will focus on ingredients, their flavors, and how and why to stir several together into a sauce, soup or ragoût. We offer these recipes as a guideline. They should be the basis for inspiration, but not taken as an absolute, since there are so many variables in everyone's market. Who knows when the first fingerling potatoes might work their seductive magic, or exactly when you'll be completely smitten, as we were one day, when a farmer delivered some handsome, glistening purple-pink Japanese eggplants? Always inspiring and easy to use, the eggplants turned up on that evening's menu as an eggplant duo of grilled and puréed eggplant served with grilled Oregon Albacore tuna. This approach to cooking goes beyond seasonality and offers the serendipitous delight of cooking with spontaneity and integrity.

Great cookbooks are about more than mere recipes. Just as a great pop song forces you to get up and dance or play air guitar, a great cookbook is one that forces you into the kitchen.

We hope this book will make you think about things differently and play air spatula.

The Concepts of Sustainable Cuisine

*"...harmony with nature is possible only if we
abandon the idea of superiority over the natural world."*

— BILL MOLLISON, *Introduction to Permaculture*

FOOD IS A BASIC NECESSITY. It's something all of us deal with in some form every day. The majority of us have become removed from involvement and participation with the food we buy, cook and consume. We rarely, if ever, sit around the dinner table discussing who grew our vegetables or how our meat was raised. But we feel that this should be part of our conversation and our awareness. Our choices and those of the retailers and wholesalers we buy from affect the environment, the economy and everyone's quality of life. We believe it is important to be aware of and concerned about where our food comes from.

Everything we do, either individually or collectively, has an impact on our environment and its future. In this light, we believe we should align our choice of ingredients with the natural cycle of the seasons. Food that is in season is at the peak of nutrition and flavor. In season, ingredients are bountiful, making them more available, cheaper and at their peak of perfection. It is also a fundamental fact of cooking that no cook, however creative and capable, can produce a dish better than the quality of the raw ingredients he or she uses. We should all try to shorten the route from the farm to our table. The results can be seen both in the quality of the food you cook, as well as far beyond your dining table.

The Sustainable Kitchen is about responsible and sustainable eating. When it comes to food, we can talk about environmental, economic and social sustainability.

By eating sustainably we can have a huge impact on the environment. Small farms that produce a wide variety of crops allow for greater biodiversity than do massive monocultures. By buying locally, we lessen the environmental costs associated with the transportation of food — costs such as increased air pollution, the use of fossil fuels, and damage to roadways and the oceans. Refrigeration of food that needs to be transported a long way uses energy and can involve the use of ozone-depleting gases that ultimately affect the whole planet. None of these environmental costs are recognized by most consumers or accounted for in the price of food.

Environmental sustainability also relates to protecting our imperiled seafood supply. To ensure the health of our oceans and a diverse supply of seafood for the future, all nations must provide better, integrated management over the procuring and processing of seafood. Our personal belief is that a majority of fish-farming or fish aquaculture systems actually promote ecological destruction and further protein loss in the ocean ecosystem. Consumers, along with chefs, need to ask the same questions that the Chefs Collaborative "Fish Pick" raises when they purchase fish: Is it farmed or is it wild? If it was farmed, was it raised with an appropriate vegetarian diet and according to environmentally sound methods? If wild, where was it caught? How was it caught? Should it be caught, or protected because the species is threatened? Does it have a high bycatch percentage that adversely impacts other marine animals?

Similarly, we need to ask questions about where our meat comes from and how the animals were raised and slaughtered. Livestock needs to be humanely treated, fed the purest natural feeds (with no animal by products or waste), never given growth hormones or sub-therapeutic antibiotics, and raised on land cared for as a sustainable resource.

For our own cooking guidelines, we support "polyculture," a system long practiced in China and Japan. Becky Goldburg, a senior scientist with Environmental Defense, a nonprofit organization dedicated to solving urgent environmental problems, states that "polyculture is the farming of many species of plants and animals together in one system in order to make optimum use of water and nutrients and to minimize farm wastes." When the home cook begins to question the food chain and demand appropriate answers, then we will all be on the way to preserving the food supply for future generations.

Sustainability goes far beyond environmental effects. Economic sustainability, another goal of responsible eating, refers to the principle of keeping food dollars in the local community so they can contribute to the maintenance and development of regional food production and the local economy. Local farmers and citizens often achieve this by setting up Community Supported Agriculture (CSA) groups in their communities. CSAs are a system of local agriculture whose roots reach back 30 years to Japan, where a group of women, concerned about an increase of food imports and the corresponding decrease in the farming population, initiated a direct growing and purchasing relationship between their community group and local farms. This arrangement is called "teikei" in Japanese, meaning "putting the farmers' faces on food."

The CSA concept traveled to Europe and eventually to the U.S., where in 1985, Indian Line Farm in the Berkshire foothills of eastern Massachusetts was established as the first Community Supported Agriculture farm in North America. Today, there are over 1,000 CSA farms across the US and Canada with members and growers sharing the costs, risks and bounty of growing food. Membership ranges from 15 to 150 families per farm, each making a financial commitment to support the farm throughout the year by signing up and purchasing shares, either in one lump sum before the seeds are sown in early spring, or in several installments throughout the growing season. In return for their investment, CSA members receive fresh, locally grown, usually organic produce once a week from late spring through early autumn from "their" farm.

Many CSAs are expanding their offerings to include such foods as honey, fruit, meats, poultry and eggs, thereby increasing their viability. Networks of CSA farms are also forming to develop associative economies by growing and providing a greater range of products in a cooperative fashion and to protect the future of the small to medium-size farm.

Our food choices also have a large impact on our society and on our communities. Through eating sustainably we can promote the physical, spiritual, cultural and economic health of farm families and communities. To do this we need to educate people of all generations about the benefits of locally grown food; for small farms to continue, we need to educate people on how to grow food. Many CSA farms offer and require apprenticeships. For some farms they are an integral component of a successful operation. Apprenticeships offer valuable hands-on education and continue the back-to-the-land movement. This concept also teaches future generations that "food" comes from the land, not from the grocery store. Early exposure to caring for the Earth will enable children to better nourish themselves and others. Home gardens, wherever possible, along with school gardens, should be a required part of school education.

Sustainability is a long-term goal. Modern factory-farm-style American agriculture has produced high crop yields, but at what cost? Sustainable and seasonal cuisine, on the other hand, brings many benefits, not the least of which is great taste. It is also great fun to know that you are cooking and eating great food grown or harvested by local people. Just as we have developed relationships with the farmers in our valley, we believe all consumers must develop relationships with the people who are growing, farming and raising the products they eat and enjoy. Farmers are the people who should be driving your diet and what's on your dinner table. Think "outside the box" and be open to the moment when you go to the market, even if it's the neighborhood supermarket. The traditional Italian cook understands this philosophy. You do not go to the market looking for red snapper or cod. You go seeking the fish that looks the best and you choose that fish for dinner. A particular group of products or vegetables may be at its best the very day you're shopping — and maybe you never imagined that particular combination — but when you let the flavors of seasonal produce and raw ingredients speak for themselves and inspire your cooking, the flavor will always be outstanding.

Robert Weir of the Grateful Dead said that music and cooking are very similar: they're all about blending and taste. For us, great cooking is akin to *a cappella* music. The blending of voices or ingredients is more

Principles of Sustainability

- Celebrate the joys of local, seasonal and artisanal ingredients.
- Understand the source of the ingredients — the way they have been grown, raised or caught.
- Support sustainable agriculture and aquaculture, humane animal husbandry practices and well-managed fisheries.
- Purchase from purveyors whose conservation practices lessen our impact on the environment.
- Choosing sustainable food products is about more than helping the environment. It's about sustaining the heritage and the economy of whole communities. Respecting local economies, traditions and habitats are important parts of participating in a sustainable food system.

than the sum of their parts. Good cooking is not about how tall you can make the plate, but about what tastes best and what flavors complement and marry well with each other. Of course, we also have a wonderful time in the process of discovering and inventing these partnerships and blending their voices. We want to encourage you to discover and enjoy that spirit of playfulness in the kitchen.

Translating Sustainability to Action

It's not enough to discuss the concepts and philosophy of responsible, sustainable eating. It's equally important to act. In the following pages of *The Sustainable Kitchen* we give practical recommendations that anyone can follow to become involved and participate fully in a lifestyle of sustainable cooking. And for those who are already aware and appreciate the values of sustainable cooking, we offer our experience and recipes as further inspiration.

- Cook seasonally; do not buy fruits and vegetables out of season.
- Always buy locally whenever possible and buy directly from the grower or from a source as close as possible to where the product is grown.

- Join a CSA or work with a local farmer who will supply you with seasonal produce of your choosing.
- Support farmers' markets and farm stands.
- The next time you are in your supermarket talk to the produce manager. Tell the manager of your concern about pesticides and let him or her know you would prefer to buy local or regional produce and certified organic food if possible.
- Ask your grocers and suppliers about the farms where the meat and poultry they sell is raised and how it is raised. If they do not know, ask them to find out. Support grocers and butchers who get their supplies from farmers who do not use factory-farming techniques.
- Ask how the fish you buy is caught, either by using sustainable practices or by practices damaging to the environment, and whether it is wild or farm raised.
- Learn which fish species are endangered from over fishing.
- Read labels; find out what ingredients or additives are in the food you are eating.
- Plant a garden and/or help set up a school or a community garden.
- Complete the cycle by composting and recycling.
- Educate yourself about food, understand the issues, and let your legislators know how you feel about food management issues and which rules and regulations are important to you.

Notes to the Cook

"Simplicity should never be confused with lack of sophistication."

— ALEXANDER FOGES

AS WE MENTIONED PREVIOUSLY, the recipes in this book should be a guideline, not an absolute. They have been tested and re-tested but you, as the cook, must be aware of all the factors that go into making a particular dish a success. The weather, the age of various ingredients and the type of equipment in your kitchen all may affect the final outcome. A recipe can be viewed as a piece of music open to various interpretations and styles. Each person will bring their own experiences to the kitchen. The dish will only be a success if you obtain the highest quality ingredients that you can afford, take the time to cook with precision, taste and season as you go and add the one ingredient not specifically mentioned but always assumed — love. The idea is to cook only to enhance the natural flavor of the product.

Carefully read the entire recipe once or twice, including the Substitutions and Options section, before beginning preparation. We have divided the recipes into several sections to make them easy to follow:

HEAD NOTES / EXPLANATION: Here you will find information regarding the specific ingredients, the people behind the ingredients and our chef's experience and techniques. Together with the Substitutions and Options section, this gives the "how and why" of the recipe.

RECIPE WITH SERVING SUGGESTIONS: Our recipes have been written with specific, clear, concise and easy-to-follow instructions and ingredients. Suggestions for presenting the finished dish and serving instructions are recommended for both a casual presentation or, if desired, a more elegant look.

ADVANCE PREPARATION: Advance preparations, if possible, have been listed and are encouraged. Any recipe changes will be noted if the flavors or tastes are affected.

SUBSTITUTIONS AND OPTIONS: Valid substitutions have been included, along with specifics about how to make the substitute ingredients and techniques work. In addition, we offer other options for serving the completed dish or additional accompaniments for the dish.

WINE AND WINE BEVERAGE NOTES: Wine and beverage notes include additional explanations of how and why the flavors of each dish work. We concentrate on matching the flavors of the food with the flavors of the wine. We have included vintage dates for most wine recommendations. Many wineries have "house styles;" if a particular vintage is unavailable, choose the most recent release. Things do change from year to year, so let your palate be your guide.

In the "We thought we should mention" department:

- All juices are freshly squeezed.
- All salt is kosher salt unless otherwise noted.
- All pepper, white or black, is freshly ground.
- All spices are freshly ground from the whole spice unless otherwise noted.
- All vegetables are washed thoroughly before use.
- Eggs are Grade A, large size.
- Butter is unsalted, sweet butter.

We expect you'll notice that the recipes and ingredients in this cookbook have a slight Pacific Northwest slant to them. That's because we live, cook and buy our products primarily in Oregon. We use these products throughout the book and we elaborate on specific topics and ingredients, as well as add appropriate tips for selected recipes. We present profiles of local farmers, ranchers, foragers and various other purveyors that supply our restaurant to give you a sense of the people behind the products and to illustrate their point of view and concerns. We hope this will encourage you to seek out your own local purveyors in order to experience the joys of the local, seasonal and handcrafted ingredients in your particular area.

Why buy locally?

It's simple. Locally grown food tastes better and is better for you because it has probably been harvested within days — if not hours — of reaching your dinner table. As the length of time from harvest to table increases, sugars turn to starches, plant cells shrink and break down, and produce loses its vitality and nutrients.

Local products preserve genetic diversity. Local produce is grown for flavor, color and an ability to provide a long season of harvest. In contrast, the modern industrial agriculture system with its factory-style farms cultivates produce with tough skins in order to survive packing and handling along the way to the grocery store. These products are typically picked underripe in order to have a long shelf life.

Most local farmers and small ranchers do not have access to, or refuse to use genetically modified seed and grain, growth hormones and antibiotics, believing that they can raise better quality products without them.

Local farmers and purveyors who sell directly to consumers cut out the middleman and therefore get full retail price for their food — which means farm families can afford to stay on the farm, doing the work they love.

Local foods support a clean environment. Cover crops prevent soil erosion and replace nutrients used by the crops. Cover crops also capture carbon emissions and help to prevent global warming.

Simply put, by supporting local farmers and ranchers today, you can help ensure that there will be farms in your community tomorrow.

Basics

WE HAVE TRIED to limit the number of professional culinary terms and to clearly explain instructions every time we use them in a recipe. The following list of basic recipes, cooking terms and techniques will help explain, in further detail, what we are trying to achieve.

BAIN-MARIE — In French this means "water bath," and involves placing a container (pan, bowl, etc.) over a large, shallow pan of boiling water in order to surround the food with gentle heat.

BOIL — Julia Child, in her book *From Julia Child's Kitchen*, defines seven stages of heating water as follows:

Tepid:	85°F to 105°F.
Warm:	115°F to 120°F.
Hot:	130°F to 135°F
Poach:	180°F to 190°F. This is the point at which the water starts to move. Julia Child calls this stage a "shiver." James Beard referred to it as "feeble ebullition."
Simmer:	190°F to 200°F. Bubbles start to show in the water. This is the point at which most stews are cooked and at which braising is done. (See below for a more complete definition of simmering.)
Slow boil:	205°F. Slow rising bubbles form in the liquid.
True boil, full boil or rolling boil:	212 °F. This is the point at which a liquid is heated to its boiling point, until bubbles break the surface. "Boil" also means to cook food in a boiling liquid.

BLANCHING — This is a process by which an ingredient is cooked in a large amount of salted, boiling water and then "shocked" by being placed in an ice-water bath in order to stop the cooking process and set the color.

BYCATCH — This term refers to the fish and other marine life that are inadvertently caught along with the targeted species in a fishery. Much of the bycatch is discarded dead at sea, and includes seabirds, marine mammals, turtles, juveniles of the targeted species, and even fish sought after in other fisheries. It is estimated that one quarter of the global fishery catch is discarded each year as bycatch.

CAPERS — The flower bud of the caper bush, *Capparis spinosa*, is native to the Mediterranean basin, but its cultivation range stretches from the Atlantic coasts of the Canary Islands and Morocco to the Black Sea, to the Crimea and Armenia, and eastward to the Caspian Sea and into Iran. The buds are picked, sun-dried and then pickled or stored in salt. In Italy, capers are graded on a scale from 7 to 16, which indicates their size in millimeters. In French-speaking countries, capers are graded using the terms "nonpareilles" for the smallest, most delicate and highly prized to "surfines," "capucines," "fines" and the largest, "gruesas."

Caper berries, about the size and shape of a grape, are the pickled fruit of the caper bush and are sold with the stem still on. They are somewhat starchy and seedy, and have a less intense flavor than capers.

CHIFFONADE — In French this means "made of rags." It refers to a fine strip, approximately 1/16-inch wide, usually cut from a rolled-up leafy vegetable.

CHOCOLATE — We constantly give thanks for the bean from the *Theabroma cacao* tree, the source of chocolate. Appropriately, in Greek *theobroma* means "food of the gods." If you intend to bake regularly, you will need several types of chocolate. Like coffee, chocolate is susceptible to moisture and absorbs external odors. Buy small amounts and store it, well wrapped, in a well-ventilated area free of odors, and at a temperature between 54°F and 68°F, or in a freezer. Allow frozen chocolate to come to room temperature before using it in a recipe. We recommend using a good brand of real chocolate, not chocolate-flavored products. We use Scharffen Berger chocolate from California, Cocoa Barry from France, and Callebaut from Belgium.

- **BITTERSWEET CHOCOLATE** — Often called "dark" chocolate, bittersweet chocolate has a high percentage of cocoa solids, usually 60 percent to 75 percent, with little or no sugar. It has a rich, intense and slightly bitter taste.

- **MILK CHOCOLATE** — Milk chocolate contains powdered or condensed milk and generally about 20 percent cocoa solids. It has a mild, creamy and sweet taste.

- **SEMISWEET CHOCOLATE** — Similar to bittersweet chocolate, semisweet chocolate will contain a minimum of 35 percent cocoa solids and will have varying amounts of sugar, vanilla and emulsifiers.

- **WHITE CHOCOLATE** — This is not really chocolate at all. It does not contain any cocoa solids but is made with cocoa butter. It often contains sugar, milk and vanillin. It is sweet, rich and smooth. Take care when melting white chocolate because it has a lower melting point than other chocolates.

- **UNSWEETENED CHOCOLATE** — This is chocolate in its rawest form. It is pure chocolate containing half cocoa butter and half cocoa solids with no sugar.

- **COCOA POWDER** — This is a highly concentrated powder made from pure cocoa solids after most of the cocoa butter has been extracted.

CRÈME ANGLAISE — Custard sauce, or crème anglaise, is one of the building blocks of the pastry kitchen. It can be terrific as a sauce or used as a base for ice cream. Hundreds of variations can be created simply by adding different flavorings, extracts or spices. The key to making crème anglaise is how long you cook it. There is a fine line between a smooth, elegant sauce and scrambled eggs.

3 egg yolks	1½ cup heavy cream or milk
¼ cup granulated sugar	½ vanilla bean, split and scraped
pinch iodized salt	or 1 teaspoon pure vanilla extract

Whisk together the egg yolks, sugar and salt in a stainless steel mixing bowl until creamy. Set aside.

Place the cream and the vanilla bean with seeds in a heavy-bottomed saucepan. Bring the cream mixture to a boil. Remove from heat and slowly whisk the cream mixture into the egg mixture.

Pour the cream/egg mixture back into the saucepan and place over low heat. Cook the custard, stirring constantly, until it begins to thicken, approximately 5 minutes. The custard should coat the back of a spoon. DO NOT let it boil. Place the custard sauce over an ice bath. When cool, strain and refrigerate. The sauce will keep for 2 to 3 days covered in the refrigerator.

Makes approximately 2 cups

CRÈME FRAÎCHE — Crème fraîche is France's favorite form of cream for cooking. It is thicker, richer and has a more complex flavor than fresh sweet cream. Here is a recipe for crème fraîche:

2 tablespoons cultured buttermilk
2 cups heavy cream (pasteurized, not ultra-pasteurized or sterilized, and with no additives)

Combine the buttermilk and cream in a saucepan and heat only to 85°F on an instant-reading thermometer. Pour into a clean glass jar. Partially cover and let stand at room temperature (between 65°F and 75°F) for at least 8 hours and up to 24 hours, or until thickened. Stir and refrigerate at least 24 hours before using.

The crème fraîche will keep up to 2 weeks in the refrigerator.

DEGLAZE — This involves using a liquid (water, wine, stock or juice) to dissolve caramelized particles left on the bottom of a roasting or sauté pan. This liquid is then usually used to make a sauce.

FINELY CHOPPED — This means to cut into very small, usually non-uniform pieces approximately ⅛-inch square.

FOLD — To fold is to cut through a mixture with the edge of a spatula, sliding the spatula along the bottom of the bowl and bringing it up at the side so that you lift the lower portion of the mixture and fold it over the upper portion. Give the bowl a quarter turn and repeat the motion until the blending is complete. The object of folding is to carefully mix the batter without losing air.

INFUSE — To infuse is to add flavor to a liquid by steeping it with a complementary flavor. The ingredients used to infuse flavor usually do not remain in the liquid, but are removed before serving.

JULIENNE — This is a technique used to cut a vegetable into a thin matchstick shape, approximately ⅛-inch by ⅛-inch by 2 inches.

MANDOLINE SLICER — We have put this on our list of required kitchen equipment. A mandoline slicer is a compact, hand-operated slicing tool with various adjustable blades and cutting attachments. Our rule when using one is Safety First. We recommend using a chain-mail-type butcher's glove or oyster glove instead of the pusher/guard that comes with the slicer. This will ensure your fingers are protected from the sharp cutting blade (and your medical insurance remains low).

MAPLE SUGAR — This is a sugar made from dehydrated maple syrup that is 93 percent sucrose and 1 percent to 3 percent invert sugars. It is expensive, but it is perhaps the most richly flavored of all sugars and worth the price. (See Sources and Information for suppliers.)

MIREPOIX — Mirepoix is a blend of vegetables — usually onions, carrots, celery and sometimes leeks — often added to other preparations. Sometimes the vegetables are slowly cooked in butter or oil before adding.

OLIVE OIL — Coveted around the world, olive oil is obtained exclusively from the fruit of the olive tree using mechanical or some other physical means for the harvest that does not alter the oil in any way. As with wine, the flavor is determined by many factors: the olive variety, ripeness, how the fruit is handled, climate, soil and cultivation method. One hundred percent pure olive oil has not undergone any treatment other than washing, decanting, centrifuging and filtering. It excludes oils obtained by the use of solvents or other methods and those mixed with oils from other sources. Virgin olive oils are made by cold pressing the olives; their flavor most resembles the flavor of the variety of olive.

For the best and freshest oils, buy olive oil in small quantities and as close to the source as possible. Keep the oil in a tightly closed container, away from heat and sunlight and in a dark cool place.

- **EXTRA VIRGIN OLIVE OIL** — Extra virgin olive oil refers to the first cold pressing of the olives. The result is oil with an impeccable fruity taste and aroma. The acidity, expressed in oleic acid, may not exceed 1 percent. Extra virgin olive oil accounts for less than 10 percent of oil in most olive oil producing countries.

- **VIRGIN OLIVE OIL** — Virgin olive oil has a perfect balance of flavor with a generic olive aroma and a maximum acidity of 2 percent.

- **ORDINARY VIRGIN OLIVE OIL** — Ordinary virgin olive oil has good flavor and an aroma, with a maximum acidity level of 3.3 percent. Ordinary virgin olive oil may be fine for sautéing or where flavor is not wanted or needed.

- OLIVE OIL — Olive oil is a low-cost blend of refined and virgin oil with a maximum acidity of 1.5 percent. This less expensive refined oil is often mixed with a flavorful virgin-style oil.
- REFINED OLIVE OIL — Refined olive oil is produced by refining virgin olive oils to eliminate high acidity levels and/or other defects. Refined olive oils will have a maximum acidity of 0.5 percent. Over half of the oil produced in the Mediterranean area is of such poor quality that it must be refined to be an edible product. Note that no solvents have been used to extract the oil, but it has been refined with the use of charcoal and other chemical and physical filters. This product was previously labeled "pure olive oil."
- POMACE OLIVE OIL — Pomace olive oil is a mixture of pomace oil and virgin olive oil with a maximum acidity 1.5 percent.
- POMACE OIL — Pomace oil is oil made from the ground olive flesh and olive pits (paste) after pressing. Any oil that hasn't been removed by pressure can then be extracted using steam and solvents. It is considered an inferior-grade oil and is primarily used for soap making or industrial purposes.

PASTA DOUGH — All you need to make pasta is flour and moisture. This basic pasta dough incorporates eggs and olive oil in order to make a soft dough that is perfect for raviolis or other filled pasta.

3-4 cups all-purpose flour or bread flour	pinch kosher salt
5 eggs	½ teaspoon extra virgin olive oil

Begin by placing 3 cups of flour on the surface of a wood table or cutting board. Make a well in the center of the flour. Break the eggs into the center of the well. Add salt and oil. Using a fork, beat together the eggs, salt and oil. Using one hand, gradually incorporate the flour from around the edge of the well into the egg mixture. Use your other hand to support the outside of the well. Stir with your fingers to begin to form a dough. Continue incorporating flour until it can be gathered into a fairly stiff ball. If the dough is soft or too moist, add additional flour, little by little, until a soft, supple consistency is achieved. If dough is too dry, add a little water until proper consistency is achieved.

Knead the dough by placing it on a lightly floured surface and pressing flat with the heel of your hand, folding it over and pressing again. Continue kneading 5 to 8 minutes or until the dough is elastic and silky. Cover the dough with plastic wrap and let it rest at room temperature for 30 minutes.

Makes 1 pound of fresh pasta

RENDER — To render is to melt fat over low heat so that it separates from any meat, which, during the rendering process, will turn brown and crisp.

SALT — Salt is the most important ingredient used at The Peerless Restaurant. The following quote by Malcom de Chazal sums up our philosophy: "Salt is the policeman of taste: it keeps the various flavors of a dish in order and restrains the stronger from tyrannizing over the weaker."

- KOSHER SALT — Kosher salt is pure refined rock salt with large crystals, also known as coarse salt or pickling salt. Because it does not contain magnesium carbonate, it will not cloud liquids and sauces to which it is added. Kosher salt is traditionally required for "koshering" foods that must meet Jewish dietary guidelines. Our favorite blend is Diamond Crystal, because of the size of the grains.

- ROCK SALT OR HALITE — Rock salt is mined from natural deposits and varies in color from colorless when pure, to white, gray or brown. It is not as refined as other salts and comes in chunky crystals. Rock salt is used predominately as a bed on which to serve shellfish, or when combined with ice, to make ice cream in crank-style ice cream makers.

- SEA SALT — Sea salt generally comes from coastal marshes, basins and other areas where seawater has been trapped and is allowed to naturally evaporate. It comes in a range of colors and crystal sizes and contains trace minerals. *Fleur de sel* or "flower of salt" is the top layer of sea salt raked from the waters around Guérande in France. We use sea salt as a flavor-enhancing garnish in order to make a final "explosion" of flavor.

- TABLE SALT OR IODIZED SALT — Table salt is a fine-grained refined salt with additives that make it free-flowing and prevent caking. It is mainly used in cooking and as a table condiment. Iodized salt is table salt with added sodium iodide. Iodized salt will make clear liquids and sauces cloudy. We prefer to use kosher salt or sea salt in our cooking.

SAUTÉ — Meaning "to jump" in French, sautéing refers to cooking a food quickly in a small amount of fat over direct high heat.

SAVORY TART DOUGH

2 cups all-purpose flour
1 teaspoon kosher salt

6 ounces cold butter, cut into small pieces
2 ounces ice water (or more as needed)

Place flour on the surface of a wood table or cutting board. Add salt to flour. Using a fork or a pastry blender, cut or mix butter into flour until pea-sized nuggets are formed. Add the ice water a bit at a time to flour/butter mixture, mixing the dough with your hand to incorporate the water. The dough should hold together if pressed between your fingers. If needed, add another tablespoon or two of ice water in order to just form a ball of dough. The dough should not be sticky.

Refrigerate dough for 30 minutes or until dough feels firm to touch. The dough may be wrapped and stored in the freezer for up to one month.

Makes one 12-inch tart shell

NOTE: Handle dough as little as possible so the flour does not build up any gluten and make a "tough" crust. This dough uses all butter and will produce a rich-tasting but slightly tough crust. Some people use part butter and part vegetable shortening. In order to produce vegetable shortening, vegetable oil is hydrogenated — meaning hydrogen atoms were added so that the oil stays solid at room temperature. We do not believe in using hydrogenated shortening because it increases the bad fat content (saturated-fat and trans-fat), thus potentially increasing your risk of heart disease. Also, most commercial vegetable shortenings are made with from genetically modified vegetables.

SIFT — To sift is to pass dry ingredients through a wire mesh strainer to remove lumps, or to combine and aerate ingredients.

SILPAT MAT — This is a silicone-coated, fiberglass-mesh baking mat meant to be placed on top of baking sheets. It eliminates the need to cut parchment paper or to grease and flour baking sheets. Nothing sticks to the mat; it is very pliable and can be used up to 500°F.

SIMMERING — This term refers to cooking an ingredient in a liquid, or maintaining the temperature of a liquid just below the boiling point. Water simmers at approximately 190°F to 200°F. Simmering a reduction sauce allows the water in the liquid to evaporate, the flavors to concentrate, and the liquid to remain clear. Allowing the liquid to boil will emulsify the fats, sugars and proteins in the sauce therefore making the liquid cloudy.

SMALL DICE — This means to cut into a cube-shape, approximately ¼-inch by ¼-inch by ¼-inch.

SWEAT — To sweat is to cook a food slowly, usually a vegetable, uncovered over low heat with very little fat until the ingredient is soft and translucent and has no color.

TEMPERING — Tempering is the process of heating chocolate to a specific temperature, so that the cocoa butter it contains is brought to the most stable crystalline form, resulting in hard, shiny chocolate. Different chocolates have different tempering temperatures.

VANILLA SUGAR — Fragrant and flavorful sugar can be made by burying split vanilla beans in granulated sugar. The mixture is stored in an airtight container for about a week before the vanilla bean is removed. The result is a delicious vanilla-flavored sugar that can be used as an ingredient or decoration.

VEGETABLE STOCK — Unlike protein-based meat stocks that need time to extract flavor and gelatin, vegetable stocks need a relatively short cooking time, about 45 minutes of simmering, to give up their flavor.

4 carrots, cut into large dice

4 ribs celery, cut into large dice

2 medium yellow onions, cut
   into large dice

1 leek, cut into large dice

4 Roma tomatoes, cut into large dice

6 cloves garlic, peeled

2 tablespoons olive oil

2 tablespoons whole black peppercorns

2 bay leaves

4 sprigs fresh thyme or
   1 teaspoon dried cut thyme

2 russet potatoes, peeled and cut into large dice

1 cup white wine

3 quarts water

Preheat oven to 425°F. In large bowl, toss together carrots, celery, onion, leek, tomatoes, garlic and olive oil. Spread mixture evenly on large baking sheet. Roast in preheated oven, stirring every 10 minutes, until browned, about 40 minutes.

Transfer roasted vegetables to large soup pot and add peppercorns, bay leaf, thyme, potatoes, wine and water. Bring to boil. Reduce heat to low, and simmer 45 minutes to an hour.

Strain stock, pressing out as much liquid as possible from vegetables. Use stock immediately or refrigerate.

Makes approximately 2 quarts

BASIC VINAIGRETTE

1 teaspoon Dijon mustard

3 tablespoons red wine vinegar

juice of ½ lemon

Kosher salt and cracked black pepper, to taste

¼ cup vegetable oil

½ cup extra virgin olive oil

Place the mustard, vinegar, lemon juice, salt and pepper in a small stainless steel bowl. Slowly drizzle in both oils, whisking constantly, until ingredients are combined. Taste and adjust seasoning.

NOTE: This vinaigrette is a temporary emulsion and will need to be whisked or shaken just before serving.

ADVANCE PREPARATION: You may keep this dressing up to two weeks in a sealed container in the refrigerator.

SUBSTITUTIONS AND OPTIONS: Almost any type of vinegar (sherry, balsamic or herb infused) will work in this recipe. We prefer a neutral oil, vegetable oil or a vegetable/olive oil blend for this vinaigrette to allow the flavor of the vinegar to show through. Using all extra virgin olive oil will add too much olive flavor and mask the vinegar's flavor.

Makes approximately 1 cup

VINEGAR — The French word *vinagre,* from which we derive the word vinegar, originally meant sour wine, but now it includes all liquids where alcohol is turned into acetic acid. Making vinegar is a two-stage process using almost any liquid containing sugar. The first stage is brought about by the action of yeasts, that change natural sugars to alcohol under controlled conditions. This is called the alcoholic fermentation. The second stage results from the action of a group of bacteria (*acetobacter*) upon the alcohol, converting it to acid. This is the acetic or acid fermentation that forms vinegar.

- TRADITIONAL BALSAMIC VINEGAR — Production of traditional balsamic vinegar is governed by the quasi-governmental Consortium of Producers of the Traditional Balsamic Vinegar of Modena (Consorzio Tra Produttori Dell'aceto Balsamico Tradizionale Di Modena). Products produced under its supervision come with a seal from the Consorzio ensuring they have met stringent standards in a blind-tasting by five experts. Aceto balsamico is not a wine vinegar but a grape vinegar, made from the fresh-pressed white and sugary Trebbiano grapes grown on the hills around Modena. The juice is matured by a long and slow vinegarization process through natural fermentation. The vinegar is concentrated by progressive aging in a series of casks made from oak, ash, cherry wood, mulberry and juniper without the addition of any other spices or flavorings.

- COMMERCIAL BALSAMIC VINEGAR — Commercial balsamic vinegar is not subject to the geographical and technological restrictions of traditional balsamic vinegar. There is no rule regarding how long the commercial product should be aged, and there are no restrictions on the material from which the storage vats are made.

- WHITE BALSAMIC VINEGAR — This was created due to the realization that the color of traditional balsamic vinegars tended to dominate more delicate dishes. The vinegar "must" is not caramelized during processing, thus producing a vinegar with a golden white color and a light, sweet taste.

- CIDER VINEGAR — Cider vinegar is usually made from apple cider or apple mash, with a process similar to that used for commercially produced wine vinegars. It has a sharp, strong flavor and a soft honey color.

- FRUIT VINEGAR — Just as in wine vinegar production, the better the quality of the fruit the better the vinegar produced. Fresh fruit is pressed, fermented into fruit wine, and then processed into vinegar.

- MALT VINEGAR — Malt vinegar is an aged and filtered product obtained from the acetous fermentation of a distilled infusion of malt. (Malt is what results when grain is steeped in water and allowed to germinate.) This vinegar is made in the same way as commercially produced wine vinegars. Good malt vinegar is left to mature for several months before being bottled. It has a strong flavor and medium acidity.

- SHERRY VINEGAR — Sherry vinegars are made from a blend of sherry wines, just as is fine sherry, and are left to mature in the wood for a long time. They develop a fat, rich flavor with a mellow complexity and medium acidity.

- RICE OR RICE WINE VINEGAR — Rice wine vinegar is the aged and filtered product obtained from the acetous fermentation of sugars derived from rice. There are three basic types of Chinese rice vinegar — black, red and white — all with fairly low acidity. Black rice vinegar is very popular in southern China, where Chinkiang vinegar, the best of the black rice vinegars, is made. It has a dark color with a deep, almost smoky flavor. Red rice vinegar is not as dark as black vinegar and has a sweet/tart flavor. White rice vinegar is light in color and has a clean, delicate, mild flavor.

- WINE VINEGAR — The best wine vinegars come from the best wines. In the traditional Orléans method (named after the town in France), wine is left in wooden casks for two to six months and is slowly turned into vinegar. It is then filtered into other casks and left to mature for a period of months or years. Vinegars made by the slow Orléans method are as complex and flavorful as fine wines and just as expensive.

  The commercial process of making wine vinegar involves wine being slowly poured over wood chips in giant vats. As the wine trickles down through the chips, it takes on some of the flavor of the wood and the airborne *acetobacter* uses oxygen in the air around the loosely packed wood chips to oxidize the alcohol in the wine and turn it into acetic acid. In the commercial process the more subtle flavors and nuances of the original wine are lost. Wine vinegars possess a wide range of acidity.

ZEST — This term refers to the citrus skin without any of the bitter white pith beneath the skin. Our favorite kitchen tool is a microplane that we use to make finely chopped citrus zest, to grate whole spices, or to shred cheese.

Appetizers and Side Dishes: To Stimulate the Palate

"Appetizers are the little things you keep eating until you lose your appetite."

— JOE MOORE

APPETIZERS ARE SMALL SAVORY TIDBITS served hot or cold, originally meant to stimulate the appetite and make the meal to follow more appealing. For us, appetizers are more than just enticements. They're often an opportunity to serve a progression of petite courses inspired by the bounty of the season and the whim of the moment. At home and when we dine out, we often make a complete meal out of sharing several "appetizers" instead of having the traditional progression of set courses.

We hate rules but if you need one when planning a menu, remember to serve the raw before the cooked, the cold before the hot, and the simple before the complex. Seafood has a clean crispness that we believe lends itself perfectly to starting your culinary adventure.

POACHED HALIBUT CHEEKS • DUNGENESS CRAB-RICOTTA RAVIOLI
ROGUE CREAMERY BLUE CHEESE TART • ASPARAGUS CUSTARD

SWEET CORN AND SHIITAKE PORCINI MUSHROOM CUSTARD • SUMMER VEGETABLE SLAW
STEAMED MANILA CLAMS WITH MERGUEZ SAUSAGE

WEATHERVANE SEA SCALLOPS IN A CITRUS MARINADE WITH SWISS CHARD AND DILL-CAVIAR CREAM
MAPLE-APPLE BRANDY CURED WILD KING SALMON WITH MAPLE-MUSTARD DRESSING
POTATO-ONION TART TATIN

OYSTER AND SEAFOOD DIPPING SAUCES: • CHAMPAGNE MIGNONETTE SAUCE • BLOODY MARY GRANITÉ
VIETNAMESE DIPPING SAUCE • GINGER-SOY DIPPING SAUCE • PEERLESS COCKTAIL SAUCE
CORNMEAL FRIED OYSTERS WITH A SALAD OF ORGANIC GREENS AND LEMON-CAPER AIOLI
THREE OYSTER STEW • CARAMELIZED ASSORTED ROOT VEGETABLES
WINTER SQUASH AND FINGERLING POTATO HASH
PARSNIP-POTATO RÖSTI

Poached Halibut Cheeks

Halibut, which can grow to over 400 pounds, are among the largest fish in the sea and the largest of all the flatfish. They have a translucent white flesh with an incredible moisture content. Halibut "cheeks" are literally the meat taken from the outside of the gill covers. Succulent and meaty, they have an almost lobster-like sweetness and a firm, thread-like texture similar to skate.

Halibut cheeks are usually the same price or less expensive per pound than halibut fillets, but you may have to special order them from your fish supplier. You can substitute small pieces of halibut fillet, but it is worth the extra effort to seek out halibut cheeks. Remember, to help sustain our ocean's resources we need to use every part of the fish. An added benefit is that the flavor of the halibut cheeks is superior to regular fillet.

1 green zucchini, cut into julienne
1 yellow squash, cut into julienne
1 medium yellow onion, cut into thin half moons
1 red pepper, cut into thin strips
1 fennel, fronds finely chopped and reserved, bulb cut in half and cut into thin half moons
2 cloves garlic, finely chopped

8, 2-ounce Alaskan halibut cheeks, cleaned
kosher salt and white pepper, to taste
1 cup dry white wine
juice of one lemon
1 small hot red chili, finely chopped or ¼ teaspoon red chili flakes (optional)
2 tablespoons extra virgin olive oil

Spread the cut zucchini, squash, onions, red pepper, fennel and garlic on the bottom of a large sauté pan. Season the halibut cheeks with salt and pepper. Place the cheeks on top of the vegetables. Pour white wine and lemon juice over halibut and sprinkle with chili.

Place the pan over medium heat. When liquid begins to boil, reduce heat to a simmer. Cover the pan and continue until the cheeks are cooked, about 6 to 8 minutes (making sure the liquid is simmering, not boiling). Remove cheeks and vegetables. Keep warm.

Pour poaching liquid into a blender. With blender on high, slowly add the olive oil until an emulsion has formed. Taste and adjust seasoning.

TO SERVE: Divide the vegetables evenly among four bowls. Place 2 halibut cheeks on top of vegetables and pour sauce over the cheeks. Sprinkle reserved chopped fennel over the cheeks as garnish.

ADVANCE PREPARATION: The vegetables can be cut several hours in advance and kept covered in the refrigerator until ready to use.

SUBSTITUTIONS AND OPTIONS: Poaching adds additional flavor and helps keep the cheeks moist. Instead of poaching, these cheeks can be lightly dusted with flour and sautéed in butter or oil. Serve the sautéed cheeks over blanched seasonal vegetables or with mashed potatoes.

WINE NOTES: The summer vegetables and rich-tasting halibut cheeks require a fragrant, slightly spicy Sauvignon Blanc or Fumé Blanc-based wine finished with a touch of oak. Recommended: 2001 Dry Creek, Reserve, Fumé Blanc, Dry Creek Valley, California; or 2002 Henri Bourgeois, La Porte du Caillou, Sancerre, Loire, France.

Makes 4 appetizer servings

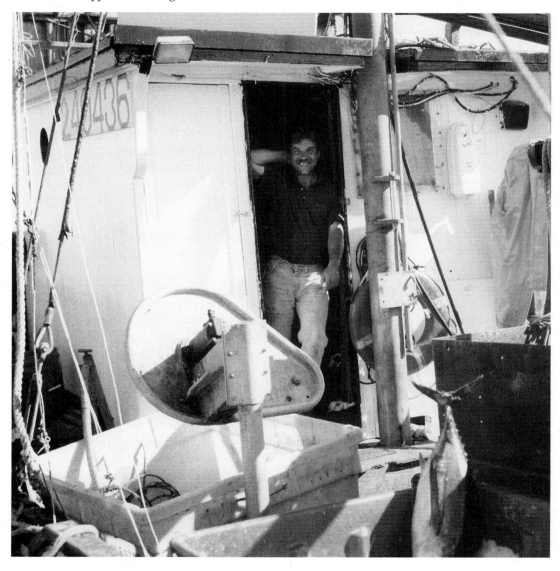

Dungeness Crab-Ricotta Ravioli

Cooking a dinner doesn't always mean looking for the fastest and easiest way to get a decent meal on the table. These raviolis are simple to make but will take a little time to assemble. It's worth the effort and this is the perfect opportunity to get the whole family involved in the fun of filling, folding and sealing these little packages of flavor. Remember, do not overfill the ravioli; this dish is as much about the pasta as it is about the filling.

This filled pasta shows how to balance flavors within a single dish: the sweetness and oceanic saltiness of the crab is balanced by the creaminess of the cheese and the butter and is rounded out by the slight heat of the coriander, the acidity of the lemon and the brightness of the tarragon.

RAVIOLI

1 pound fresh Dungeness crab meat, drained of excess water
1 cup fresh ricotta cheese, drained
½ cup freshly grated dry Monterey Jack or Parmigiano-Reggiano cheese
juice and the grated zest of ½ lemon
1 shallot, finely chopped

1 teaspoon fresh tarragon, finely chopped
¼ teaspoon ground coriander seed
¼ teaspoon freshly grated nutmeg
white pepper, to taste
1 recipe egg pasta dough, rolled out to thin sheets (see page 17)

SAUCE

4 tablespoons butter
juice of ½ lemon
1 tablespoon tarragon, finely chopped

kosher salt and ground white pepper, to taste
additional freshly grated dry Monterey Jack cheese for serving

TO PREPARE THE RAVIOLI: In a medium-size bowl, combine the crab, ricotta, Monterey Jack, lemon juice, lemon zest, shallot, tarragon, coriander, nutmeg and pepper. Gently stir well to mix thoroughly, being careful not break up the crab meat too much. Taste and adjust seasonings.

Cut the pasta sheets into 4-inch by 8-inch rectangles. Place one tablespoon of the crab mixture on half of each rectangle. Lightly wet two edges of the pasta around the filling with water. Fold over the pasta, like a book, to make a 4-inch by 4-inch square. Press the edges and around the filling of each ravioli to seal and to squeeze out any air bubbles.

NOTE: Only wet half of the pasta square; pasta sticks to water but water doesn't stick to water.
Bring a large pot of salted water to a boil.

TO PREPARE THE SAUCE: In a large sauté pan over medium heat, add the butter. Cook until the butter starts to turn light brown and begins to smell like toasted nuts. Remove the pan from the heat and add the lemon juice, tarragon, salt and pepper.

TO SERVE: Add the ravioli to the boiling water and cook until the pasta is tender, about 4 to 6 minutes. Drain the ravioli, reserving 1 to 2 tablespoons of the cooking water. Return the sauté pan with the butter sauce back on the heat. Add the cooked ravioli and reserved pasta cooking water to the pan and toss to coat the pasta with the sauce. Season with salt and pepper.

Place four raviolis on each plate. Pour a little sauce over each of the raviolis and sprinkle cheese over the top.

ADVANCE PREPARATION: The ravioli may be made ahead, placed on a sheet pan between pieces of parchment paper and frozen. Once frozen, carefully place the raviolis in a sealed bag and store them in the freezer for up to a week. When ready to serve take them from the freezer and put them directly into the boiling water. Do not thaw them ahead of time or the ravioli will become soggy.

SUBSTITUTIONS AND OPTIONS: You may substitute egg roll, wonton and gyoza (pot sticker) wrappers for the pasta dough. The texture of the final dish will be slightly more "chewy" but will still yield a delicious result. Additionally, other cooked seafood or shellfish, such as cooked bay shrimp, cooked lobster meat, smoked or cured salmon or leftover cooked fish from last night's dinner, can be used in place of the crab.

WINE NOTES: On warm spring and summer evenings we enjoy drinking wines made from the Spanish white grape Albariño because they are refreshing with tangy citrus and slightly herbal flavors. The creamy texture of the wine will match the cheese in the filling and the butter in the sauce while balancing the lemon and herb. Recommended: 2002 Bodegas del Palacio de Fefiñanes, Rias Baixas, Albariño, Spain; 2002 Havens, Albariño, Napa Valley, California.

NOTE: In 1999, Havens Wine cellars made the first commercially offered Albariño in America (all of 15 cases) and then registered the variety with ATF in 2000.

Makes 8 appetizer servings, about 32, 4-inch square ravioli

Rogue Creamery Blue Cheese Tart

We originally developed this recipe to show off the versatility and flavor of domestic cow cheeses. Blue cheese and pears are a classic dessert combination. We have incorporated this flavor profile in a savory tart perfect for a spring afternoon or even a Sunday brunch. It is like having dessert for an appetizer. How can that be bad?

1 recipe savory tart dough (see page 18)
1 tablespoon butter
1 small yellow onion, finely chopped
1½ cups heavy cream
2 whole eggs

1 egg yolk
4 ounces Rogue Creamery blue cheese, crumbled
kosher salt and white pepper, to taste
pear compote (see page 203)

TO PREPARE THE TART SHELL: Preheat oven to 400°F.

Place dough on a floured board. Using a rolling pin, roll dough out from the center until it forms a circle about ½-inch thick. Turn dough over and roll until you form a circle about 1/8-inch thick and 12-inches in diameter. Press the dough into a 12-inch tart pan and trim off the excess pastry. Prick the entire surface of the dough with a fork. Refrigerate for 30 minutes.

Blind bake the tart shell by placing the tart pan on a baking sheet. Line the dough with foil or parchment and fill it with dried beans or pie weights. Bake for 10 minutes. Remove beans and bake an additional 10 minutes or until the bottom is a light golden brown. Remove from oven and cool tart shell on a rack for 30 minutes before filling.

TO PREPARE THE FILLING: In a medium-size sauté pan over medium heat, melt the butter. Add the onions and season with salt and pepper. Sauté until tender but not colored, about 8 to 10 minutes. Remove onion and allow to cool completely.

In medium-size bowl, combine onions, cream, eggs, egg yolk and cheese. Mix until well combined. Season with salt and pepper. Spoon the custard into pre-baked tart shell. Place filled shell on a baking sheet. Bake in 400°F oven for 15 to 20 minutes or until custard is just set. Remove tart from oven and place on a cooling rack to cool.

TO SERVE: Remove tart from tart pan. Cut tart into 8 wedges and serve with pear compote.

ADVANCE PREPARATION: The tart can be made a day ahead, refrigerated and reheated in a 250°F oven for 20 to 30 minutes or until warm.

SUBSTITUTIONS AND OPTIONS: This recipe will work with almost any blue cheese or even any semi-soft or soft cheese. We recommend either a domestic blue or a domestic chèvre-style fresh goat's milk cheese. You can substitute puff pastry, usually available in the freezer section of your market, for the tart dough. Allow the frozen puff pastry to come to room temperature, roll it out, prick it with a fork and bake according to the tart dough instructions.

WINE NOTES: The saltiness of the cheese and the rich, slightly spicy, fruitiness of the pear compote require a wine with crisp, clean balanced flavors. A wine with a honey-like sweetness, some acidity and a pear flavor will balance the richness of the strong cheese. Recommended: 2000 Schubert, "Dolce", Martinborough, New Zealand; or for a wine with less residual sugar, 2001 Ponzi, Pinot Gris, Willamette Valley, Oregon. For a fun light sparkling wine try a 1999 Prunotto, Moscato d'Asti, Piedmont, Italy, a wine meant to be consumed in large mouthfuls.

Makes one 12-inch tart or 8 appetizer servings

True-Blue Cheeses:

*David Gremmels and Cary Bryant
of The Rogue Creamery*

"We want to make the finest blue cheese in the world," says David Gremmels. It's a statement he doesn't make lightly. He knows he and his partner, Cary Bryant, have tall cheesemakers' boots to fill: 70 years worth with the cheesemaking legacy of Thomas and Ignacio Vella, the legendary father and son team of master Italian-American cheesemakers.

David and Cary took over the cheesemakers' mantle in 2002 from Ignacio Vella, inheriting history as well as a cheesemaking facility. Tom, who died in 1998 at age 100, opened the Rogue Creamery plant in 1935 after founding the Sonoma (Calif.) Cheese Company in 1931.

The Rogue Creamery's blue cheeses have been famous since their introduction in 1957. Returning from France with new knowledge and genuine *Penicillium roqueforti* cultures, the magical mold that blesses all classic blue cheeses, Tom released his first prize-winning Oregon Blue Vein Cheese The rest, as Ig fondly says, is Oregon cheesemaking history.

But drive too fast through Central Point, Oregon, midway between San Francisco and Portland in the Rogue Valley, and you'll miss the vintage 1930s-style concrete building where David and Cary continue the Vella's cheesemaking legacy. Here, cheesemaking follows strict old world methods and recipes. Handmilled and cheddared raw milk cheeses are produced using the open vat cheesemaking process and traditional artisanal cheesemaking techniques. All milk comes from local, pasture-fed cows, half Holstein and half Jersey.

The Creamery's line now includes five exemplary blue-veined cheeses made in the classic style, including David and Cary's award-winning 2003 introduction, Crater Lake Blue. There's also a range of Cheddar cheeses and squeaky cheese curds flavored with pesto, jalapeño peppers, paprika and other tastes. All are made in small volume batches, artisan fashion. "We give our cheeses attention that large cheesemakers cannot duplicate," says David. "Turning them every day, tasting them every week, and with Ig, we have the best mentor we could imagine."

The results speak for themselves. A taste of velvety Oregonzola or Extreme Blue, or any Rogue Creamery Blue for that matter, seduces taste buds and satisfies a craving few cheeses can fill. "Our guests adore these cheeses when we feature them as part of our artisan cheese plate, or use them as an ingredient," says Stu. "They're part of Oregon's culinary history, as well as praised for their fabulous taste." ᦰ

Asparagus Custard

This custard and the Sweet Corn and Shiitake Mushroom Custard that follows are both savory versions of a Spanish flan or a Japanese *chawan mushi*. No matter what you call them, our versions of these light, silky custards are bursting with flavor. They are relatively quick to make, but we recommend that you allow the necessary time for the ingredients to infuse into the cream base.

Select asparagus stalks that are firm, straight, uniform and have spears with tightly closed, compact tips. Asparagus spears start to lose flavor and moisture as soon as they are harvested; for this reason, imported asparagus (from out of state or out of the country), while still good, tends to lack flavor.

10-12 4-ounce metal or ceramic ramekins or molds
2 teaspoons butter, melted
1 bunch green asparagus spears, standard size, about 1 pound
2 tablespoons butter
1 medium yellow onion, roughly diced
2 cups heavy cream
1 cup whole milk
7 whole eggs
¼ teaspoon nutmeg, freshly ground
¼ teaspoon Tabasco Sauce
1 teaspoon tarragon, finely chopped
kosher salt and white pepper, to taste

Preheat oven to 300°F. Brush the melted butter over the insides of the ramekins. Set aside.

Cut off the tips of the asparagus, about the first 2½-inches, and set aside. Cut the asparagus stems into small pieces. In a medium-size sauté pan over medium heat, melt the butter. Add the onion and asparagus stems and season with salt and pepper. Cook until the vegetables are soft and translucent but not colored, about 8 to 10 minutes. Add the cream and milk.

Bring the cream and milk mixture to a boil. Turn off the heat. Let the mixture infuse for 15 minutes and then purée it in a blender until smooth. In a large mixing bowl using a whisk, mix the eggs, nutmeg, Tabasco and cream/milk mixture. Pass the custard mixture through a fine strainer, pushing down on the solids to extract all of the liquid. Add the tarragon and season with salt and pepper.

Place the ramekins into a large, ovenproof pan with high sides. Pour the custard into the prepared ramekins and place the pan in the oven. Fill the large pan half full of hot water. Be careful not to splash any water onto the custards. Cover the large pan with aluminum foil and bake for 45 minutes to 1 hour. The custards are finished when, if gently shaken, they are just set.

TO SERVE: Fill a large, stainless steel pot three-quarters full with salted water, and bring to a boil. Add the reserved asparagus tips and cook for 3 to 4 minutes or until the asparagus is tender. Unmold the custard onto individual plates. Place cooked asparagus tips around the custards.

ADVANCE PREPARATION: The custard base can be made several days ahead and kept refrigerated until you are ready to use it. The cooked custards can be made a day ahead, refrigerated and reheated in a water bath or a steamer when you are ready to serve. Cook 10 to 15 minutes or until a skewer placed in the center of the custard comes out warm.

SUBSTITUTIONS AND OPTIONS: The custard mix may be steamed in almost any size or shape of oven-safe container. A large soufflé dish (approximately 9 inches in diameter) will make a great entrée-size recipe. Additionally, the custards can be served hot, warm or cold; and served in the dishes that they were cooked in or unmolded for a more elegant presentation. One alternative is to make a classic French Royale. Steam or bake these custards in a larger soup bowl, allow the custards to set and pour a warm, clear soup broth over them.

If serving the custards chilled, serve with mixed baby greens and basic vinaigrette (see page 20).

WINE NOTES: You will need an acidic white wine with mineral flavors to hold up to the asparagus and cut through the richness of the cream. Recommended: 2001 La Poussie, Sancerre, Loire, France, or 2001 Tablas Creek, Esprit de Beaucastel Blanc, Paso Robles, South Coast, California (Château de Beaucastel's American effort).

Makes 10 to 12 individual 4-ounce custards

Sweet Corn and Shiitake Mushroom Custard

The corn-mushroom flavors in this custard resemble *Huitlacoche,* also known as "corn smut" or "maize mushroom." Huitlacoche is an edible black fungus which grows on ears of corn and makes the kernels swell to ten times their normal size. The fungus is harvested and treated as a delicacy. In Central America, the earthy and somewhat smoky fungus is used to flavor quesadillas, tamales and soups.

10-12 4-ounce metal or ceramic ramekins
    or molds
1 teaspoon butter, melted
2 tablespoons butter
3 cups fresh corn kernels, approximately
    4 to 5 large ears of corn
1 cup shiitake mushrooms, sliced, stems
    included
2 cups heavy cream

1 cup whole milk
7 whole eggs
¼ teaspoon curry powder
¼ teaspoon nutmeg, freshly ground
¼ teaspoon cumin seed, freshly ground
kosher salt and white pepper, to taste
¼ cup pickled shiitake mushrooms,
    drained (see page 196)

Preheat oven to 300°F. Brush the melted butter over the inside of the ramekins. Set aside. Cut the corn kernels from the cob and scrape the cobs with a back of a knife to extract "corn milk." Reserve the cobs.

In a medium-size sauté pan over medium heat, melt the butter. Add 2½ cups of the corn kernels and shiitake mushrooms and season with salt and pepper. Cook until the vegetables are soft and translucent but not colored, about 10 to 12 minutes. Add the cream, milk, corn cobs and corn milk.

Bring the corn/cream mixture to a boil. Turn off the heat. Let the mixture infuse for 15 minutes. Remove the cobs from the pan. Purée the corn/cream mixture in a blender until smooth. In a large mixing bowl using a whisk, mix the eggs, curry powder, nutmeg, cumin and corn/cream mixture. Pass the custard mixture through a fine strainer, pushing down on the solids to extract all of the liquid. Taste and adjust seasoning.

Place the ramekins into a large, ovenproof pan with high sides. Pour the custard into the prepared ramekins three-quarters of the way up the sides. Add the remaining ½ cup of corn kernels to the ramekins and place the pan in the oven. Fill the large pan half full of hot water. Be careful not to splash any water onto the custards. Cover the large pan with aluminum foil and bake for 45 minutes to 1 hour. The custards are finished when, if gently shaken, they are just set.

TO SERVE: Unmold the custard onto individual plates. Place pickled shiitake mushrooms on top of each custard.

ADVANCE PREPARATION: The custard base can be made several days ahead and kept refrigerated until you are ready to use it. The cooked custards can be made a day ahead, refrigerated and reheated in a water bath or a steamer when you are ready to serve. Cook 10 to 15 minutes or until a skewer placed in the center of the custard comes out warm.

SUBSTITUTIONS AND OPTIONS: The custard mix may be steamed in almost any size or shape oven-safe container. A large soufflé dish (approximately 9 inches in diameter) will make a great entrée-size recipe. Additionally, the custards can be served hot, warm or cold; and served in the dishes that they were cooked in or unmolded for a more elegant presentation. One alternative is to make a classic French Royale. Steam or bake these custards in a larger soup bowl, allow the custards to set and pour a warm, clear soup broth over them.

If serving the custards chilled, serve with mixed baby greens and the basic vinaigrette (see page 20).

If available, substitute sautéed fresh porcini mushrooms or pickled porcini mushrooms for the shiitake mushrooms. The porcinis will add a clean, earthy flavor and very distinctive aroma to the finished dish.

WINE NOTES: A creamy German-style Riesling matches particularly well with dishes that mix some earthy flavors, including mushrooms and onions, with naturally sweet flavors, such as fresh corn and a slight spiciness, represented by the cumin. The wine need not be totally dry. A touch of sweetness matters little if there is enough acidity to offset it. Recommended: 2002 Müller-Catoir, Spätlese Trocken Pfalz Haardter, Riesling, Bürgergarten, Germany; or 2001 Woodward Canyon, Dry Riesling, Columbia Valley, Washington.

Makes 8 to 10 individual 4-ounce custards

Summer Vegetable Slaw

This dish has become a July Fourth tradition at the Peerless. It's a perfect side dish for summer picnics since it's an ideal accompaniment to grilled meats. The slightly acidic mustard dressing is a refreshing contrast to crunchy, colorful vegetables like red and yellow peppers, radishes, fennel, onion and cabbage.

Change the vegetables based on the season, keeping in mind that it is best to have a variety of colors, textures and flavors. Avoid any vegetable that will bleed, such as red beets, or that will overpower the other flavors in this dish. The key is to cut the vegetables in roughly the same size and shape.

VEGETABLE SLAW
(You will need approximately 1 pound of any combination of the following vegetables.)

1 red bell pepper, seeds removed and julienned

1 yellow bell pepper, seeds removed and julienned

1 head radicchio, core removed and cut into chiffonade

½ small head Napa cabbage, core removed and cut into chiffonade

1 green zucchini, cut in half, seeds removed and julienned

1 yellow squash, cut in half, seeds removed and julienned

1 bulb fennel, core removed and julienned

½ daikon radish, julienned

1 large red onion, cut into half moons

1 bunch green onions, cut on a bias about 1 inch long

¼ cup mint leaves, cut into chiffonade

¼ cup basil leaves, cut into chiffonade

1 tablespoon cilantro leaves, finely chopped

mustard dressing

kosher salt and white pepper, to taste

MUSTARD DRESSING
Makes 2½ cups

2 tablespoons Dijon mustard

2 tablespoons honey

¾ cup apple cider vinegar or rice wine vinegar

¾ cup extra virgin olive oil

¾ cup vegetable oil

kosher salt and white pepper, to taste

TO PREPARE THE SLAW: In a large stainless steel bowl, combine vegetables, herbs and enough mustard dressing to lightly coat the vegetables. Cover and refrigerate for at least one hour. Taste and adjust seasoning.

TO PREPARE THE DRESSING: Place mustard, honey, vinegar, salt and pepper in a small stainless steel bowl. Slowly drizzle in both oils, whisking constantly, until ingredients are combined. Taste and adjust seasoning.

TO SERVE: When ready to serve, drain any excess liquid from the vegetables and place on serving dish.

ADVANCE PREPARATION: Make the slaw and refrigerate at least 1 hour and up to 6 hours before serving. The vegetables will wilt and become soggy if allowed to marinate in the dressing for longer than 6 hours.

SUBSTITUTIONS AND OPTIONS: To infuse a touch of heat to this dish, add chili oil or a julienned fresh hot chili to your taste.

WINE NOTES: This dish needs a crisp, herbal Chenin blend with a touch of sweetness to hold up to the acid in the dressing and the mixture of savory bright herbs. Chenin Blanc is the forgotten grape; it's summer in a glass. Recommended: 2002 Andrew Rich, "Tabula Rasa," Chenin Blanc, Oregon; or 2001 Vinum, CNW Cuvée, Chenin Blanc, California.

Makes approximately 8 cups

Steamed Manila Clams
with Merguez Sausage

One of the most flavorful and easiest ways to cook clams is to steam them in a fragrant liquid. It may seem a strange combination but the sweet tomatoes, spicy sausage and rich olive oil balances the briny shellfish perfectly. At the restaurant, we make our own merguez (North African lamb sausage seasoned with garlic and hot spices). For those who choose not to make their own, we recommend purchasing a good quality merguez, Spanish chorizo or Portuguese linguiça (spicy smoked garlic sausage).

64 Manila or littleneck clams, approximately 3 pounds

16 sun-dried tomatoes, approximately 1 ounce

½ pound merguez, chorizo or other spicy sausage, cut into thin slices

1 small red onion, cut into thin half moons

2 tablespoons parsley, finely chopped

4 ounces white wine

1 tablespoon extra virgin olive oil

kosher salt and cracked black pepper, to taste

Scrub the outside of the clams thoroughly under cold running water to remove any sand and grit.

Place all ingredients in a medium pot with a tight-fitting lid. Cover and place over medium heat. Simmer for 10 to 15 minutes, until the clams have opened. Discard any clams that do not open.

TO SERVE: Divide the clams, tomatoes, sausage and onions into four warm bowls. Pour the broth over. Serve with plenty of crusty country-style bread for "sopping up" the delicious broth.

ADVANCE PREPARATION: Clams will remain alive from 7 to 10 days when stored in the refrigerator at 35°F to 40°F. Rinse the clams in cold water to remove any grit or dirt, drain any excess water and store them in a bowl in the refrigerator with a damp towel placed on top. Live shellfish needs to breathe so never store them in an airtight container and never cover them in fresh water. The shells should be firmly closed and if any gape slightly, give them a light tap – they should close back up.

SUBSTITUTIONS AND OPTIONS: Clams fall into two categories: hard-shell and soft-shell. Any hard shell clam or even mussel, will work for this recipe. The gray, hard-shell clams found in bays, tidal flats and on beaches of the east coast are all members of the same species. Atlantic hard-shell clams (also called qua hogs) are sold according to size: *Button* clams are the smallest, *Littlenecks* are the next smallest, about 14 per pound, *Topnecks*, come 10 to 12 per pound, *Cherrystones* are medium-size, at 8 to 10 per pound and *chowder clams* are the largest. Our favorite east coast clam is the *Mahogany* clam. They have maroon shells and orange colored meat, are about the same size as west coast *Manila* clams.

If you choose a west coast hard-shell clam, select *Manila* clams. We prefer them because we think they are sweeter than Eastern clams because they have lots of glycogen, the carbohydrate common to all clams. Most importantly, choose a variety that is harvested as close to you as possible.

WINE NOTES: Most unoaked dry white wines are good choices with clams. We like a Mâcon for its clean flavors. If you choose a sausage that is particular spicy try a Vouvray or Viognier. Recommended: 2000 Pine Ridge, Chenin Blanc-Viognier, California is an interesting change-of-pace white at a try-me price; or 2000 J. A. Ferret, Les Vernays Cuvée Spéciale, Pouilly-Fuissé, Burgundy, France.

Makes 4 appetizer servings

Weathervane Sea Scallops in a Citrus Marinade with Swiss Chard and Dill-Caviar Cream

Weathervane scallops are a West Coast scallop variety that we love to feature on the menu whenever we find them. Indigenous to Alaskan and Canadian waters, the Weathervane scallop harvest is only a fraction of the size of the East Coast scallop production. We encourage you to make the effort to seek out this sweet nutty-tasting shellfish.

This dish celebrates the pure scallop flavor that is unique to the seafood world. The citrus overtones enhance the delicate scallop taste and will round out an accompanying wine, making it seem more mature. We know the caviar in this recipe is an extravagance, but its salty character adds a sophisticated balance to the sweetness of the shellfish and the creaminess of the crème fraîche. Only a small amount is needed so you can indulge here and use the rest at a special Sunday brunch.

8 Alaskan Weathervane sea scallops (dry packed or in the shell), muscle on side removed.
½ cup extra virgin olive oil
¼ cup tangerine or orange juice
¼ cup grapefruit juice
1 shallot, finely chopped
½ teaspoon fleur de sel or other coarse sea salt
cracked black peppercorns (cracked pink peppercorns
    may be added for additional color), to taste
½ cup small Swiss chard leaves or baby greens
kosher salt and white pepper, to taste
¼ cup crème fraîche or sour cream (see page 15)
1 teaspoon dill, chopped
2 teaspoons American sturgeon caviar

Cut each scallop in half horizontally and set aside.

To make dressing, in a small stainless steel bowl, whisk together oil, juices and shallot. In another stainless steel bowl, mix together crème fraîche, dill and caviar and set aside.

Place the scallops in ¾ cup of the dressing. Marinate the scallops for up to 20 minutes, turning every 5 minutes or so.

TO SERVE: Lightly toss the chard with the remaining ¼ cup of the dressing. Remove the scallops from their dressing and place over the greens. Sprinkle the fleur de sel and cracked peppercorns on top of scallops. Drizzle caviar and crème fraîche mixture around the plate.

ADVANCE PREPARATION: The scallop marinade/dressing may be made several days ahead. Marinate the scallops and dress the greens just before serving.

SUBSTITUTIONS AND OPTIONS: East Coast wild Atlantic scallops may be substituted. However, many of the Atlantic wild scallops are dredged, which is a habitat-damaging method. Additionally, poor management has caused overfishing and species depletion. If you choose Atlantic scallops we recommend either diver, hand-harvested sea scallops; net-farmed Atlantic sea scallops from Newfoundland; or bay scallops from Nova Scotia because they are grown on suspended racks and cause less harm to the environment than dredged scallops. No matter which you choose, make sure the scallops are either in their shell or "dry packed," not treated or soaked with sodium tripolyphosphate (STP). The freshness of the shellfish is the most important part of this recipe.

WINE NOTES: Choose a wine to highlight the citrus flavor in the appetizer. The citrus in the marinade brings out the pure flavors in the wine and rounds out the fattiness of the shellfish. Caviar can enhance the mineral taste of the wine, but the dill and cream will balance the flavor. The final note of the slightly bitter raw chard brings the entire dish together. Choose a Sauvignon Blanc from a region like the Columbia Valley in Washington State or Marlborough in New Zealand that exhibits citrus elements, or go all out and splurge on a blanc de blanc champagne. Do you think Champagne and caviar might work together? Recommended: 2001 Chateau Ste. Michelle, Horse Heaven Vineyard, Sauvignon Blanc, Columbia Valley, Washington; or 1998 Cloudy Bay, Sauvignon Blanc, Marlborough, New Zealand; or NV, Agrapart & Fils, Blanc de Blanc Brut, Avize, France.

Makes 4 appetizer servings

American Sturgeon Caviar

Caviar is roe (eggs) from sturgeon, a primitive species of fish native to the northern hemisphere. Considered a culinary delicacy since the 15th century, the eggs are sieved to remove fatty tissues and membranes, and then lightly salted. A single large sturgeon can produce hundreds of pounds of roe. We recommend farmed sturgeon caviar currently being raised in California (see the Sources and Information section for Sterling Caviar from Stolt Sea Farm in Elverta, California). The nutty, creamy flavor of American white sturgeon caviar resembles Osetra caviar from the Caspian Sea but is harvested in an ecologically friendly method from sturgeon successfully reared in a protected environment. Be aware that Caspian Sea caviars (Beluga, Osetra and Sevruga) are growing increasingly scarce — and more expensive — due to overfishing, pollution and poaching of endangered sturgeon stocks. ❧

Maple-Apple Brandy Cured Salmon
with Maple-Mustard Dressing

This is one of our favorite versions of the classic Swedish dish *gravlax* — a salt, sugar and herb cured, preserved salmon originally buried in the ground ("in the grave"). Our cure has a higher percentage of salt than usual in order to give a firmer texture to the finished product.

We serve this gravlax in the autumn when the King salmon are spawning and the maple trees are wearing their brilliant autumn foliage. Use only the freshest wild salmon you can find. If you must, you can use salmon that has been frozen for at least 72 hours at -4°F or lower. Even though cured, this salmon is technically still raw and must remain refrigerated. Note that it will keep only 10 days to 2 weeks.

CURED SALMON

¾ cup kosher salt

⅓ cup maple sugar or brown sugar (see the
  Sources and Information section)

1½ cups dill, coarsely chopped

2 tablespoons cracked white peppercorns

1 wild King salmon fillet (about 3 pounds),
  skin on, pin bones removed

4 tablespoons Clear Creek Distillery
  Eau-de-Vie de Pomme or other apple
  flavored brandy or liquor

MAPLE-MUSTARD DRESSING

⅓ cup apple cider vinegar or white
  wine vinegar

1 tablespoon maple syrup

1 teaspoon whole grain mustard

1 shallot, minced

1 cup vegetable oil

kosher salt and white pepper, to taste

TO PREPARE THE CURED SALMON: In a medium-size glass or stainless steel bowl, mix together the salt, sugar, dill and peppercorns.

Place the salmon skin-side down in a deep glass, stainless steel or ceramic pan large enough to hold the entire salmon fillet. Spread the salt mixture over the salmon, pressing down gently to push mixture into the flesh of the fish. Drizzle brandy over salmon.

Cover salmon with plastic wrap. Place another pan on top of salmon and weigh this pan down lightly using several large cans or a brick.

Refrigerate for 24 hours. Remove from refrigerator, turn the salmon over and baste with the excess liquid. Replace the weight and refrigerate the fish again for an additional 24 hours.

Salmon is cured when the flesh is firm to the touch. If needed, turn, baste, weigh down and refrigerate fish an additional day. It may take up to 4 days to completely cure.

When fully cured, wash off salt mixture by running fish under cold water. Dry well with a lint-free towel. Wrap salmon in plastic and refrigerate until ready to serve.

TO PREPARE THE DRESSING: In a small bowl, combine vinegar, syrup, mustard and shallot. Whisk in oil to make a thick sauce and refrigerate.

TO SERVE: Place salmon skin-side down on a cutting board. Slice salmon using a long, thin, sharp knife by holding the knife parallel to the salmon. Slice on a 45° angle into very thin slices. Cut toward the tail, beginning about 3 inches from the tail. Serve with Maple-Mustard dressing, baby green salad and toasted brioche or French bread.

ADVANCE PREPARATION: The salmon will take 2-4 days to cure depending on the thickness of the fillet. Once cured, the salmon will keep up to two weeks in the refrigerator. The dressing can be made several days ahead. Whisk the ingredients together again just before serving.

SUBSTITUTIONS AND OPTIONS: Any Pacific salmon will work for this recipe but the flavor of wild King salmon is best. Additionally, any high fat content fish like sturgeon or even Pacific black cod will also work in place of the salmon. If you choose a farmed-raised fish, make sure it has been raised with an appropriate vegetarian diet and according to environmentally sound methods.

BEVERAGE NOTES: Since the salmon is cured in Clear Creek Distillery Eau-de-Vie de Pomme, Apple Brandy from Oregon it only seems right to serve it with the dish. Owner-distiller Steve McCarthy crushes and ferments whole apples, distills, and then ages the liquor in old cognac barrels made from Limousin oak following the traditional customs of the calvados makers of Normandy, France. The end result is an amber, smooth "American Calvados," with a special flavor from the high-quality Oregon fruit used.

Makes 15 to 20 appetizer servings

Oregon's Eau-de-Vie Master:
Steve McCarthy and Clear Creek Distillery

Stride through sun-dappled pear orchards with Steve McCarthy and you're with a man who is both intense and intensely knowledgeable about his craft, which some say is an art form. Steve has been distilling the sweet essence of pears and apples from Hood River orchards into brandies, eau-de-vie and Italian-style grappas for close to 20 years. He says it connects him with the earth. His signature item is the fabled Clear Creek "pear in a bottle" eau-de-vie where a mature pear is actually grown inside a wine bottle — much like the old ship-in-a-bottle feat — and the glass bottle later filled with eau-de-vie liquor.

"I noticed that some years the orchards would be full of pears, lots of good, sound fruit and others years not. In order to be prosperous in the bad years, we needed ideas. It's common in Europe — where in some places all they can grow is goats — to take whatever they have and make something from it," Steve says. "Preserving fruit by making a brandy out of it was common long before refrigeration was an option. Even bad wine can transform itself into decent cognac."

And make something of it, McCarthy has. He took himself off to Europe in the early '80s to research equipment and learn the brandy-making process, visiting people "who made what I liked." Then he set up his own distilling operation back in Portland, one step, two oak barrels, and one orchard at a time.

"You couldn't get Williams pear brandy in the US at the time," he says. Trees for this pear variety, a cousin to the Bartlett pear, took five years to mature. First he made a grappa and then a kirsch. One product led to another and still does.

It's almost a year-round operation, depending on the harvest season.

"Steve's brandies were a legend in the restaurant world before we even moved back to Oregon," says Mary. "Our chef friends would talk reverently about them and we knew they were 'a must' on our wine list."

As Steve knows, it's not just taste that keeps his brandies on menus. Each sip is the essence of summer, clear and pure, the round sweetness of perfectly ripe fruit, a joy to the mouth and a link to sunlit orchards. ⌒

Oysters

"As I ate the oysters with their strong taste of the sea and their faint metallic taste that the cold white wine washed away, leaving only the sea taste and the succulent texture, and as I drank their cold liquid from each shell and washed it down with the crisp taste of the wine, I lost the empty feeling and began to be happy and to make plans."
— Ernest Hemingway, *A Moveable Feast*

Oysters lead a pretty cushy life. Most oysters on the US market, and many of the clams and mussels, are farm-raised. They are raised in estuaries, those incredibly productive zones where nutrient-rich fresh and salt water meet and mingle. Twice a day tides rise and fall, carrying ocean plankton inland and organic nutrients from the land outward. Oysters feed at their leisure, filtering up to eight gallons of salt water per hour to collect food in the form of detritus, tiny phytoplankton and the even smaller nanoplankton. An intertidal oyster doesn't need to hunt for food; it can simply relax and wait for the tide to bring the next serving. An oyster's entire reproductive cycle is based on water temperature — not mood. When the water gets warm enough, oysters become reproductive and spawny. Thus, we recommend that you only purchase oysters from certified beds and from waters that are 55°F or colder.

There are three factors that contribute to the taste of oysters: species, method of cultivation and location of cultivation.

SPECIES

Edible species of oysters can be divided up into two genera, the genus *crassostrea* and the genus *ostrea*. Oysters in the genus *crassostrea* have cupped shells that house the bulk of the meat. Fertilization occurs outside the shell. Oysters in the genus *ostrea* have flatter shells and fertilization takes place inside the female shell.

PACIFIC (*Crassostrea gigas*) — Native to Japan. *Gigas* are the most common oyster in the world, making up over 90 percent of all oysters produced. They are fast-growing, with an oblong shape and a deep cup. They are a highly adaptable species and have been brought into areas that either have no commercial oyster crop or where the native oysters have, for some reason, failed.

ATLANTIC (*Crassostrea virginica*) — Native to eastern United States, Gulf Coast and Canada. Approximately 85 percent of all of the oysters grown in the United States are Atlantic oysters. They have a round, somewhat flat, shell. A large amount of these oysters are processed in various ways and never reach the table as half-shell oysters.

KUMAMOTO (*Crassostrea sikamea*) — Native to the Far East; cultivated in the Pacific Northwest. "Kumos" are a very slow-growing oyster.

PORTUGUESE (*Crassostrea angulata*) — Native to northwestern Europe.

SYDNEY ROCK (*Crassostrea commercialis*) — Native to Australia.

OLYMPIA (*Ostrea lurida*) — the only oyster Native to the West Coast United States.

Olympia oysters are extremely small in size with a tiny, round shell and a metallic taste.

EUROPEAN FLAT (*Ostrea edulisi*) — Native to northwestern Europe. European flats have a flat, round shell with a coppery taste.

CHILOE (*Ostrea chilensis*) — Native to Chile.

COON OR GULF (*Ostrea frons*) — Native to southeastern United States.

PEARL OYSTERS gold-lip (*Pinctada maxima*), black-lip (*Pinctada margaritifera*) and penguin oyster (*Pteria penguin*) — These are inedible oysters from which fine pearls are obtained.

METHOD OF CULTIVATION

While wild oysters grow on rocks, those that are cultivated are raised naturally in different ways. Some oyster growers buy oyster larvae and place the larvae in huge fiberglass tanks, along with strings of adult oyster shells. Others put oysters, the size of peas, in floating wire cylinders, where the rolling tides smooth and round their shells. They are then transferred to flats of wire bags attached to iron trestles where they continue to grow until they are large enough to be harvested. Still others place seed oysters in wire bags attached to racks. The ebb and flow of the tides continuously rotates the oysters inside the bags with a movement similar to a washing machine.

LOCATION OF CULTIVATION

Oysters of the same species (or different species) take on a subtle and sometimes not-so-subtle difference when grown in different beds. The action of tides, salinity of the water, availability of food, presence of algae, the amount of fresh water coming into the saltwater marshes, and the mineral content are all contributing factors that cause the variance in oysters' shape, color and flavor.

PURCHASING OYSTERS

When purchasing live oysters, choose oysters that close tightly when handled. Discard oysters that remain open or have damaged shells. Live oysters are usually sold by the dozen. Freshly shucked oysters will smell like the sea and the liquor will be clear.

STORING OYSTERS

Oysters will remain alive from 7 to 10 days when stored in the refrigerator at 35°F to 40°F. Store live oysters cup-side down (flat side up) to keep them in their own liquor, and cover

Tasting oysters

There are three factors to consider:

SALINITY (*degree of saltiness*)	TEXTURE	FINISH
Mild	Crunchy	Mineral
Medium	Creamy	Buttery
Salty		Fruity
		Vegetable

with a damp towel. Live oysters need to breathe so never store them in an airtight container and never cover them with fresh water. Shucked oysters are graded and sold according to size and range from the largest, called "selects," to the smallest, labeled "extra small." Store fresh, shucked oysters on ice or in the coldest part of the refrigerator and use within five days of purchase.

SHUCKING OYSTERS

STEP 1: Scrub the oyster to get rid of any mud or grit.

STEP 2: Protect your hand by draping a towel over your open palm, or use a mesh oyster glove. Hold the oyster firmly in one hand and the oyster knife in the other, making sure the deeper cup of the oyster is at the bottom. Slip the knife blade of the oyster knife between the top and bottom shell right by the hinge on back.

STEP 3: Once the knife has penetrated the shell, run the knife all the way around the inside of the oyster cutting the muscle attached to the top of the shell.

STEP 4: Using a twisting motion, pry the top and bottom shells apart. Be gentle but firm so you don't lose any of the liquor inside.

STEP 5: Cut the oyster free from its shell. It will be connected by a tough knob on its underside, the adductor muscle. Slide your knife under the body of the oyster and sever the muscle. Discard the top shell. ◡

Oyster and Seafood Dipping Sauces

When serving oysters on the half shell as a first course, allow 6 to 12 oysters per person. Although we prefer to eat oysters on the half shell either unadorned or with a squeeze of lemon or a drop of Pernod, we have included several dipping sauces to complement the oysters' pristine saltiness.

CHAMPAGNE MIGNONETTE SAUCE

1 shallot, finely chopped
½ cup champagne vinegar
½ cup champagne

1 teaspoon cracked black pepper
1 tablespoon lemon juice

Combine all ingredients and refrigerate.

SUBSTITUTIONS AND OPTIONS: You may leave out the champagne and use a total of 1 cup of champagne vinegar. A good-quality white wine vinegar may also be substituted for the champagne vinegar.

Makes 1 cup

BLOODY MARY GRANITÉ

2½ ounces vodka
5 ouncesounces tomato juice
1 tablespoon grated fresh horseradish
  or 1 teaspoon prepared horseradish
½ ounce lemon juice

1 teaspoon Worcestershire sauce
½ teaspoon celery seed
½ teaspoon cracked black pepper
1 teaspoon Tabasco
1 small dried hot red chili, crushed (optional)

Combine all ingredients and stir together. Pour into a shallow, non-reactive metal pan.

Place in freezer and stir every 15-30 minutes. Scrape with a large fork once frozen to create "grains."

Makes 1 cup

VIETNAMESE DIPPING SAUCE (*Nuoc Cham*)

3 cloves garlic, finely minced
3 tablespoons sugar
1 small fresh, small red chili, seeded and
  finely chopped

1 tablespoon fresh ginger root, minced
3 ounces lime juice
4 ounces *nouc mam* (Vietnamese fish sauce)

Combine the garlic, sugar chili and ginger and crush the mixture to a paste. Add the lime juice and fish sauce and stir to blend. A mortar and pestle works the best.

Makes 1 cup

GINGER-SOY DIPPING SAUCE

1 shallot or small yellow onion, peeled and finely chopped
1 small sweet apple, peeled and cut into small dice
¼ cup fresh ginger, peeled and grated

½ cup soy sauce
4 tablespoons white rice vinegar
1 tablespoon toasted sesame oil
1 teaspoon granulated sugar

In a blender, combine the onion, apple, ginger, soy sauce, rice vinegar, sesame oil and sugar. Blend until smooth.

Makes 1 cup

PEERLESS COCKTAIL SAUCE

½ cup chili sauce
¼ cup ketchup
1 tablespoon grated fresh horseradish or 1 teaspoon prepared horseradish
1 teaspoon lemon juice
1 teaspoon Worcestershire sauce

½ teaspoon dry mustard
½ teaspoon cracked black pepper
1 teaspoon Tabasco Sauce
¼ teaspoon kosher salt

Combine all ingredients and mix well.

Makes 1 cup

Cornmeal Fried Oysters
with a Salad of Organic Greens and Lemon-Caper Aioli

Stu has always been a fan of Oyster Po' Boy sandwiches — the classic fare from New Orleans — a French baguette, hollowed out and stuffed with fried oysters and lots of tartar sauce. This is our tribute but with a slight twist. This version is an appetizer course, but the size could easily be doubled and the dish served as an entrée.

CORNMEAL FRIED OYSTERS

½ cup all-purpose flour
½ cup stone-ground yellow cornmeal
½ cup cornstarch
¼ teaspoon cayenne pepper

¼ teaspoon kosher salt
18 oysters, shucked and drained
1 cup vegetable oil

LEMON-CAPER AIOLI

11 slices white bread, crusts removed,
   cut into small pieces
3 tablespoons white wine vinegar or milk
4 cloves garlic, finely chopped
1 egg yolk

¼ teaspoon kosher salt
1½ cups olive oil
2-4 ounces lemon juice
1 teaspoon capers, nonpareilles, roughly
   chopped

GREENS

6-8 slices all-natural bacon, cut into small dice
10-12 ounces organic mixed greens, cleaned

12 caper berries, with stems
kosher salt and cracked black pepper, to taste

TO PREPARE THE OYSTERS: To make the coating mixture, combine the flour, cornmeal, cornstarch, cayenne pepper and salt in a bowl. Toss several oysters at a time in the coating.

Heat the oil in a deep skillet over medium heat until a thermometer registers 350°F. Fry the oysters in small batches for 1 minute on each side. Drain and remove to a plate lined with paper towel. Keep warm.

TO PREPARE THE AIOLI: Soak the bread pieces in the vinegar or milk for 5 minutes or until saturated with liquid. Remove and place the bread and garlic in a mortar and grind with a pestle to mash into a very smooth paste. Pound in the egg yolk and salt. Using a whisk, slowly whip the olive oil into the egg mixture, little by little, until a thick emulsion is formed. Stir in lemon juice. Aioli should have the consistency of a dressing. Thin aioli with warm water if necessary. Add capers.

TO PREPARE THE GREENS: Render the bacon by placing it in a medium-size sauté pan over medium heat and cook, stirring frequently, about 12 to 15 minutes, until crisp. Remove bacon and drain on paper towels.

TO SERVE: Toss the greens with salt, pepper, bacon and half of of the aioli. Divide the greens evenly onto six plates. Place hot oysters and caper berries around the greens and drizzle with remaining aioli.

ADVANCE PREPARATION: The aioli may be made ahead and kept for several days in the refrigerator. This recipe yields more aioli than needed for the salad; the extra aioli makes a great spread for sandwiches.

SUBSTITUTIONS AND OPTIONS: You may substitute prepared mayonnaise with lemon juice, garlic and capers for the aioli, but the flavor will not be as complex or rich. You may purchase shucked oysters, but nothing beats the freshness of oysters right out of their shell.

WINE NOTES: Choose a crisp white wine with a little sweetness and enough spice to cut through the aioli. A new world Melon with a mineral/melon finish or a smoky-sweet winter bock beer are good choices. Recommended: 2001 Eugene Wine Cellars, Melon, Willamette Valley, Oregon; or Doppelbock, Widmer Brewing Co., Portland, Oregon.

Makes 6 appetizer servings

Three Oyster Stew

The three oysters in this stew refer to the shellfish, the oyster mushroom and salsify. The salsify we are referring to is actually called Scorzonera, but can also be labeled Black Salsify, Black Oyster Plant or Viper Grass. It is a regular-shaped, non-tapering root vegetable with a muddy-brown exterior that when peeled reveals a cream-colored, slightly sticky interior. Salsify has a delicate flavor resembling artichoke hearts and coconut milk, and is in the same plant family (*Compsitae*) as endive.

This stew is fairly simple to make but has a complex and rich flavor. Use either Pacific or Atlantic freshly shucked oysters and, for our taste, the saltier the better. Add a salad and a light fruit dessert and you have a complete meal.

2 salsify	1 cup heavy cream
2 tablespoons butter	juice of 1 lemon
1 leek, white part only, finely diced	1 plum tomato, peeled, seeded and diced
1 shallot, finely diced	12 French baguette or sourdough baguette
1 rib celery, finely diced	toast rounds
¼ pound oyster mushrooms	fresh tarragon, chopped, to taste
½ cup white wine	fresh chives, chopped, to taste
24 oysters, shucked, liquor reserved	

We suggest wearing gloves when peeling salsify to prevent discoloring your hands. Peel the salsify and cut it into 1½-inch to 2-inch long matchstick pieces. To prevent the root from oxidizing and turning brown, place the cut pieces of salsify into a plastic or stainless steel container and cover with water that has the juice of one lemon added.

In a medium-size sauté pan over medium heat, melt the butter. Add the leeks, shallots, celery and mushrooms. Sauté until tender but not colored, about 8 minutes. Add the salsify, wine and oyster liquor. Cook the mixture over medium heat until half the liquid remains. Add the heavy cream and reduce the liquid until the sauce is slightly thickened. Add the lemon juice, oysters and tomato and cook until just warm, 2 to 3 minutes. Do not let the liquid boil.

TO SERVE: Spoon the stew into center of soup plate. Arrange toast around and sprinkle with chives and tarragon.

ADVANCE PREPARATION: You may prepare each step of the stew recipe, except adding the lemon juice, oysters and tomatoes, two to three days in advance. Just before serving, bring the stew base to a boil, reduce heat to a simmer and add the remaining ingredients.

SUBSTITUTIONS AND OPTIONS: You may substitute other cultivated mushrooms or wild mushrooms for the oyster mushrooms, but the texture will not be as chewy and the flavor will be more earthy. Parsnips will make a good substitute for the salsify, but the stew will have a slight sweetness not found in the salsify. Clams or mussels in their shell will make a good alternative to the shucked oysters.

WINE NOTES: Oysters and champagne are a classic match. We prefer a sparkling rosé to match the earthy, mushroom flavors in the stew, or an oaky Chardonnay to play off of the cream in the stew. Recommended: 1998 Soter, *Beacon Hill*, Brut Rosé, Willamette Valley, Oregon; or NV Billecart-Salmon, Brut Rosé, Mareuil-Sur-Ay, France. For a still wine choose a 2001 Chateau St. Jean, Chardonnay, Sonoma Valley, California.

Makes 6 appetizer servings

Potato-Onion Tart Tatin

A "Tart Tatin" is a famous French upside-down apple tart made by covering the bottom of a shallow baking dish with butter and sugar, then apples and finally a pastry crust. While baking, the sugar and butter create a delicious caramel that becomes the topping when the tart is inverted onto a serving plate. The tart was created by two French sisters who lived in the Loire Valley and earned their living making it for their neighboring townfolk. The French call this dessert *tarte des demoiselles Tatin*, "the tart of two unmarried women named Tatin."

We love to add our own twists to classic dishes. To make a savory version, we use potatoes and onions instead of apples. The key to this dish is the caramelization of the natural starches in the potatoes and the use of duck fat. You can substitute butter, but trust us when we say the flavor will not be nearly as decadent.

8 tablespoons duck fat

2 medium yellow onions, peeled and thinly sliced

8 large russet potatoes, peeled, sliced in half lengthwise and cut into ¼-inch thick half moons

kosher salt and white pepper, to taste

1 sheet puff pastry, large enough to cut out a 12-inch diameter circle

Preheat oven to 400°F.

In a 12-inch nonstick, ovenproof pan, melt the duck fat. In a large bowl, combine onions, potatoes, melted duck fat, salt and pepper. Toss to coat the vegetables with the fat.

Place the 12-inch nonstick pan over medium heat. Place potato mixture in pan and spread evenly over the bottom. Turn potato mixture frequently until the vegetables are translucent and soft, about 20-25 minutes.

While potatoes are cooking, roll out the puff pastry until it is approximately ⅛-inch thick and large enough to make a 12-inch diameter circle. Prick the entire surface of the puff pastry with a fork. Cut out a 12-inch diameter circle of pastry.

Place pastry on top of potato mixture, pat down and place pan in oven. Cook approximately 10-12 minutes or until pastry is golden brown.

Remove tart from oven and allow sit at room temperature for 15 to 20 minutes. Invert tart onto a plate and allow to cool completely. When tart is completely cold, cut into pie-shaped wedges.

TO SERVE: Place wedges on a baking sheet and place in 400°F oven. Cook until the edges are golden brown, about 5 minutes, and turn over. Continue cooking until the other side is golden brown and the center is warm, an additional 5 minutes.

ADVANCE PREPARATION: The tart is best when made a day ahead, unmolded, and allowed to sit overnight in the refrigerator before cutting and reheating.

SUBSTITUTIONS AND OPTIONS: Any combination of root vegetables will work as long as at least ¼ of the vegetable mixture is potatoes. Any fat (butter, vegetable oil, etc.) will work, but we recommend the use of duck fat or goose fat for its sweetness and "glue factor." You can render your own duck fat or it can be purchased from any of the game and specialty meat suppliers listed in the Sources and Information section.

WINE NOTES: For the best pairing, match the wine with the main component of the meal. If serving this recipe as a dish by itself, find a wine with a hint of sweetness and a buttery finish to match to the sweetness and richness of the duck fat and pastry. Recommended: 2001 Paul Blanck, Riesling, Alsace, France; or 2001 Longoria, Fe Ciega Vineyard, Pinot Noir, South Coast, California.

Makes one 12-inch tart

Caramelized Assorted Root Vegetables

Roasting vegetables is an age-old technique that releases natural sugars. By combining several vegetables and cooking them slowly until they are caramelized and sweet, we take that method one step further and achieve an enticing medley of flavors and textures. You could serve these humble root vegetables alone or with almost any roasted meat, game or poultry. The recipe can be doubled or tripled if necessary, but divide the mixture between several pans so the cooking process is not affected.

4 ounces pearl onions or cipollini onions	2 Yukon Gold or other waxy potatoes
1 head garlic	4 tablespoons extra virgin olive oil, plus more
4 carrots	if needed
2 parsnips	kosher salt and cracked black pepper, to taste
2 turnips	

Preheat oven to 350°F.

Fill a medium-size saucepan ⅔ full with water and set over high heat. Bring water to a boil. Add onions and boil 1 minute or slightly longer to loosen skins. Remove onions with a slotted spoon and let cool. When onions are cool enough to handle, use a paring knife to loosen skins, then slip the skins off and discard. Set onions aside.

Separate the head of garlic into cloves, and lightly smash each clove using the side of a large knife to loosen the skin. Remove the skin and set garlic cloves aside.

Peel carrots and parsnips, then cut into pieces about 2 inches long.

Peel turnips and potatoes, halve lengthwise, then cut each half into 1-inch thick slices. Set all vegetables aside.

In a large, heavy roasting pan or in a large, ovenproof sauté pan, heat olive oil over medium-high heat until almost smoking. Add the vegetables and sauté, stirring, for 5 minutes. Remove the pan from heat and season vegetables with salt and pepper.

Transfer pan with vegetables to oven. Roast, stirring every 5 minutes, until vegetables are lightly browned and tender when pierced with a knife, 30 to 35 minutes. If the vegetables start to stick to the bottom of the pan while roasting, add 1 to 2 tablespoons additional oil and toss again.

Remove pan from oven, taste and adjust seasoning.

ADVANCE PREPARATION: These vegetables are best served immediately after they come out of the oven, but if you prefer, you can roast them ahead and reheat them just before serving.

SUBSTITUTIONS AND OPTIONS: Any root vegetables will work; you may omit or add vegetables to suite your tastes and what is available in the market.

WINE NOTES: For the best pairing, match the wine with main component of the meal. If serving this recipe as a dish by itself, find a white wine with cedar and toast in the finish to match to the caramelization of the vegetables — smoky not oaky. Recommended: 2001 Chateau Montelena, Chardonnay, Napa Valley, California; or 2000 Domaine Laroche, Chablis, Les Blanchots, Burgundy, France.

Makes 4 side dish servings

Winter Squash and Fingerling Potato Hash

A "hash" is a dish of chopped or minced food, usually meat and vegetables that have already been cooked once. The mixture is browned by frying or is reheated in a sauce. This recipe elevates hash from leftover to a vegetarian star in its own right.

We recommend mixing several different varieties of winter squash. Choose a Butternut squash for its sweetness and orange color, a Delicata squash for its creaminess and pale yellow flesh, and a Banana squash for its beautiful golden color.

4 tablespoons butter or olive oil
4 cups winter squash, peeled and cut into small dice
2 cups fingerling potatoes, cut into small dice
1 small yellow onion, cut into small dice
1 small celeriac, peeled and cut into small dice
1 turnip, peeled and cut into small dice
1 tart green apple, peeled and cut into small dice
¼ cup fresh sage leaves, cut into chiffonade
kosher salt and cracked black pepper, to taste

Place a large sauté pan over medium heat. Add the butter or oil. Add the squash, potatoes, onion, celeriac, turnip and apple to the pan. Season with salt and pepper. Cook, stirring occasionally, until the vegetables are soft, translucent and golden brown, about 15 to 20 minutes. The vegetables should develop a crust while retaining their shape. Add the sage, taste and adjust seasoning.

ADVANCE PREPARATION: This hash can be cooked a day ahead and reheated at serving time. Place a tablespoon or two of butter or oil in a large sauté pan over medium heat and cook hash until hot.

SUBSTITUTIONS AND OPTIONS: You can substitute any waxy type potato such as Yukon Gold, Yellow Fin or red.

WINE NOTES: The sweet/tart taste of the apple helps to balance the earthiness of the potatoes and squash. Choose a red wine with some toasty notes to play off of the vegetable crust and a slight herbal note to enhance the sage in the hash. Recommended: 1999 Bodega San Pedro de Yacochuya, Cafayate, Salta Argentina; or 2000 Abacela, Malbec, Umpqua Valley, Oregon.

Makes 8 side dish servings

Parsnip-Potato Rösti

In Switzerland rösti means "crisp and golden." The term refers to foods, usually shredded potatoes, that are sautéed on both sides until crisp and browned. The only thing holding this succulent potato "cake" together is the starch from the potatoes and love. We adore the juxtaposition of its crisp outer crust with a creamy inner texture.

3 parsnips, peeled
4 large russet potatoes, peeled

8 tablespoons butter
kosher salt and cracked black pepper, to taste

Preheat oven to 350°F.

Shred parsnips and potatoes on a box grater or in a food processor fitted with a grating attachment. Melt half of the butter. In a large bowl, combine parsnips, potatoes and melted butter, and season with salt and pepper.

In a 12-inch nonstick pan over medium heat, melt remaining butter. Place parsnip mixture in pan and spread evenly. Cook until bottom is golden brown and a cake is formed. Turn cake over and place pan in oven. Cook approximately 15 minutes or until bottom is golden brown and parsnip mixture is cooked all the way through.

Remove cake from pan and allow rösti to cool slightly. Serve by cutting rösti into wedges.

ADVANCE PREPARATION: The rösti is best served immediately after it comes out of the oven.

SUBSTITUTIONS AND OPTIONS: Any combination of root vegetables will work as long as at least ¼ of the vegetable mixture is potatoes.

BEVERAGE NOTES: Ask anyone of German descent if beer and potatoes go together. Indian Pale Ales have a light amber color, aggressively hoppy flavor and aroma, and a slight malty sweetness that will match with the root vegetables and the crusty texture of this cake. Recommended: Bridgeport Brewing Company, India Pale Ale, Portland, Oregon; or Dogfish Head Craft Brewery, Indian Brown Ale, Lewes, Delaware.

Makes one 12-inch large rösti or 20 two-inch individual röstis

Salads and Soups: To Expand Your Cravings

*"To make a good salad is to be a brilliant diplomat
— to know how much oil to put with one's vinegar."*

— OSCAR WILDE

OUR SELECTION OF SALADS AND SOUPS in this chapter exhibit such a depth of flavor that many qualify as a light meal. Not surprisingly, salads have become more than just fillers or side dishes. They give a cook the opportunity to show off ingredients at the peak of their flavor. Soups offer the chance to match the simple, pure freshness of seasonal ingredients with complex accents and a little technique to form a more intricate dish. Remember that it is about flavor and the blending of ingredients to make a finished dish that is more than the sum of its parts.

Important notes about Salads and Soups

- Make sure your greens are clean and dry. In order to remove excess moisture, we recommend using a salad spinner after lightly soaking or washing your greens in ice water. Vinaigrettes and dressings will not adhere to wet lettuce and the flavor of the salad will be weak and watery.

- Season as you go. Most of the ingredients in these recipes are natural and not purchased pre-made. That said, they require seasoning at each step of the recipe. Salt and pepper the greens, the vinaigrette and the garnish for a particular salad.

- Serve chilled food on chilled plates and hot food on hot plates.

- Taste, taste, taste. Taste the components of the salad or soup separately, including the greens, dressings, and garnishes. Then taste the completed dish to make sure the proper balance has been achieved.

Spring

Dungeness Crab and Fuji Apple Salad with Curry Mayonnaise
White and Green Asparagus Salad with Citrus Vinaigrette
Butterhead Lettuce with Spring Radishes, Peas and White Balsamic Dressing
Roasted Beet and Rhubarb Soup
Chilled Sweet Pea Soup
Spring Vegetable Soup with Garlic Whistles

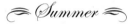

Summer

Heirloom Tomato Salad with Grilled Red Torpedo Onions and Pesto Vinaigrette
Yellow Tomato Gazpacho with Avocado-Tomato Salsa
Roasted Elephant Garlic Soup with Grilled Japanese Eggplant and Basil Purée

Autumn

Fuyu Persimmon and Duck Salad with Hazelnut-Sherry Vinaigrette
Salad of Rabbit Legs Braised in Red Wine with Mustard Greens and Sun-Dried Tart Cherries

Winter

Salad of Winter Greens with Shaved Fennel and Celeriac
Hot-Smoked Salmon Salad with Horseradish-Mustard Dressing
Cream of Potato, Leek and Jerusalem Artichoke Soup with Jerusalem Artichoke Pickles

Dungeness Crab and Fuji Apple Salad with Curry Mayonnaise

This recipe, a delicious, easy-to-make alternative to crab cakes, showcases the sweet-saltiness of the West Coast's favorite, Dungeness crab. The flavor of the dish is pleasantly complex without the recipe being complicated for the cook to make. We can say with assurance that the final result is definitely greater than the sum of its parts.

We've also included our recipe for an elegant, easy curry mayonnaise. If you're in a crunch for time, simply substitute purchased mayonnaise and add curry powder to taste.

CRAB SALAD

1 pound fresh, cleaned Dungeness crab meat, drained of excess water
½ Fuji apple, peeled and cut into small dice
½ stalk celery, cut into small dice
½ European cucumber, seeds removed and cut into small dice
1 shallot, cut into small dice
¼ bulb fennel, cut into small dice

1 teaspoon fennel fronds (tops), finely chopped
1 teaspoon lemon zest, finely chopped
juice of ½ lemon
4 tablespoons curry mayonnaise
kosher salt and white pepper, to taste
1 cup spicy greens (such as arugula, mustard greens or cress)

CURRY MAYONNAISE

1 teaspoon curry powder
1 egg yolk
1 teaspoon lemon juice

½ cup vegetable oil
kosher salt and white pepper, to taste

TO PREPARE THE SALAD: In a large stainless steel bowl, combine crab, apple, celery, cucumber, shallot, fennel and fennel fronds. Add lemon zest, lemon juice and mayonnaise and gently fold ingredients together, trying not to break up the crab too much, until well combined and evenly covered with the mayonnaise. Season with salt and pepper.

TO PREPARE THE MAYONNAISE: Place the curry powder, egg yolk and lemon juice in a small stainless steel bowl. Slowly whisk in oil until ingredients thicken and a creamy consistency is formed. If the consistency is too thick, slowly add small amounts of cold water until the mixture resembles a spreadable mayonnaise. Season with salt and pepper.

TO SERVE: On a chilled plate, place crab salad on a bed of spicy greens and top with a spoonful of remaining curry mayonnaise and sliced European cucumbers.

ADVANCE PREPARATION: The mayonnaise may be made ahead and kept in a sealed container for several days in the refrigerator. This recipe yields more curry mayonnaise than needed for the crab salad, but it's a special treat to have on hand. The extra mayonnaise makes a delicious spread for sandwiches.

SUBSTITUTIONS AND OPTIONS: Jonah crab meat is the best substitute in this recipe because it has a similar sweetness and appearance to Dungeness crab (see page 64). If substituting lump meat from Blue crab, the salad will have a more buttery flavor and a less stringy texture. This is not a bad thing, just different.

You may substitute other sweet apple varieties like Macintosh or Delicious, but do not use tart varieties such as Granny Smith. The additional sourness will throw off the balance of flavors.

WINE NOTES: Choose a Riesling with crisp acidity and hints of green apple and citrus. Recommended: 2001 Holloran Winery, "La Pavillon," Riesling, Willamette Valley, Oregon; or 2002 Pikes, Riesling, Clare Valley, South Australia.

Makes 4 appetizer servings

Crab

The messy cracking and sucking on the shells of boiled whole crab has always created a fun-loving, picnic-like atmosphere at our house. We recommend eating the crab species that are found closest to where you live so they have the greatest chance of being "just caught." Even better, make friends with a crab fisherman and go catch them yourself. Whole, live crab should feel heavy for their size and be extremely active. Cooked whole crabs should be bright red, while cooked crab meat should be white, somewhat translucent and smell and taste of the sea, not of ammonia.

Atlantic Coast

BLUE CRAB

A resident of the Atlantic Ocean from Cape Cod south to Florida and into the Gulf of Mexico, this crab species is most prevalent along the Chesapeake Bay.

Blue crabs appear along the Eastern Shore in the spring just before warm weather begins. Blue crab meat is sold either fresh or pasteurized. After the crabs are steamed, the meat is picked over and then packed into cans, sorted as either "lump meat" (solid, whole lump meat from the body), "flake meat" (small pieces of meat from the body), or "claw meat" (meat from the claws that is usually brown in color). Whole Blue crabs yield approximately 15 percent meat in proportion to their body weight.

Blue crab meat has a sweet, buttery flavor, but its texture depends on what part of the crab the meat comes from.

NOTE: During their normal growing cycle, all crabs must shed their shells. A soft-shell crab is a Blue crab that has shed its hard outer shell. For five to six hours, until its hard outer shell grows back, the crab has only a soft shell. Soft-shell crabs (once cleaned) are usually eaten whole and are never picked over for meat. Soft-shell crabs must be cooked and eaten immediately or the soft shell takes on an undesirable leathery characteristic.

JONAH CRAB

This crab species is native to the Atlantic Ocean from Nova Scotia to Long Island. It appears in clear, open water and is most abundant during the spring.

The Jonah crab, also known as "Peeky Toe crab," is in the same family as the Dungeness crab, but has less meat than its West Coast cousin. We have found that Jonah crab, if available, is the best Atlantic Ocean crab substitute for the Pacific Dungeness crab.

STONE/SPIDER CRAB

Stone crab is a type of Spider crab found in the Atlantic Ocean from North Carolina southward through the Florida Keys and into the Caribbean. Its rock-like, oval-shaped outer shell inspires its name.

Stone crab season begins on October 15 and ends on April 15. To protect the Stone crab species, commercial fishermen are only allowed to keep one claw and release the rest of the catch. This does not harm the crab and in no way inhibits the crab's feeding capabilities, since claws are used for only defensive purposes. It can take up to two years for the crab to regenerate another claw.

Stone Crab claw meat is sweet and delicate with a flavor and texture similar to the claw meat of the Maine lobster. Stone crab claws are usually sold cooked and sometimes frozen.

Pacific Coast

DUNGENESS CRAB

A native of cold Pacific Ocean waters from Mexico to Alaska, the majority of Dungeness crabs are harvested near San Francisco and along the Oregon and Washington coast. The harvest season begins in November and runs through August. Production usually peaks in December through March.

The Dungeness crab fisheries are considered to be well-managed and are one of the world's most sustainable large-scale commercial crab fisheries. To protect the breeding population only male crabs larger than a set minimum size can be harvested and fishing is prohibited during the breeding season. At other specific times of the year only certain Native American populations may harvest crabs. The circular pots used to catch Dungeness crab are highly selective traps, meaning that bycatch is not an issue with these fisheries.

Dungeness crab meat is sold either fresh or frozen (crabs are steamed, the meat is picked and then canned), as "leg meat" (usually the most prized and most expensive), or as "broken leg meat" or "body meat." Whole Dungeness crabs yield approximately 25 percent meat in proportion to body weight.

Dungeness crab meat has a light, slightly nutty flavor and a delicate sweetness.

ALASKA KING CRAB

This crab species inhabits the Pacific Ocean off the coast of British Columbia north through Northern Alaska.

There are three commercial King crab species: Red King crabs, Blue King crabs and Golden King crabs. Each species is harvested from late autumn through early winter.

King crab is sold either whole or as "legs and claws" (individual whole legs and claws that have been separated at the shoulder), "split legs" (individual whole legs that have been split in half lengthwise), "select portions" (the meatiest section of the leg, considered by crab lovers to be the most desirable part of the crab), or "broiler claws" (single claws scored around the top so the shell can be easily removed to expose the tender white meat).

King crab meat is firm and sweet with a bright membrane and white flesh. Red King crab is the most prized of the three species.

SNOW CRAB

A native of the North Pacific, this species is found primarily in Alaskan and Canadian waters. The Alaskan Snow crab harvest usually runs mid January through March. Both the King crab and Snow crab fisheries are closely managed by Alaska Department of Fish and Game. Snow crab meat is a good substitute for King crab, but its subtle flavor is less sweet than King crab and the meat is not as red. ❧

White and Green Asparagus Salad with Citrus Vinaigrette

Asparagus is a member of the lily family, a cousin to onions, leeks, shallots and chives. The large spears come from younger plants (they start producing sprouts in their third year) while small sizes come from older plants or plants that have been planted closer together.

White asparagus is not genetically different from green asparagus. It is any asparagus grown in the dark, under the soil or under an opaque cover. It is more tender, milder, and nuttier in flavor than green asparagus. Stu was first exposed to white asparagus while he was working and traveling in France; it was everywhere in the spring, not just in the fine dining restaurants. With a little detective work, we've found someone growing white asparagus in almost every city where we have worked.

We prefer to use "standard" size or "jumbo" size asparagus for this recipe. Avoid the "pencil" size asparagus as they are too thin and their flavor and texture will get lost in this salad. The key to this recipe is to blanch the asparagus by first cooking the white asparagus and then the green asparagus in salted boiling water. Make sure you "shock" each type of asparagus separately by placing in an ice-water bath to stop the cooking process and set the color.

SALAD

¼ pound all-natural bacon, cut into small dice

12 each white asparagus

12 each green asparagus

4 cups baby spinach leaves, washed

4 ounces citrus vinaigrette

kosher salt and white pepper, to taste

1 teaspoon pink peppercorns, crushed (optional)

CITRUS VINAIGRETTE

1 shallot, finely diced

1 fresh small hot red chili, seeded and finely diced or ½ teaspoon hot red chili flakes

1 tablespoon sugar

1 tablespoon tomato paste

2 tablespoons orange juice, freshly squeezed

2 tablespoons lemon juice, freshly squeezed

2 tablespoons Moro orange (blood orange) juice, freshly squeezed

¾ cup vegetable oil

kosher salt and white pepper, to taste

Makes approximately 1 cup

TO PREPARE THE SALAD: Render the bacon by placing it in a medium-size sauté pan over medium heat and cook, stirring frequently, about 12 to 15 minutes, until crisp. Remove bacon and drain on paper towels.

Clean both white and green asparagus by trimming the ends, leaving each stalk about 4 to 5 inches long. Using a vegetable peeler, peel the bottom of the asparagus stalks to form even-shaped spears.

NOTE: Save the ends of the asparagus to make the Asparagus Custard recipe (see page 33).

Fill a large, stainless steel pot, three quarters full with salted water and bring to a boil. Add the white asparagus and cook until the stalks can easily be pierced with a point of a knife. Plunge the asparagus into an ice-water bath. When cold, drain and pat dry. Repeat the process with the green asparagus and reserve.

In a large bowl, combine spinach and bacon. Season with salt and pepper. Drizzle 2 ounces of vinaigrette over and toss until well combined and the greens are evenly covered.

TO PREPARE THE VINAIGRETTE: Combine all ingredients, except vegetable oil, in a stainless steel saucepan. Bring to boil, reduce to a simmer and simmer until liquid is reduced by half, about 3 to 5 minutes. Allow liquid to cool slightly.

Place liquid in a blender. With blender running, add vegetable oil in a slow stream and blend until emulsified. Taste and adjust seasoning.

TO SERVE: In the center of each plate alternately arrange three asparagus spears of each color to form a "Lincoln Log" triangle. Place spinach-bacon mixture in the center of the triangle. Drizzle the remaining 2 ounces of vinaigrette around the plate and sprinkle with crushed pink peppercorns.

ADVANCE PREPARATION: You may make this dressing up to two weeks ahead and store it in a sealed container in the refrigerator. The bacon can be rendered several days before serving. Let it return to room temperature before adding to the salad. The asparagus can be blanched and chilled a day ahead.

SUBSTITUTIONS AND OPTIONS: If you cannot find white asparagus, use all green asparagus. Substitute regular Valencia oranges for the Moro oranges. Note that pink peppercorns are not true peppercorns (dried berries of the *Piper nigrum* plant), but are actually dried berries from the *Baies rose* plant. They are optional, but will add a sweet, aromatic and subtle juniper flavor to the dish. If you cannot find them, substitute crushed juniper berries.

WINE NOTES: Asparagus has a reputation for being a wine killer. However, a white wine with tangy citrus notes, a creamy texture and finished with spice will round out the bacon and citrus flavors in the salad. Recommended: For a sparkling wine try NV Pacific Echo, Brut, Medocino County, California; or for a still wine try 2001 René & Vincent Dauvissat, Chablis Séchet, Burgundy, France.

Makes 4 appetizer servings

Butterhead Lettuce with Spring Radishes and Peas with White Balsamic Dressing

This is a "knife and fork" salad with a "creamy" style dressing. Think of it as a flavorful, more sophisticated spring version of the truck stop favorite iceberg lettuce salad with ranch dressing. The white balsamic dressing is a staple at the restaurant. Since this recipe makes more dressing than you need, consider sharing some with friends or use it as dip for raw vegetables.

WHITE BALSAMIC DRESSING

Makes approximately 2 cups

¼ pound snow or snap peas, cleaned

¼ pound English peas, removed from pod

6 each radishes, thinly sliced

2 heads Butterhead or other head lettuce such as Bibb or Boston

4 ounces white balsamic dressing

¼ cup sliced almonds, toasted

kosher salt and cracked black pepper, to taste

SALAD

2 egg yolks

1 shallot, finely diced

1 teaspoon kosher salt

¼ teaspoon white pepper

¾ cup extra virgin olive oil

¾ cup vegetable oil

½ cup white balsamic vinegar

TO PREPARE THE DRESSING: Mix together the olive oil and vegetable oil. In the bowl of an electric mixer with a whip attachment, combine the egg yolks, shallot, salt and pepper. On medium speed whip the egg mixture and then slowly add half the oil mixture, a little at a time. When the mixture begins to resemble a thick mayonnaise add a little of the vinegar. Continue slowly adding oil and then vinegar until all the liquids have been fully incorporated. Taste and adjust seasoning.

TO PREPARE THE SALAD: Fill a large, stainless steel pot, ¾ three quarters full with salted water and bring to a boil. Add the snow peas and cook until tender. Plunge the peas into an ice-water bath. When cold, drain and pat dry. Repeat the process with the English peas and reserve.

In a large bowl, combine both peas and radishes. Season with salt and pepper. Drizzle two tablespoons of dressing over and toss until well combined and the vegetables are evenly covered.

TO SERVE: In the center of each plate, place half a head of Butterhead lettuce. Drizzle remaining vinaigrette over lettuce. Place peas over lettuce and sprinkle almonds on top and around. Serve with additional dressing and additional fresh cracked black pepper.

ADVANCE PREPARATION: You may make the dressing up to one week ahead and store it in a sealed container in the refrigerator. The peas can be blanched and chilled earlier in the day but they will begin to lose their color if prepared a day or more ahead.

SUBSTITUTIONS AND OPTIONS: White balsamic vinegar is processed differently than regular balsamic vinegar, where the vinegar "must" is caramelized during processing, thus producing a rich, golden color. White balsamic is used for aesthetic reasons, so as not to color sauces and dressings. Substitute white wine vinegar or champagne vinegar.

WINE NOTES: The creamy-style dressing, buttery lettuce and almonds sing out for a rich, creamy Chardonnay with nutty flavors and a juicy finish. Recommended: 2001 Hamilton Russell, Walker Bay, Chardonnay, Overberg South Africa; or 2001 Landmark, Overlook, Chardonnay, Sonoma, California.

Makes 4 appetizer servings

Oddball Heirlooms:

Kris Hoien of Spirit Ranch

"I like the oddball stuff," says Kris Hoien, who grows 40 different varieties of vegetables and salad greens, mostly heirloom varieties gleaned from a variety of seed catalogs or carried over from the previous year. "I'm always searching for antique tomatoes and beans no one's heard of."

Her 44-acre farmstead lies in a beautiful, partially forested canyon running alongside Yale Creek due west of Jacksonville, Oregon. On an August afternoon, five acres of terraced hillside are lush with rust and gold sunflowers standing tall to shade peppers and Japanese eggplant. Golden corn tassels shimmer in a warm breeze while squash and melon plants sprawl lazily in the heat. Heirloom tomatoes serve as red and yellow punctuation marks, and spiky gray-green garlic and onion spears crisscross loam earth. All plants were started from seed in her greenhouse.

When Kris shows up at the kitchen door to deliver her produce we have the surprise of opening the box to whatever veggies are ripe. One week it's pristine white cauliflower, the next a bonanza of tomatoes: Striped Purple, Brandywine, Sweet 100's, or another exotic heirloom variety. Another week may bring a medley of summer beans. Kris is one of a handful of farmers who will grow produce and herbs especially for us. Who else would want Tongue of Fire beans and cardoons along with carrots and celery?

Kris has been farming for 10 years and Spirit Ranch is one of the Rogue Valley's original CSA (Community Supported Agriculture) farms. She began with 28 members and now supplies 50 shareholders, plus several local restaurants and growers' markets. Along with vegetables, she also raises egg-laying chickens, broiler chickens, pasture-raised beef, flowers for bouquets and shiitake mushrooms.

"I like the idea of CSA farms, the concept of people being connected to a farm," Kris says when talking about the program. "It's like Christmas for a lot of subscribers when we deliver their box each week."

On one of our first spring visits to Spirit Ranch, Kris gave us a tour of her greenhouse. She mentioned she'd started some head lettuce, but said, "I know you usually like those individual small leaf varieties." The minute we laid eyes on her small Butterhead lettuces, we knew we'd found the perfect "knife and fork salad." We claimed every succession of lettuces she had that spring and almost cried when the first hot weather arrived. ❧

Roasted Beet and Rhubarb Soup

Beets are not just for borscht and rhubarb is not just for dessert. The rhubarb in this recipe is used to harmonize with the other flavors in this soup and to round out the acidity in the wine and vinegar. Even if you are not a beet fan, we believe the color and flavor of this soup will make you a convert.

6 large red beets, scrubbed, tops removed
2 stalks rhubarb, leaves removed, roughly chopped
1 medium yellow onion, roughly chopped
2 teaspoons garlic, roughly chopped
1 teaspoon fresh ginger root, peeled and roughly chopped

½ cup red wine
2 tablespoons balsamic vinegar
8 cups water, vegetable stock or chicken stock
1 bay leaf
kosher salt and white pepper, to taste

Preheat oven to 350°F.

Wrap beets in aluminum foil and place in oven. Roast for approximately one hour or until beets are easily pierced with a knife. Remove from the oven, unwrap foil and wait until cool enough to handle, then rub off the peel. Roughly chop 5 of the beets for the soup and cut the one remaining beet into matchstick-size pieces to use for garnish. In a large stock pot, place roasted beets, rhubarb, onion, garlic, ginger, red wine and balsamic vinegar. Bring to a boil. Reduce heat and simmer until wine-vinegar mixture is reduced by half. Add the water or stock, bay leaf, salt and pepper and simmer, approximately 45 minutes to 1 hour or until vegetables are tender.

Remove bay leaf. Working in batches, purée soup in a blender until smooth. If soup is too thick, add hot water or stock until the desired consistency is achieved. Before serving, taste and adjust seasoning.

NOTE: Be careful when blending this soup. Hot liquids have a tendency to "explode" out of a blender when being puréed. We recommend using an immersion-type hand blender. This allows you to bring the blender to the soup instead of the soup to the blender.

TO SERVE: Pour soup into warm bowls. Place the reserved matchstick-size beets in the center of each bowl and serve with toasted, sliced baguette rounds rubbed with olive oil and garlic.

ADVANCE PREPARATION: As with many of our soups, the flavors become better and more complex if the soup is made several days ahead and allowed to rest in the refrigerator.

SUBSTITUTIONS AND OPTIONS: This soup can be served hot or cold.

WINE NOTES: Choose a wine with modest tannins, slight dark berry flavors and a little acidity. Recommended: 1999 Edgefield, Alder Ridge Vineyard, Cabernet Sauvignon, Columbia Valley, Oregon; or 2002 Domaine Cuvée Classique, Rosé, Bandol, France.

Makes 6 appetizer servings, approximately 1 quart

Chilled Sweet Pea Soup

This soup is basically a very flavorful chilled pea juice — very simple and very refreshing. The success of this dish rests with the farmer; the sweeter the pea, the better the flavor. If you have a juice extractor, then omit the puréeing and straining step. Make sure you still follow the blanching step to brighten and set the color of the vegetables and to take away the slightly raw taste.

2 pounds English peas in the pod (approximately 5 cups)

1 bunch green onions or spring onions with tops, roughly chopped

½ cup mint leaves

½ cup lemon balm leaves (optional)

juice of half a lemon

2 dashes Tabasco Sauce (approximately ½ teaspoon)

kosher salt and white pepper, to taste

½ cup English peas, removed from pod — used for garnish

2 ounces crème fraîche or sour cream (see page 15)

6 pea shoots (optional)

Fill a large, stainless steel pot, three quarters full with salted water and bring to a boil. Add the peas and cook for 30 seconds. Plunge the peas into an ice-water bath. When cold, drain and pat dry. Repeat the process with the green onions, mint and lemon balm. Repeat the same process for the peas that were removed from the pod to be used for garnish in the soup. Important: Save the ice-water bath.

Working in batches, purée soup in a blender using enough reserved ice-water until the mixture is smooth. Altogether, the soup will use approximately 5 cups of ice-water. Strain mixture through a fine mesh strainer by pressing the solids with a wooden spoon in order to extract as much liquid as possible. Add the lemon juice and Tabasco. Season with salt and pepper. Refrigerate two hours.

Before serving, taste and adjust seasoning.

TO SERVE: Pour soup into chilled bowls. Add reserved peas for garnish. Place a dollop of crème fraîche in the center of the soup and top with pea shoots.

ADVANCE PREPARATION: This soup should be made and served on the same day. Soups, in general, will taste better given a day to oxidize in the refrigerator; however, this soup will actually lose the desirable bright green color and flavor.

SUBSTITUTIONS AND OPTIONS: You may substitute sugar snap peas or snow peas for the English peas. The soup can be served cold or hot, but we prefer the refreshing crispness of the chilled version. The Avocado-Tomato Salsa recipe included in the Yellow Tomato Gazpacho recipe also makes a wonderful addition (see page 80).

WINE NOTES: The herbal flavor of this soup needs a well-balanced white wine with intense floral and spicy aromas and a touch of citrus. Recommended: 2000 Hoodsport Winery, Gewürztraminer, Washington; or 2002 Navarro, Old Vine Cuvée, Chenin Blanc, Mendocino, California.

Makes 6 appetizer servings, approximately 1 quart

Spring Vegetable Soup
with Garlic Whistles

We love to make this simple, fresh-tasting soup to welcome spring. You can easily make this soup year-round by changing the ingredients based on what is in season and your whim. Let the vegetable stock act as the neutral base and build flavors around the seasonal vegetables that suit your taste. We have included a recipe for roasted vegetable stock in the Basics section, but you can use a purchased natural vegetable stock or broth.

Garlic whistles or garlic scapes are the looping flower tops of the hard stem garlic plant before they bloom. They are usually available only in late May through early June. Garlic whistles are much more mild-flavored than regular garlic bulbs, imparting just a hint of garlic to your dish. They can be treated like asparagus and steamed or blanched, or treated like a green onion and diced, shaved or sliced raw.

½ cup English peas removed from the pod

6 spears standard-size green asparagus spears, cut into ½-inch pieces

6 garlic whistles, cut into ½-inch pieces or use 1 teaspoon finely minced garlic

6 baby carrots, cut in half lengthwise or ½ cup peeled carrots, julienned

1½ quarts vegetable stock (see page 19)

½ cup hardy spring greens, stems removed, roughly chopped

6 spring onions, ends trimmed, cut in half lengthwise

2 Roma tomatoes, peeled, seeded and cut into ¼-inch dice

kosher salt and white pepper, to taste

1 tablespoon chopped savory herbs (parsley, thyme, oregano and sage)

In a large stainless steel stock pot, add the vegetable stock and bring to a boil. Reduce to a simmer. Add the peas, asparagus, garlic whistles and carrots to the simmering stock. Cook 4 to 5 minutes until the vegetables are just tender. Add the greens, spring onions and tomatoes. Season with salt and pepper.

TO SERVE: Pour soup into warm bowls. Sprinkle the chopped herbs on top of each bowl.

ADVANCE PREPARATION: The finished soup should be put together just prior to serving. The vegetable stock base can be made up to a week ahead and refrigerated, or frozen up to a month ahead.

SUBSTITUTIONS AND OPTIONS: Select the vegetables based on what looks the best and has the best flavor in your market or garden. Use summer squash, corn, bell peppers and basil in the summer months or use autumn mushrooms, potatoes and roots in the autumn months.

Cooked pasta, such as *farfalle* (butterflies or bow ties), *conchigliette* (small shells) or *orecchiette* (little ears) can be added if you want to include a starch. For an elegant presentation, add shaved summer or winter black truffles (Oregon, French or Italian truffles) and a splash of truffle oil just prior to serving.

BEVERAGE NOTES: The beverage match will change based on the vegetables included. The spring version calls for a crisp, refreshing balanced wine or a beer with a hint of citrus. Recommended: 2002 Brancott, Marlborough Reserve, Sauvignon Blanc, New Zealand; or 2001 Mason, Sauvignon Blanc, Napa, California; or Blue Star Great American Wheat Beer, North Coast Brewing Company, Fort Bragg, California; or Samuel Adams Weiss Bier, Boston Beer Company, Boston, Massachusetts.

Makes 6 appetizer servings, approximately 1½ quarts

Heirloom Tomatoes

They are round, oval, torpedo and squat-shaped. They are found in every color of the rainbow including yellow, red, orange, green, white and striped. They are as small as grapes and as large as baseballs. They don't taste like cardboard, water or potatoes. They are a fruit — not a vegetable — and a relative of the eggplant and the pepper. They are thin skinned, very juicy, misshapen, split/crack/break easily, taste great, but are often less than perfect in appearance. "They" are heirloom tomatoes.

Modern tomato hybrids found in most supermarkets were developed to meet marketers' demands — not necessarily consumers' preference — for uniform appearance, shelf life, and the ability to withstand mechanical harvesting, long storage and shipment. Flavor was sacrificed and we were the losers. But many

early tomato varieties survived, in a dazzling range of colors, shapes and flavors, handed down as "heirlooms" by dedicated growers raising old varieties in home gardens and on small family farms.

Heirloom produce refers not to a specific age or variety, but to varieties grown from seeds that are not sterile and will reproduce true to type. That's where the surprise of color and size comes into play. Heirloom varieties usually are approximately fifty years old (although no specific age is required to qualify) and generally produce very flavorful offerings. Growing heirloom tomatoes is a labor of love and farmers are known to save heirloom seeds from year to year and from generation to generation. In contrast, anyone growing the hybrid varieties, typically sold in supermarkets, needs to purchase seeds each year.

Our favorite part of dealing with heirloom produce varieties is the flavor, of course. But we find the names of these old varieties of tomatoes almost as exciting. How could anyone resist names like Nebraska Wedding Tomato, Yellow Taxi, Cheetam's Potato Leaf, Djena Lee's Golden Girl, Green Zebra, Cherokee Purple, Lemon Boys or Tommy Toe? Different heirloom tomato varieties will grow better in different climate zones. Thus, not all heirlooms will be available everywhere in the country. If you think you want to grow some of these wonderful tomatoes, ask your neighbors, go to a farmer's market, or ask your local nursery for recommendations.

Tomatoes mature from the bottom of the plant upward so pick from the bottom first. If you're buying at the market, select tomatoes that have a deep color and a subtle texture when lightly squeezed. Avoid bruised, soft or cracked fruits. Don't judge ripeness by color alone, either. Look for rich smell, texture and of course taste. Your nose will know.

If you want to keep that rich taste and texture, never store tomatoes in the refrigerator. The cold temperature will cause their metabolic rate to slow and all ripening to stop, and the delicate flavors will start to decline.

A Short List of Our Favorite Heirloom Tomato Varieties

ARKANSAS TRAVELER — These are medium-sized, light red or dark pink tomatoes.

BLACK KRIM — Named for the island of Krim in the Black Sea, these Russian heirloom tomatoes are slightly flattened, 4-inch to 6-inch globes with dark, greenish-black shoulders that can turn almost chocolate-black with enough heat and sun.

BRANDYWINE — This pink-skinned tomato is considered by many to be the best tasting of all tomatoes.

CHEROKEE PURPLE — Originally raised by the Cherokee Indian tribe, these tomatoes have incredible flavor. The plants are heat tolerant and vigorous, and produce medium-size to large meaty tomatoes with a flattened shape. The tomato's color has been described as dusky pink with dark shoulders, purple, and pinkish brown with the interior ranging from purple to brownish red.

EVA PURPLE BALL — This variety consistently shows up on lists of the best heirloom tomatoes because of its excellent disease resistance and flavor. The tomatoes are small to medium-size with a purple or pink cast.

GREEN ZEBRA — These small to medium-size tomatoes, in various shades of yellow to yellowish-green stripes, have firm flesh and a sweet zingy flavor.

JAUNE FLAMMEE — These beautiful apricot-shaped tomatoes are golden-yellow with a contrasting reddish interior and excellent flavor.

ROSE — This is a wonderful variety, often compared to Brandywine because of its excellent flavor, with a large meaty fruit and a deep pink color.

TASTY EVERGREEN — Aptly named, this variety has flesh and gel that remain green inside when ripe, and has a strong, sweet flavor. The skin of these medium-size to large tomatoes ripens from green to light yellow-brown.

TOMMY TOE — Each plant produces hundreds of apricot-sized fruits over a long season.

YELLOW TAXI — These baseball-sized, lemon yellow tomatoes are meaty and weigh between four and six ounces and ounces. The fruits are attractive, sweet-flavored, low in acid and easy to grow. ❧

Heirloom Tomato Salad
with Grilled Red Torpedo Onions and Pesto Vinaigrette

Heirloom tomatoes have enough flavor to be a light appetizer on their own. All you need to do is slice and sprinkle them with a little sea salt. One of Mary's earliest memories is eating a plate of just picked, still warm from the sun heirloom tomatoes from her family's garden.

This fruit salad (remember tomatoes are a fruit) showcases what we think summer is all about: intense flavor, colorful ingredients and playful flavor combinations. The resulting tastes are refreshing and complex without being pretentious or difficult to make. Find as many different heirloom tomatoes as possible. The range of flavors and textures will surprise you.

SALAD

2 red Torpedo onions, peeled, cut into half moons and thinly sliced

¼ cup olive oil

1 pound various heirloom tomatoes (approximately 4 to 6 tomatoes)

kosher salt or coarse sea salt and cracked black pepper, to taste

¼ cup pesto vinaigrette

basil leaves for garnish

PESTO VINAIGRETTE

1 clove garlic, peeled

kosher salt, to taste

¼ cup toasted pine nuts (optional)

2 cups fresh basil leaves, stems removed

4 tablespoons red wine vinegar

¾ cup extra virgin olive oil

cracked black pepper, to taste

Makes approximately 1 cup

TO PREPARE THE SALAD: Preheat a grill.

Toss the onions in a bowl with the oil and season with salt and pepper. Remove the cores from the tomatoes and cut them in various shapes and sizes (wedges, round slices, half-moons, etc.), and reserve. Place onions on the grill over medium heat and grill until the onions are tender and caramelized, about 10 minutes.

TO PREPARE THE VINAIGRETTE: In the bowl of a food processor, purée garlic and salt until a paste is formed. Add pine nuts and basil and process until a fine paste is formed. With motor running, add vinegar and then slowly add oil in a thin stream until the mixture is emulsified. Taste and adjust seasoning.

TO SERVE: Arrange the tomatoes on plates. Season with salt and pepper. Place several slices of grilled onions on top of the tomatoes and drizzle with pesto vinaigrette. Arrange several basil leaves on and around tomatoes and sprinkle with additional cracked black pepper.

ADVANCE PREPARATION: The onions can be grilled ahead of time and refrigerated. Bring them to room temperature before adding to the salad. Don't store tomatoes in the refrigerator as this will make their texture grainy and mealy, and they'll lose flavor. As with most produce, buy only what you need. Store tomatoes on the counter between 55°F and 70°F.

SUBSTITUTIONS AND OPTIONS: We prefer Tropea Red Torpedo onions because they are mild with a burst of onion flavor. Tropea is a town in the Italian province of Calabria facing the Tyrrenian Sea and is famous for its pungent, football-shaped, red onion. Any medium-sized red onion can be substituted for the Red Torpedo onions.

Any ripe, flavorful tomato can be used in this recipe, but the taste of this dish rests on the shoulders of the farmer.

Other herbs can easily be substituted for the basil in the pesto vinaigrette. A good rule to follow is to use half parsley leaves and half other herbs; otherwise the pesto will overpower the delicate sweetness of the tomatoes.

WINE NOTES: Tomatoes are difficult to pair with wine. A New Zealand-style Sauvignon Blanc or Fumé Blanc with slightly tart citrus, pepper, grass and mineral flavors or a sparkling dry rosé will cut through the acidity of the tomatoes. Recommended: 2002 Thornbury, Sauvignon Blanc, Marlborough, New Zealand. For something that connotes elegance try a 1998 Schramberg, Sparkling Brut Rosé, Napa Valley, California.

Makes 4 appetizer servings

Yellow Tomato Gazpacho
with Avocado-Tomato Salsa

One bright August morning Steve Florin of Dancing Bear Farm dropped off the season's first heirloom tomatoes. As brilliant in color as sunshine, not only were these tomatoes exploding with true tomato flavor, they inspired a welcome diversion when the thermometer outside was pushing 100°F. How fast can a chef think "cold soup?"

Traditional gazpacho is a Spanish chilled soup from Andalusia using red tomatoes and soaked bread. Our version uses Yellow Taxi tomatoes and omits the bread. A Yellow Taxi tomato is a low-acid, meaty, sweet heirloom slicing tomato, with a lemon-yellow skin. It is fairly easy to grow in cooler climates.

YELLOW TOMATO GAZPACHO

6 Yellow Taxi tomatoes or other yellow heirloom tomatoes, ripe

2 cloves garlic, peeled

1 English or regular waxy cucumber, peeled, seeded and cut into large pieces

1 yellow pepper, seeded and cut into large pieces

1 red onion, cut into large pieces

½ small hot red chili, seeded, cut into large pieces or to taste

¼ cup red wine vinegar

3 ounces extra virgin olive oil

kosher salt and white pepper, to taste

4 each red and yellow cherry tomatoes, cut in half, for garnish

AVOCADO-TOMATO SALSA

2 avocados, preferably Haas, flesh cut into small dice

1 small hot red chili, seeded, cut into small dice

1 small red onion, cut into small dice

1 red heirloom slicing tomato, peeled, seeded and diced

1 tablespoon cilantro, finely chopped

juice of one lime

¼ cup extra virgin olive oil

kosher salt and cracked black pepper, to taste

TO PREPARE THE SOUP: Working in batches, purée all ingredients, except for the cherry tomatoes, in a blender until smooth. Strain mixture through a fine mesh strainer into another bowl by pressing the solids with a wooden spoon in order to extract as much liquid as possible. Season with salt and pepper. Refrigerate two hours or overnight.

Before serving, taste and adjust seasoning.

TO PREPARE THE SALSA: Combine all ingredients in a stainless steel bowl and refrigerate at least 20 minutes.

TO SERVE: Place salsa in the center of chilled soup bowls. Ladle soup around the salsa and garnish with red and yellow cherry tomatoes halves.

ADVANCE PREPARATION: We recommend making this soup a day ahead. The flavors are better and more complex given a day of rest in the refrigerator.

SUBSTITUTIONS AND OPTIONS: This soup can be made with either red or yellow tomatoes as long as they are ripe. The flavor of the soup depends entirely on the taste of the tomatoes.

Ripe tomatillos can be substituted for the heirloom tomatoes in the salsa. They will add a citrus flavor element that will balance the richness of the avocado.

WINE NOTES: Because we recommend using low-acid tomatoes, this soup is very wine-friendly. Try a Napa Valley Sauvignon Blanc or a dry Austrian-style Riesling with a hint of fruit and enough acid to hold up to the tomatoes. Recommended: 2002 Voss, Sauvignon Blanc, Napa Valley, California; or 2000 Chateau St. Michelle-Dr. Loosen, Eroica, Riesling, Columbia Valley, Washington.

Makes 4 appetizer servings, approximately 3 cups

Broccoli Lover Grows Up, Becomes Farmer:

Steve Florin of Dancing Bear Farm

It was all because of fennel. "When a farmer shows up at your back door bearing glorious green-white fennel bulbs, you don't turn him away," Stu says. The farmer was Steve Florin, a teddy bear of a man with a graying beard and ready smile. "Stu lit up when he tasted the fennel!," Steve tells about that first meeting. "Most stuff chefs get is three to four days old. This was barely 24 hours out of the garden."

That serendipitous fennel relationship has evolved and now includes peppers, tomatoes, yellow snap beans, chicory, beets, Jerusalem artichokes, nine varieties of tomatoes, watermelon, strawberries, arugula blossoms, potatoes and more — a veritable seed catalog of produce. Add eggs from chickens running merrily around four acres of pasture and it's bliss for the Peerless pastry cook. It all comes from Dancing Bear Farm in Williams, in the beautiful Applegate Valley east of Medford.

Although he grew up in the suburbs of Chicago, Steve says, "I've always been a hobbyist farmer. I was one of the few kids who liked asparagus and broccoli." He also has degrees in environmental engineering and works in a medical lab.

Steve made the leap from avocation to genuine farmer after he found the right land: 20 acres with water rights and usable buildings including a trailer and a 1,000-square-foot barn. It was a common case of over-grazed pasture in poor shape; once part of a large dairy farm, the land had been used for haying, sheep grazing and cattle. After two years of intensively reworking the soil, building an 800-square-foot greenhouse, and installing an irrigation system, Steve planted his first crops on a rejuvenated five acres. He was certified organic by Oregon Tilth from day one.

"The difference between gardening and farming is that you can spend all day taking care of a garden when it's 30 feet, but you can't take all day on 30 feet when you have 5 acres," says Steve. "It's been a learning experience, that's certain," says Steve. "But I've believed for a long time that flavor and taste are key, and that it's possible to eat seasonally and eat very well. This farm proves it."

Here's to beliefs becoming reality. The back door at The Peerless will always be open whenever the fennel farmer comes to call. ❧

Roasted Elephant Garlic Soup
with Grilled Japanese Eggplant and Basil Purée

Elephant garlic is actually closely related to the leek and thought by some to be the wild ancestor of the leek. The bulbs are very large and can weigh more than a pound. They have a flavor that is milder than regular garlic and develops a rich sweetness when roasted.

4 heads elephant garlic
¼ cup olive oil
4 leeks (white part only), roughly chopped
1 medium yellow onion, roughly chopped
1 russet potato, peeled and roughly chopped

½ cup white wine
8 cups chicken stock, vegetable stock or water
kosher salt and white pepper, to taste
1 Japanese eggplant, thinly sliced and grilled
¼ cup basil purée (see page 199)

Preheat oven to 350°F.

Cut off top ¼ inch of each garlic head. Place garlic heads in small shallow baking dish and drizzle oil over. Bake until golden, about 1 hour. Cool slightly.

Press individual garlic cloves between thumb and finger to release cloves. In a large sauce pan, place garlic, leeks, onion, potato and wine. Bring the wine to a boil, reduce to a simmer and cook until the wine is reduced by half its volume. Add the stock or water, salt and pepper and simmer 30 minutes, stirring occasionally. Cool slightly.

Working in batches, purée the ingredients in a blender until smooth. If soup is too thick, thin by adding additional stock or water. Taste and adjust seasoning.

TO SERVE: Ladle soup into warm bowls. Place grilled eggplant in the center of each bowl and top with basil purée.

ADVANCE PREPARATION: As with many of our soups, the flavors become better and more complex if the soup is made several days ahead of time and given a day of rest in the refrigerator.

SUBSTITUTIONS AND OPTIONS: You can substitute regular hard neck garlic for the elephant garlic, but the final soup will have a slightly more sharp and pungent flavor. This soup can be served hot or cold. Cream can be added, but we feel this puréed soup already has a cream-like consistency and richness without the added fat. The eggplant and basil add an additional herbal smokiness that balances the sweetness and creaminess of the garlic.

WINE NOTES: The rich roasted sweetness and creaminess of the roasted garlic requires a wine with the similar characteristics and a kiss of oak. Recommended: 2000 Adea, Chardonnay, Willamette Valley, Oregon; or 2000 Whiterock, Organic Chardonnay, Napa Valley, California.

Makes 6 appetizer servings, approximately 1 quart

Fuyu Persimmon and Duck Salad
with Hazelnut-Sherry Vinaigrette

What in the world is a Fuyu persimmon? The Fuyu is a non-astringent persimmon variety. It is sweet and delicious when it becomes orange to orange-red in color and is still firm. The Native American persimmon grown in the southern US and the more common pointed Hachiya persimmon are astringent varieties that do not lose their bitterness until the fruit becomes soft.

Why do we care? Ripe Hachiya persimmons are great for making cooked dishes such as chutneys, relishes or even pies. The Fuyu persimmon is perfect for this salad because its sweetness will cut through and balance the richness of the duck while maintaining its crisp texture.

DUCK

2 duck breasts, boneless, skin-on, trimmed of excess fat

kosher salt and cracked black pepper, to taste

HAZELNUT-SHERRY VINAIGRETTE AND SALAD

Makes approximately 1 cup

4 tablespoons sherry vinegar

kosher salt and black pepper, to taste

6 tablespoons hazelnut oil

6 tablespoons vegetable oil

3 cups spicy baby greens

2 Fuyu persimmons, cut in half and then cut into wedges

1 cup hazelnut-sherry vinaigrette

¼ cup toasted hazelnuts, roughly chopped

TO PREPARE THE DUCK: Place a large, cast-iron pan over medium heat. Score the duck breasts by cutting through the skin in a criss-cross pattern without cutting the meat. Season the breasts with salt and pepper. Place duck breasts, skin side down in the hot pan. Cook the breasts until the fat has been rendered and the skin is crisp, about 10 to 15 minutes. Constantly drain the fat from the pan as it renders out of the skin. Turn the breasts over onto the meat side and cook an additional 5 minutes or until the meat is red but is warm on the inside.

Remove the duck from the pan and drain on paper towels. Let the duck breasts rest for at least 5 minutes before slicing.

TO PREPARE THE VINAIGRETTE AND SALAD: Place the sherry vinegar, salt and pepper in a small stainless steel bowl. Slowly drizzle in hazelnut oil and vegetable oil, whisking constantly, until ingredients are combined. Taste and adjust seasoning.

Place the greens in a medium-size stainless steel bowl. Gently toss the greens with half of the vinaigrette. Season with salt and pepper.

TO SERVE: Place the duck breasts skin-side down on a cutting board. Cutting in the opposite direction from the grain of the meat, cut each breast into thin slices. Place a quarter of the greens in the center of each plate. Place several wedges of persimmon on one side of the watercress. Place several slices of duck breast on the opposite side of the persimmons. Sprinkle hazelnuts over the greens and drizzle remaining vinaigrette around the plate.

ADVANCE PREPARATION: The duck breast can be sautéed ahead of time and served chilled, if you prefer.

SUBSTITUTIONS AND OPTIONS: Brown Turkey figs or Black Mission figs make a wonderful sweet, fruity addition to this salad. For the duck breast, we recommend using a Margret duck breast from a female Muscovy duck. Long Island (Pekin) or Moulard duck breast will also work for this recipe, but we believe the Muscovy has better flavor and texture. Muscovy breast meat is extremely lean and the skin of this duck variety has 50 percent less fat than the Moulard or Pekin duck varieties.

To cook the duck, we recommend using a cast-iron pan because of its even heating properties and its virtually indestructible nature. If you use an aluminum or stainless steel sauté pan, watch the duck breasts carefully to make sure their skin is being evenly rendered.

You may substitute smoked duck breasts purchased from specialty game suppliers (see Sourcese and Information section) for the cooked duck.

WINE NOTES: A toasty, oaky-style Chardonnay from California or a Burgundy-style Pinot Noir from Oregon will match the accompanying flavors in the salad without getting lost behind the richness of the duck. Recommended: 2001 Shafer, Red Shoulder Ranch, Chardonnay, Carneros, California; or 2001 McKinley, "Special Selection," Pinot Noir, Willamette Valley, Oregon. For a sexier match try a dry sherry with nutty, caramelized flavors and a clean, long finish: Berrys', Fine Dry Oloroso Sherry, Spain.

Makes 4 appetizer servings

Salad of Rabbit Legs Braised in Red Wine
with Mustard Greens and Sun-Dried Tart Cherries

Rabbit is a delicious, low-fat alternative to chicken or other poultry. Rabbit is slightly sweet, more flavorful than poultry, and extremely versatile. Make sure you purchase farmed rabbit raised in a controlled environment without growth hormones or antibiotics.

Note that because rabbit is very lean, it has a tendency to dry out if improperly cooked. Braising will both protect the meat and impart multiple layers of flavor.

BRAISED RABBIT LEGS

6 rabbit hindquarters, thigh bone removed
all-purpose flour, for dusting
kosher salt and white pepper, to taste
3 tablespoons vegetable oil
1 small onion, cut into small dice
1 carrot, cut into small dice
1 stalk celery, cut into small dice
3 cloves garlic, peeled

1 tablespoon sun-dried tart cherries
1 herb sachet (cheesecloth bag or coffee filter made into a bag containing 1 bay leaf, 1 tablespoon black peppercorns & 1 sprig fresh thyme)
rabbit bones, roasted, if available
1 cup red wine (use wine from soaking cherries from salad recipe below)
2 cups brown chicken stock or water

DRESSING

2 tablespoons reduced rabbit braising liquid from above, room temperature
1 tablespoon sherry vinegar

3 tablespoons extra virgin olive oil
1 each shallot, roughly chopped
kosher salt and black pepper, to taste

SALAD

¼ pound shiitake mushrooms, about 18 mushrooms, stems removed (note: the stems can be added to the vegetable mixture used for braising the rabbit legs)
2 tablespoons vegetable oil

2 tablespoons sun-dried cherries, soaked in red wine until soft — approximately 30 minutes
6-8 cups mustard greens, approximately ½ pound
kosher salt and black pepper, to taste

TO PREPARE THE RABBIT LEGS: Preheat oven to 325°F.

Season the rabbit legs with salt and pepper and dust them with flour. Place a large, 12-inch sauté pan over medium-high heat. Add the oil and when hot, add the rabbit legs and cook until golden brown on all sides. Remove the legs and most of the fat.

Place pan with the remaining fat back over medium heat and add the onion, carrot, celery and garlic. Cook the vegetables until they are slightly colored, about five minutes. Add the sun-dried cherries, herb sachet, rabbit bones and wine to the pan and cook to reduce the liquid until half of the volume remains. Add the rabbit legs back to the pan and add enough stock or water to just cover the meat. Bring stock to a boil and then cover and place pan in oven.

Braise by letting the rabbit cook, covered, in the oven 45 minutes to 1 hour or until meat is tender but just before it begins to fall off the bone. Remove meat from pan and keep warm by placing it in a covered pan in a warm (150°F to 200°F) oven. Using a fine strainer, strain the cooking liquid into a saucepan. Simmer the liquid until half of the volume remains, about 25 to 30 minutes. Use liquid in the salad dressing recipe or save to use as a sauce for another rabbit dish.

TO PREPARE THE DRESSING: In a blender, blend rabbit braising liquid, sherry vinegar, extra virgin olive oil, shallot, salt and pepper until smooth.

TO PREPARE THE SALAD: Cut the shiitake mushrooms into quarters. Place a small sauté pan over medium heat. Add the oil and allow it to get hot. Add the mushrooms, salt and pepper and sauté until lightly brown and the mushrooms are tender, about 10 minutes.

TO SERVE: Toss the sun-dried cherries, mushrooms and greens with half of the dressing. Place greens on center of a plate. Place warm rabbit legs on top of greens and drizzle additional dressing over legs.

ADVANCE PREPARATION: The rabbit can be braised 2 to 3 days in advance and will develop a more complex flavor. Cool the legs in their liquid and refrigerate. Reheat the legs, in their own liquid, when ready to use.

SUBSTITUTIONS AND OPTIONS: Chicken legs or duck legs are a good substitute for the rabbit. If using duck legs, do not dust with flour, but cook the duck legs, skin-side down until the fat has rendered and the skin is crisp. The salad is also delicious served on its own without the rabbit. If omitting the braised rabbit, substitute red wine vinegar for the rabbit braising liquid and increase the olive oil to a total of 6 tablespoons. Almost any wild or cultivated mushroom will work in this recipe, but we prefer to substitute chanterelle mushrooms when they are in season because of their earthy, dried stone-fruit flavor and firm texture.

WINE NOTES: The cherry and earthy flavors of the braising liquid and the spiciness of the mustard greens demand an intense and bright dark berry-flavored Pinot Noir with a smoky/earthy edge. Recommended: 2000 Carrabella, Pinot Noir, Willamette Valley, Oregon; or 2000 Domaine Arlaud, Bourgogne Rouge, Morey-Saint-Denis, France.

Makes 6 appetizer servings

Salad of Winter Greens
with Shaved Fennel and Celeriac

To make a salad in "off season" winter months you must be willing to try something new. In the summer, beautiful heads of iceberg, Bibb and Boston flourish. In the winter there is still plenty to choose from. Swiss chard, kales and collards thrive, as well as beet greens, turnip greens and our favorite, mustard greens like mizuna and misome. The cold and frost adds a sweetness to these greens not found in the warmer months.

Celeriac, also known as celery root, is related to and resembles stalk celery when growing in the ground. The edible portion is the swollen, knobby stem that forms at and just beneath the soil surface. The interior is smooth and white, similar to a turnip or a radish. The bulb can be eaten raw, as in this recipe, or cooked like potatoes. The celery-like leaves and stalks can be used but are more bitter than regular stalk celery.

1 small celeriac	2 cups winter greens (approximately ½ pound)
1 small fennel bulb	2 ounces basic vinaigrette (see page 20)
1 small red onion	kosher salt and white pepper, to taste

Peel the celeriac with a stationary peeler (a peeler that does not swivel) or a paring knife. Cut the celeriac into thin sheets and the cut the sheets into a fine julienne. Cut the fennel bulb in half and cut the halves into thin half moons. Peel the red onion. Cut the onion in half and cut the halves into thin half moons.

NOTE: We recommend using a mandoline slicer to cut the celeriac, fennel and red onion because it will give you the thinnest slices possible.

In a large, stainless steel bowl, combine the celeriac, fennel, red onion and assorted greens. Season with salt and pepper. Drizzle the vinaigrette over the greens and toss until well combined and the greens are evenly covered.

TO SERVE: Place the greens on a plate and arrange the vegetables over and around. Serve with additional vinaigrette and additional fresh cracked black pepper.

ADVANCE PREPARATION: The celeriac, fennel and onion can be cut several hours ahead and stored in ice-water until ready to use.

SUBSTITUTIONS AND OPTIONS: Choose any mixture of hardy or spicy lettuce such as arugula or spinach. Additional roots or tubers such as carrots or cooked potatoes will make a flavorful addition.

WINE NOTES: The spicy greens and the slightly acidic vinaigrette need a rich, tart white wine with a hint of spice. Recommended: 2001 Luna, Pinot Grigio, Napa Valley, California; or 2001 Coleman, Yamhill County, Pinot Gris, Oregon.

Makes 4 appetizer servings

Hot-Smoked Salmon Salad
with Horseradish-Mustard Dressing

For this recipe we prefer the flaky texture and richer, stronger flavor of hot-smoked rather than cold-smoked salmon (see page 103).

The horseradish-mustard dressing is little on the acidic side in order to cut through the spiciness of the winter greens and the smokiness of the hot smoked salmon. The horseradish flavor will come out in the dressing even more if the dressing is allowed to sit in the refrigerator overnight.

HORSERADISH-MUSTARD DRESSING
Makes approximately 1 cup

½ teaspoon whole grain mustard
½ teaspoon Dijon mustard
1½ tablespoons prepared creamy horseradish or 1½ teaspoon finely grated fresh horseradish
1 teaspoon garlic, finely chopped

4 tablespoons white wine vinegar or champagne vinegar
juice of ½ lemon
1 shallot, finely chopped
kosher salt and cracked black pepper, to taste
¾ cup vegetable oil

SALAD

4 Yukon Gold or other small waxy potatoes, skin on
12 baby carrots cut in half or 1 large carrot, julienned
2 heads Belgian endive, separated into individual spears

2 cups winter mixed greens (approximately ¼ pound)
4 2-ounce hot-smoked salmon medallions
¾ cup horseradish-mustard dressing
kosher salt and white pepper, to taste

TO PREPARE THE DRESSING: Place both of the mustards, horseradish, garlic, vinegar, lemon juice, shallot, salt and pepper in a small stainless steel bowl. Slowly drizzle in oil, whisking constantly, until ingredients are combined. Taste and adjust seasoning.

TO PREPARE THE SALAD: In a large saucepan, place potatoes and enough cold water to cover them by several inches. Add kosher salt to water and bring to a boil. Reduce to a simmer and cook potatoes until just tender. Drain potatoes. Cut the potatoes into quarters. In a medium-size bowl, combine warm potatoes with carrots and 2 ounces of the dressing. Gently toss to coat vegetables with dressing without breaking up the potatoes. Allow potatoes to cool in dressing.

If necessary, drain excess dressing from potatoes and carrots. In a large bowl, combine potatoes, carrots, endive and winter greens. Season with salt and pepper. Drizzle two ounces of remaining dressing over and toss until well combined and the greens are evenly covered but not overdressed.

TO SERVE: Arrange the endive spears on a plate like the spokes of a wagon wheel. Top with winter greens and vegetables. Arrange a piece of smoked salmon on top of the salad. Serve with remaining dressing and additional fresh cracked black pepper.

ADVANCE PREPARATION: You may make this dressing up to two weeks ahead and store it in a sealed container in the refrigerator. The potatoes can be made several hours in advance but make sure you combine the dressing with the warm potatoes so they can soak up the flavor.

SUBSTITUTIONS AND OPTIONS: Smoked sablefish, smoked sturgeon, smoked cod or even smoked mackerel will make a wonderful substitution. Make sure you find a brand of smoked fish that has been smoked with no preservatives, no artificial ingredients, and is from wild not farm-raised fish sources (see Sources and Information section). You can also substitute the Maple-Apple Brandy Cured Salmon recipe for the hot-smoked salmon, but the texture and the flavor profile of the salad will change.

WINE NOTES: The hot-smoked salmon presents a spicier, more floral flavor to match with wine than does cured salmon. The heady floral, spicy flavors of a dry Alsatian-style Gewürztraminer will highlight the smoky flavors in the salmon and still hold up to the horseradish. Recommended: 2001 Red Newt Cellars, Finger Lakes Reserve, Gewürztraminer, Finger Lakes, New York. For something different, the richness, balanced with sweetness of 2001 Caymus, Conundrum, California, should make your mouth do a happy dance.

Makes 4 appetizer servings

Cream of Potato, Leek and Jerusalem Artichoke Soup with Jerusalem Artichoke Pickles

Jerusalem artichokes, also known as sunchokes or *girasols*, are the tubers (underground stems) of a type of sunflower plant. They have a crisp water-chestnut-like texture and a mild radish flavor with just a hint of globe artichoke sweetness. They are extremely versatile and do not need to be peeled as long as their skin is mercilessly scrubbed.

This soup allows you to use the best of winter's bounty to its fullest. It uses a minimal amount of cream to allow the pure flavors of the roots to come through. Cream soups and sauces need an acidic element and the lemon juice and the pickled Jerusalem artichokes will add the necessary balance.

¾ pound large Yukon Gold potatoes, peeled and roughly chopped, approximately 4 potatoes

1 leek, roughly chopped and washed

½ pound Jerusalem artichokes, skin scrubbed and roughly chopped, approximately 4 medium-sized artichokes

½ medium-sized yellow onion, roughly chopped

2 cloves garlic, roughly chopped

2 quarts water or vegetable stock

kosher salt and white pepper, to taste

1 cup heavy cream

juice of ½ small lemon

In a large stock pot, place potatoes, leek, Jerusalem artichokes, onion, garlic, water or stock, salt and white pepper. Bring to a boil. Reduce heat and simmer, approximately 30 to 40 minutes or until vegetables are tender. Add the cream and simmer 10 additional minutes.

Working in batches, purée soup in a blender until smooth. Add lemon juice and before serving, taste and adjust seasoning.

TO SERVE: Pour soup into heated bowls and serve with Jerusalem Artichoke Pickles (see page 207).

ADVANCE PREPARATION: As with many of our soups, the flavors become better and more complex if the soup is made ahead and given a day of rest in the refrigerator.

SUBSTITUTIONS AND OPTIONS: This soup can be made with almost any type of potato. Celeriac or celery root can be added in addition to the other vegetables. In the spring, wild leeks (ramps) will add a woodsy, garlicky flavor alternative. Water chestnuts or radishes can be substituted for the Jerusalem artichokes. American sturgeon caviar or even shaved summer or winter black truffles (Oregon, French or Italian black truffles) can be on added on top to give a touch of extravagance to an otherwise rustic soup.

WINE NOTES: To cut through the rich creaminess of the soup and complement the roots you will need a bright and tangy wine with an herbal finish. Recommended: 2001 Brander, Santa

Ynez Valley au Naturel, Sauvignon Blanc, South Coast, California; 2001 Jean-Claude Chatelain, Sancerre Sélection, Loire, France.

Makes 6 appetizer servings, approximately 1 quart

Seafood Entrées:
Sublime Recipes from Oceans, Rivers and Seas

"The key to sublime seafood is in not the hand of the cook but in the lure
of the fisherman. It is all about how a fish is caught, handled and filleted
that ensures perfection" — Charlie Palmer

I STILL REMEMBER SITTING in a little dockside restaurant on the Massachusetts coast savoring a piece of Atlantic swordfish caught within the hour. It's hard to imagine that eating anything that tastes so good — and can be good for you — could be a major problem.

More people than ever before are choosing to eat seafood, and to meet this growing demand more and more fish and shellfish are being harvested. Some fish and shellfish stocks are doing distinctly better than others. It depends on how many fish are caught, the way they're caught, how well the fisheries are managed, and or even how long each type of fish or shellfish must live before they are able to reproduce.

The good news is that there are plenty of alternatives to depleted species like Atlantic swordfish. Your choices make a difference. Get to know your local species and your local fishermen, and support those fisheries and fish farms that are sustainable.

Spring

Pacific Halibut *a la Nage*
Pan-Seared Alaskan Sablefish with Green Garlic, Fiddlehead Ferns and Soft Polenta
Hot Alder Smoked Salmon on a Salad of Fava Beans, Fennel, Citrus and Arugula

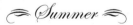

Summer

Spice-Rubbed Grilled Salmon with Savory Herb Sauce
Slow Roasted Ivory King Salmon with a Ragoût of Mushrooms, Spinach and Fingerling Potatoes
Olive Oil Poached Albacore Tuna with an Artichoke Salad and Lemon Vinaigrette

Autumn

Fennel-Crusted Halibut with Roasted Tomato Broth
White Sturgeon with Couscous and Spicy Eggplant

Winter

Steamed Pacific Cod with a Stew of Mussels and Clams

The Imperiled Seafood Supply

Considering the state of the world's oceans, it is distressing to acknowledge that severe overfishing, pollution, land abuses that affect habitats, and destructive fishing techniques have harmed ocean life and depleted many of our favorite species. No longer do people believe that fish supplies are inexhaustible. In fact, the National Marine Fisheries Service, the US federal agency that oversees domestic fisheries management, estimates that 92 domestic fish stocks are overfished today. The other major factor affecting fisheries is habitat destruction. In the case of declining wild salmon runs on the West Coast, for example, the key factors causing their decline are logging, dams across migratory rivers, intensive water use, agricultural land practices and development activities.

In many ways, government ineptitude and dishonesty have allowed our natural resources to be abused and sold off at a miniscule fraction of their worth. Corporate greed has been allowed to run roughshod over the American environment in a shortsighted search for profit. True, the demand for seafood has grown over 20 years due to population increases and recognition of the nutritional benefits. Granted, the health of the oceans is an international issue as much as a domestic one, but who will lead the way towards a greater awareness about sustainable fishing practices?

All too often the well-managed stocks of a worldwide species are lumped into the same category as the poorly managed stocks, and few learn the story beyond the negative headlines. Some, like Alaska's wild salmon fishery, are rigorously and successfully managed with strict environmental controls. Not all swordfish is endangered either — the Pacific swordfish stock is maintaining its current levels while the Atlantic stocks have been decimated — but rarely is this mentioned. Seldom is method of capture differentiated so consumers truly understand the impact of their purchases on a species. Why should hook-and-line Atlantic cod fishermen be put out of business for what the trawlers did in their greedy quest for more fish regardless of size, species or bycatch?

Some believe that aquaculture can take the pressure off depleted wild fish populations as well as meet the protein demands of an increasing world population. But in our opinion, most fish farms actually promote ecological destruction and further protein loss. Aquaculture can release concentrated waste into rivers and oceans. Farmed fish can escape and breed with wild species, spreading diseases and introducing less robust, possibly mutated fish. Sustainable aquaculture systems are closed, like those for farmed-raised striped bass and farm-raised catfish. These systems have procedures in place to prevent pollution and escapes and use, where possible, vegetarian feed or limited fish protein.

The good news is that declining wild populations can recover if their breeding habitats are protected and fishing methods are used that prevent overfishing, irresponsible bycatch and habitat destruction. Awareness and a sense of stewardship, conservation and protection are the first steps for this recovery.

The other link in the seafood sustainability chain is an informed consumer. You have a choice, and how you exercise your buying power carries weight. You can become informed about the state of the word's oceans and what fish species are plentiful and environmentally preferable. Remember that fish is a seasonal product. Become informed and learn which fish species are doing well and which are endangered. Make it a point to support restaurants that serve sustainable seafood.

Also, ask questions. Using fresh, local and sustainably caught seafood takes patience and the in-the-moment ability and spontaneity to respond to whatever the fisherman brings to market. Think of it as the Zen of seafood buying. Cultivate a relationship with your seafood supplier. Don't be afraid to go outside your immediate area or neighborhood to seek out the best. This may mean going to Chinatown or an Asian market, but at a minimum ask for someone behind the counter who knows about the fish being sold. Ask, "What can you tell me about this fish? Where does it come from? And how was it caught?" ∾

Monterey Bay Aquarium's Seafood Watch program provides up-to-date national and regional lists so consumers can make wise choices when buying seafood. The lists are updated twice a year; check **www.montereybayaquarium.org** for the most current information.

WEST COAST REGION

BEST CHOICES	CAUTION	AVOID
Abalone (Farmed)	Clams (wild-caught)	Caviar (wild-caught)
Catfish (Farmed)	Cod, Pacific	Chilean Seabass/Toothfish
Caviar (Farmed)	Crab, Imitation/Surimi	Cod, Atlantic/Icelandic
Clams (Farmed)	Crab, King (AK)	Crab, King (Imported)
Crab, Dungeness	Crab, Snow (U.S.)	Lingcod
Crab, Snow (Canada)	Lobster, American Maine (All Sources)	Monkfish
Halibut, Pacific	Mahi-Mahi, Dolphinfish/Dorado	Orange Roughy
Hoki	Mussels, wild-caught	Rockfish Rock Cod/Pacific Snapper
Lobster, Spiny/Rock (U.S., Australia)	Oysters (wild-caught)	(Pacific)
Mussels (Farmed)	Pollock	Salmon, (farmed/Atlantic)
Oysters (Farmed)	Rockfish Rock Cod/Pacific Snapper	Sharks, except U.S. West Coast Thresher
Sablefish/Black Cod (BC, AK)	(BC, AK; hook and line)	Shrimp (imported)
Salmon (CA, AK; wild-caught)	Sablefish/Black cod (CA, OR, WA)	Sturgeon (wild-caught)
Salmon (canned)	Salmon (OR, WA; wild-caught)	Swordfish (Atlantic)
Sardines	Sanddabs, Pacific	Tuna, Bluefin
Seabass, White	Scallops, Bay	
Shrimp/Prawns (trap-caught)	Scallops, Sea	
Striped Bass (Farmed)	Shark, Thresher (U.S. West Coast)	
Sturgeon (Farmed)	Shrimp/Prawns (U.S. farmed or U.S.	
Tilapia (Farmed)	trawl-caught)	
Trout, Rainbow (Farmed)	Sole (Pacific)	Monterey Bay Aquarium,
Tuna, Albacore/Yellowfin/Bigeye	Squid, CA market squid	886 Cannery Row, Monterey, CA
(troll/pole-caught)	Swordfish (U.S. West Coast)	93940 Tel: (877) 229-9990
	Tuna (canned)	1999–2003,
	Tuna, Albacore/Yellowfin/Bigeye	Monterey Bay Aquarium
	(longline-caught)	Foundation.

Pacific Halibut *a la Nage*

A chef's trick that you can easily accomplish at home is a traditional French technique for poaching fish in the oven and using the liquid as the sauce — *a la nage*. In a skillet, we place a piece of halibut, or any fish, on top of a layer of vegetables, add a flavorful liquid and cover with parchment paper. The whole dish is contained in a single pan, the method of cooking is quick and flavorful, and as a bonus there is no added fat.

1 carrot, cut into matchsticks
1 parsnip, cut into matchsticks
1 turnip, cut into matchsticks
1 stalk celery, cut into matchsticks
1 leek, cut into matchsticks
1 medium onion, thinly sliced
½ pound fingerling potatoes, red potatoes or
    yellow creamer potatoes, thinly sliced

4 5-ounce Pacific halibut fillets,
    kosher salt and white pepper, to taste
1½ cups fruity white wine such as a Pinot Gris
juice of 1 lemon
2 cups fish stock, chicken broth or water
1 tablespoon fresh parsley, chopped
1 tablespoon fresh chives, chopped

Preheat oven to 425°F.

In a skillet large enough to hold all of the fish, spread the carrots, parsnips, turnips, celery, leek, onion and potatoes in a thin layer on the bottom. Season the fish with salt and pepper. Place the halibut on top of the vegetables, making sure the halibut fillets do not touch each other.

In a small bowl, combine the wine, lemon juice and stock and pour the liquid over the fish. Make sure the liquid reaches halfway up the sides of the fish. Cover the pan with a piece of parchment paper. Place the skillet over high heat until liquid begins to simmer. Transfer the skillet to the oven and cook until the fish is cooked to the desired doneness. Fillets that are 1½ to 2 inches thick take approximately 8 to 10 minutes to reach medium — just slightly opaque in the center but still moist. Keep warm.

TO SERVE: Discard the parchment. Carefully remove the halibut from the skillet. Place the vegetables on a serving plate and place the halibut on top of the vegetables. Bring the cooking liquid to a boil on high heat and cook until the liquid thickens and just coats the back of a spoon. Add the chopped parsley and chives. Adjust seasoning and pour liquid over fish.

ADVANCE PREPARATION: The vegetables may be cut and refrigerated several hours in advance.

SUBSTITUTIONS AND OPTIONS: Any fish with firm flesh, such as salmon or wild striped bass, will work for this recipe. The best substitute is wild King salmon fwith its high fat content and meaty flesh. Salmon has a rich, sweet flavor that combines well with a touch of acid from a crisp, fruity wine or citrus juices. Any citrus and almost any wine will work with the recipe as long as it is fairly dry.

Leftover fish is perfect for a light salad, or it can be shredded and made into fish cakes or fish tacos.

WINE NOTES: We prefer the Pacific Northwest cliché match of Pinot Gris with this light but flavorful halibut dish. It's a bright wine with enough flavor and body to hold up to the fish without overpowering the delicate broth. Recommended: 2002 Paschal, Pinot Gris, Southern Oregon; or 2001 Chehalem, Reserve, Pinot Gris, Willamette Valley, Oregon.

Makes 4 entrée servings

Wild Salmon Kings:

Fishermen Direct Seafoods

Trace the blue line of the Rogue River on a map of Oregon and you'll know where the salmon swim. The river meanders south from Crater Lake, crosses the valley that shares its name and heads southwest though the coast range. Where it joins the Pacific Ocean, at Gold Beach, Oregon, just above the California border, the river widens and adds "wild" to its name. Gold Beach is a port town. It's home to around 2,500 people: loggers, service folks for tourists who come to stay in the motels and eat at the restaurants, and, naturally, fishermen.

Scott Boley, John Wilson and Jeff Werner are partners in Fishermen Direct Seafoods with four boats among them. They started the business in 1998 to cut out the costly middleman and promote fresh Oregon seafood. Not just wild Chinook salmon, but also Albacore tuna, Dungeness crab, halibut, lingcod, Petrale sole and a variety of Pacific Coast rockfish, each according to its season.

All fish are ocean troll-caught, which means each is individually caught on a separate lure, a time-consuming method yielding smaller catches. It's more expensive to catch fish one at a time and requires an experienced fisherman, but quality is guaranteed. The fish are processed within hours of being caught.

"They'll call me or I call them, and I can get fresh salmon overnight from the time it's caught at sea until it arrives in our kitchen," says Stu. "When it comes from Fishermen Direct, I know the quality is tops because it's coming right out of the water. Their fish is local; it doesn't spend days at sea or in transit."

The Fishermen Direct retail store is in the old 1930s-era Cannery Building in Gold Beach. If not at sea, the boats — the *Frances*, the *Instigator*, the *Helen Marie* and the *Diana Marie* — dock out back. Nearby is the processing center. Along with selling fresh fish, Fishermen Direct also fillets, cans, vacuum packs and freezes fish in high-quality freezers, plus packs fish to travel and ship nationwide.

"They're my local fishermen," says Stu. "On the other side of the mountains maybe, but their quality and service are as good as buying off the boat. You know the difference with the first taste." ❧

Pan-Seared Alaskan Sablefish
with Green Garlic, Fiddlehead Ferns and Soft Polenta

Found only in the north Pacific, the sablefish or black cod has rich, buttery flesh. Most of the US and Canadian catch is exported to Japan, where it is prized for sushi. Heavy fishing in the 1970s and 1980s led to a decline in sablefish populations; Alaskan and Canadian managers instituted reforms, which seem to be protecting the population. Alaska and British Columbia sablefish are a Monterey Bay Aquarium Seafood Watch List "Best Choice," because the populations are abundant and the fisheries are well-managed.

This is another recipe that signals spring across the country. Green garlic refers to immature garlic plants that are unearthed before the cloves have a chance to form. They are mild in flavor compared with mature garlic. Fiddlehead ferns are the young, edible, tightly coiled fern frond of the ostrich fern that resembles the spiral end of a violin or fiddle. The shoots are in their coiled form for only about two weeks before they unfurl into graceful greenery. They have a slightly chewy texture and a flavor similar to a cross between asparagus, green beans and okra.

POLENTA
2½ cups milk
½ cup water
1 sprig fresh thyme

kosher salt and white pepper, to taste
½ cup polenta (not instant polenta)
¼ cup chèvre-style, soft
  goat cheese

SABLEFISH
4 5-ounce sablefish/black cod fillets, skin on
2 tablespoons vegetable oil

2 tablespoons butter
kosher salt and white
pepper, to taste

VEGETABLES
2 tablespoons butter
¼ pound fiddlehead ferns, ends trimmed
¼ pound fiddlehead ferns, ends trimmed
  and blanched
¼ pound green garlic, cut into 2-inch pieces
  and blanched

¼ pound snap peas,
  cleaned and blanched
kosher salt and white
pepper, to taste

TO PREPARE THE POLENTA: Pour the milk, water, thyme, salt and pepper into a medium-size saucepan. Bring liquid to a boil. Lower heat so liquid is simmering. While constantly whisking, slowly add the polenta to the liquid. Cook polenta over low heat, continuously whisking the mixture until the polenta begins to thicken and the grains are soft, about 20 minutes. Remove thyme sprig. Stir in cheese and mix until melted. Keep warm.

TO PREPARE THE SABLEFISH: Place a sauté pan, large enough to hold all the fish, over medium heat. Season the sablefish with salt and pepper. Add the oil and butter to the hot pan. When butter begins to foam, slip the fish, skin-side down, into the pan. Sear the skin for 4 to 5 minutes or until the skin is crisp. Turn the fish over and cook an additional 4 to 5 minutes or until the flesh is opaque but still moist. Keep warm in a low-temperature oven.

TO PREPARE THE VEGETABLES: Place butter in the same pan you used to sear the sablefish. Place the pan over medium heat. When butter begins to foam but not brown, add the fiddlehead ferns, green garlic and snap peas. Season with salt and pepper. Toss vegetables in the butter until warm.

TO SERVE: Divide polenta among 4 warm plates. Place warm vegetables next to polenta and place fish on top of vegetables.

ADVANCE PREPARATION: The vegetables can be blanched a day ahead (see page 13 for explanation of blanching). If you make the polenta more than 30 minutes before serving, you may need to whisk in additional water or milk. Check seasoning if you add additional liquid.

SUBSTITUTIONS AND OPTIONS: Any firm-fleshed, oily fish, such as wild salmon, mackerel, bluefish, shad or even Yellowfin tuna will work for this recipe. Although nothing tastes exactly like a fiddlehead fern, asparagus or okra may be substituted. Julienned leeks or green onions can be substituted for the green garlic.

WINE NOTES: The rich-tasting, oily fish is balanced by the creaminess of the cheese polenta and the bulby flavor of the green garlic. Choose a bright acidic white wine with sweet pea and apple flavors to match the strong fish. Recommended: 2002 Huia, Sauvignon Blanc, Marlborough, New Zealand; or 2001 Groth, Sauvignon Blanc, Napa Valley, California.

Makes 4 entrée servings

Hot Alder Smoked Salmon
on a Salad of Fava Beans, Fennel, Citrus and Arugula

A hot-smoked fish dish has been a perennial favorite on the Peerless menu since we started. Almost any high-fat fish like salmon, Pacific cod or sturgeon is a good candidate for hot-smoking. The easiest methods for smoking at home are using an outdoor grill, a Chinese wok or a stovetop smoker such as the Cameron's Stovetop Smoker. Make sure you have a good ventilation system if you are smoking food indoors.

Mary, being a Northwest native, prefers the mild flavor of alder wood for smoking but a fruit wood like apple or pear, a hardwood like mesquite or even crushed hazelnut shells will work.

HOT-SMOKED SALMON

4 5-ounce wild salmon fillets, skin on

½ cup citrus vinaigrette (see page 66)

kosher salt and white pepper, to taste

ARUGULA SALAD

¼ pound fava beans, removed from pod

¼ pound snow peas

1 head fennel, thinly sliced (use a mandoline slicer)

1 grapefruit, skin peeled with a knife and flesh cut into segments

1 Valencia orange, skin peeled with a knife and flesh cut into segments

1 Moro orange (blood orange), cut into segments *(optional)*

1 lemon, cut into segments

3 bunches arugula

¼ cup citrus vinaigrette (see page 66)

kosher salt and cracked black pepper, to taste

TO PREPARE THE SALMON: Preheat oven to 350°F.

Place salmon fillets and citrus vinaigrette in a stainless steel bowl and marinate for 20 to 30 minutes. Remove fish from marinade and pat dry. Season salmon with salt and pepper.

Smoke the salmon, skin-side down, in a hot smoker, wok or a barbeque over alder wood for 5 minutes. Place fish in oven for an additional 5 to 6 minutes or until fish is just cooked through. Keep warm.

TO PREPARE THE SALAD: Fill a large stainless steel pot three quarters full with salted water and bring to a boil. Add the fava beans and cook for 30 seconds. Remove the beans and plunge them into an ice-water bath. When cold, drain and peel the outer coating. The outer shell should "pop" or slide right off of the bean.

Add the snow peas to the boiling water and cook for 2 minutes. Plunge the peas into an ice-water bath. When cold, drain and pat dry.

Combine fava beans, snap peas, fennel, grapefruit, oranges, Moro oranges, lemon and arugula in a stainless steel bowl.

Add citrus vinaigrette, salt and pepper and toss to coat. Reserve.

TO SERVE: Place arugula salad in the center of a plate. Place a salmon fillet on top of each salad. Drizzle additional vinaigrette around.

ADVANCE PREPARATION: Prepare all of the salad ingredients a day ahead, but do not dress the salad with the vinaigrette until you are ready to serve. Marinate, smoke and assemble the dish just before serving.

SUBSTITUTIONS AND OPTIONS: Wild King or wild Sockeye salmon are the best choices for this recipe. We do not recommend substituting farm-raised rainbow trout because the smoke and the acidic vinaigrette will overpower the delicate taste of the fish.

Grilling or sautéing will work in place of hot-smoking, but will not replicate the rich, earthy smoky flavor.

This composed entrée salad screams spring. Change the fish and the salad ingredients based on the season. Summer Coho salmon matches well with a salad of heirloom tomatoes, grilled red Torpedo onions and pesto vinaigrette (see page 78).

WINE NOTES: This dish needs a peppery Pinot Noir to match the arugula salad. Choose a wine with a high acid level and soft tannins to cut through the acid in the citrus and the smoke of the fish. Recommendation: Our friend (and dedicated Harley guy) Dean Fisher's 2001 Adea, *Dean-o's Pinot* , Pinot Noir, Willamette Valley, Oregon is designed for the patio, not the cellar; or for a great value with an eco-twist, try a 2001 Amity Vineyards, Eco Wine, organic, sulfite-free, Pinot Noir, Willamette Valley, Oregon.

Makes 4 entrée servings

Brining, Dry Curing, Cold-Smoking and Hot-Smoking

One of Stu's first jobs in a professional French kitchen was as an assistant *garde manger* — the person who handles all the cold food preparation, hors d'oeuvres and the charcuterie. He learned the traditional techniques of sausage making, curing and preserving meats. It is part science and part art. Today, we have adapted many of the time-honored techniques to suit our sustainable mindset for freshness and innovation; for us, charcuterie still holds the fascination of an alchemy that works.

Below is a short list explaining various curing techniques to help you make an informed decision next time you walk into the deli.

- BRINING is a very salty marinade, approximately 1 pound to 1½ pounds of salt to 1 gallon of liquid (20 to 30 percent salinity). Brines usually contain sugar, herbs, spices and sometimes nitrites (preservatives). Brining is a perfect technique for that Sunday afternoon chicken or the Thanksgiving turkey.

- DRY CURING uses a dry mixture, primarily salt based, to remove moisture and add additional flavor to the product. Dry cures, like brines, usually contain sugar, herbs, spices and sometimes nitrites (preservatives).

- COLD-SMOKING is a process of exposing food that has first been brined or salt cured to smoke at low temperatures (50°F to 85°F) for a fairly long period of time. The curing /brining adds flavor and extracts moisture from the food, allowing the smoke to penetrate more easily. Cold-smoked foods are actually still raw.

- HOT-SMOKING is the process of exposing food to smoke at high temperatures (over 160°F) for a fairly short period of time. Hot-smoked foods can benefit from first brining or curing, but it is not required. Hot-smoked foods are usually fully cooked when removed from the smoker.

- HARD-SMOKING refers to foods that have been heavily salted and smoked. There is very little moisture left in the food, and it often does not require refrigeration, as do other smoked products. The final product will resemble jerky. ∾

Spice Rubbed Grilled Salmon
with Savory Herb Sauce

Stu spent a bit of time working and traveling in southern France, where he picked up his affinity for Mediterranean-influenced dishes. The base of this recipe is a versatile Moroccan-flavored spice rub. One ingredient you may not be familiar with is fenugreek. Native to India and southern Europe, fenugreek consists of small stony seeds from the pod of a bean-like plant. The seeds are hard, yellowish brown and angular, and have a bittersweet, burnt-sugar flavor with a warm, penetrating and pungent aroma. Ancient Egyptians used the spice for medicinal purposes; today, fenugreek is used commercially in the preparation of mango chutneys and as a base for imitation maple syrup.

DRY SPICE RUB
Makes approximately 4 ounces

2 tablespoons ground paprika
1 teaspoon granulated sugar
1 teaspoon kosher salt
½ teaspoon ground black pepper
½ teaspoon ground ginger
½ teaspoon ground cardamom

½ teaspoon ground cumin
½ teaspoon ground fenugreek (optional)
¼ teaspoon ground cloves
¼ teaspoon ground cinnamon
¼ teaspoon ground allspice
¼ teaspoon ground cayenne pepper

SAVORY HERB SAUCE

1 cup plain yogurt, drained in a fine-mesh colander or cheesecloth for ½ hour
2 tablespoons sorrel, roughly chopped (optional)
2 tablespoons cilantro, roughly chopped
2 tablespoons parsley, roughly chopped

2 tablespoons basil leaves, roughly chopped
1 tablespoon chives, roughly chopped
1 tablespoon green onions, roughly chopped
1 teaspoon lemon juice
zest of ½ lemon, finely grated
kosher salt and ground white pepper, to taste

SALMON

4 5-ounce wild salmon fillets, trimmed, skin off

2 tablespoons vegetable oil
dry spice rub

TO PREPARE THE SPICE RUB: We recommend using whole spices, lightly roasting them, grinding in a spice grinder or coffee grinder, and then mixing them together. To roast, place spices in a dry sauté pan over medium heat. Sauté until light brown in color. Be careful not to over-roast them, as this will make them bitter.

TO PREPARE THE SAVORY HERB SAUCE: In a stainless steel or glass bowl, combine the yogurt, sorrel, cilantro, parsley, basil, chives, green onions, lemon juice and zest. Mix well. Taste and adjust seasoning.

TO PREPARE THE SALMON: Preheat a grill.

Place a small amount of the dry spice rub on a small plate. Lightly rub each salmon fillet with enough vegetable oil to just coat the fish. Press the flesh-side (side opposite of where the skin was) into the dry spice rub and thoroughly coat one side of the fish. Place salmon on a grill, dry rub side down and cook over medium to high heat, a total of 8 to 12 minutes or until still pink in the middle.

TO SERVE: Place grilled salmon on warm plates and top with a dollop of savory herb sauce.

ADVANCE PREPARATION: The dry rub can be made in advance and stored in a dry, cool place in a sealed container. The savory herb sauce can be made up to 4 days ahead and stored in a sealed container in the refrigerator.

SUBSTITUTIONS AND OPTIONS: You will need a firm-fleshed, strong-flavored fish, such as wild striped bass, black bass or even sturgeon to stand up to the strong spices in the rub. Serve the salmon with soft polenta (see page 99) or parsnip-potato rösti (see page 59) or a simple potato purée.

We are lucky enough to get goat's milk yogurt at the restaurant from time to time and prefer using it in this recipe. Cow's milk yogurt will work fine, but make sure it is plain, not non-fat, and made from organic or natural milk. The savory herb sauce makes a wonderful accompaniment for a cured or cold-smoked salmon appetizer.

WINE NOTES: The cool, bright-tasting herb-yogurt sauce will balance the spiciness of the dry rub. Choose a full-bodied, herbal and earthy red with balanced, sweet tannins. Recommended: 2001 E. Guigal, Chateauneuf-du-Pape, Rhône, France; or a classic from Randall Graham, the "Rhône Ranger" of California, a 2000 Bonny Doon Vineyards, Le Cigare Volant, California.

Makes 4 entrée servings

Slow Roasted Ivory King Salmon
with a Ragoût of Mushrooms, Spinach and Fingerling Potatoes

Ivory salmon is a luxurious white-fleshed King salmon native to certain rivers of southeast Alaska and Canada. Most salmon get their typical red or pink color from carotene in the food they eat, but white or ivory Kings are genetically predisposed with an extra enzyme to process carotene, rather than collect it in their flesh. Ivory salmon tends to be milder, silkier and more buttery in flavor than regular King. Ivory salmon may be difficult to find, but we believe they are worth the search and urge you to splurge should you encounter one at your local market.

Slow roasting fish on a bed of vegetables results in an extremely aromatic dish with a texture that literally melts in your mouth.

IVORY KING SALMON

4 5-ounce Ivory King salmon medallions, skin-off

kosher salt and white pepper, to taste

4 stalks celery, cut into 2-inch long strips
1 medium yellow onion, cut into thin slices

RAGOÛT

2 tablespoons vegetable oil
2 shallots, peeled and finely chopped
¼ pound mushrooms (wild or cultivated), cleaned and quartered
½ pound fingerling potatoes, quartered
1 pound spinach, stems removed and cut into chiffonade

2 cloves garlic, finely chopped
¼ cup white wine
¼ cup Madeira wine (optional) or use an additional ¼ cup of white wine
kosher salt and cracked black pepper, to taste

TO PREPARE THE SALMON: Preheat oven to 275°F.

Season salmon with salt and pepper. Place celery strips and onion in an ovenproof roasting pan, creating a rack for the salmon. Place salmon on top of celery/onion mixture. Place pan with salmon in oven and roast for about 12 to 15 minutes, until the salmon is just cooked in the center.

TO PREPARE THE RAGOÛT: In a medium-size sauté pan over medium heat, add vegetable oil. Add shallots and mushrooms and sauté until soft but not colored, approximately 10 minutes. Add potatoes and continue cooking until the potatoes are slightly caramelized and tender, an additional 12 to 15 minutes. Add the spinach and garlic and toss to coat in oil. Add both wines and cook until wine is almost evaporated and the pan is almost dry. Season with salt and pepper. Keep warm. Taste and adjust seasoning.

TO SERVE: Place ragoût in center of plate. Arrange salmon with celery/onion strips on top of ragoût.

ADVANCE PREPARATION: The ragoût may be made up to two days ahead and refrigerated. Add a little oil to a hot sauté pan and heat the ragoût just prior to serving.

SUBSTITUTIONS AND OPTIONS: Any salmon will work for this recipe but the flavor of wild Pacific salmon is best. If you choose farm-raised fish, make sure it has been raised according to environmentally sound methods.

Any mushroom would work for the ragoût, but given the choice, we prefer the distinctive earthiness and slight dried-apricot flavors of wild chanterelles or the firm texture of cultivated shiitake mushrooms.

WINE NOTES: Pinot Noir and salmon are fast becoming a classic match, for good reasons. You will need a wine with black stone fruit, a hint of spice and a slight earthy tone to hold up to the richness of the salmon and the mushrooms. Recommended: 2000 McKinlay, Special Select, Pinot Noir, Willamette Valley, Oregon; or 2001 Penner-Ash, Pinot Noir, Willamette Valley, Oregon.

Makes 4 entrée servings

Wild Pacific Salmon

"There's a fine line between fishing and standing on the shore like an idiot."
— STEVEN WRIGHT

Walk into any supermarket on any day and you will likely find some form of salmon. One reason for this is that salmon is one of the most versatile fish available. At the Peerless, we have prepared salmon ourselves using every method imaginable from roasting, planking, poaching, and sautéing to curing and crimping. We have served salmon hot and cold and we have sliced it, cut it into steaks, cooked it whole, wrapped it in pastry and made it into a mousse. Here is the information you need to make responsible and sustainable choices the next time you venture into the seafood department.

Since salmon stop eating once they leave saltwater, it is best to catch them when they first enter freshwater. At this point, their flesh has the highest fat and protein content. The length of time they spend in the ocean and the distance they must travel in freshwater determines the fat content. The longer and colder the river, the higher the fat content, richer the flavor and firmer the texture. Thus, salmon are generally named for the place they come from like the Copper River in Alaska (the longest, coldest river in Alaska), the Taku River in Alaska or the Columbia River on the Oregon/Washington border. Why should you care? The fatter and happier the salmon, the better the flavor.

Always choose wild salmon over farmed salmon. Wild salmon taste better and are healthier for you and for the environment. As the slogan goes, "Wild salmon don't do drugs." Most farmed salmon are kept in crowded net pens where they are prone to disease. To control various pathogens and parasites, the fish farms commonly use drugs and other chemicals. In many instances, farmed salmon escape their net cages and can endanger the health of wild fish populations. The antibiotics and other agents used can also have a negative impact on shellfish and the marine life that support other fisheries.

We believe that a majority of aquaculture (fish farming) systems actually promote ecological destruction and further protein loss. Research already shows that wild salmon are healthier for you and the environment, and are environmentally friendlier than farmed salmon. Because salmon are carnivorous, requiring fish meal in their diet, each pound of farmed salmon requires between two and five pounds of wild fish. This means a net loss of marine resources. Moreover, scientists have found evidence of dioxins and PCB contamination in the fishmeal fed to farmed salmon, raising further food safety concerns.

Knowing your salmon species, together with where and how they were caught, will help you get the best product for your money, promote sustainable cuisine and ensure that you get the most flavor from your fish. Wild salmon in the Pacific Northwest consist of five species plus Steelhead trout, an anadromous rainbow trout. In general, choose fish, whether whole or pre-cut, that are moist, shiny, firm to the touch and smell like the ocean, not like fish. Ask when and how the fish was caught, where it came from and how it has been stored. As James de Coquet said, "Salmon are like men: too soft a life is not good for them."

Chinook or King salmon are the largest of the Pacific salmon, averaging between 15 and 40 pounds. They spawn in long, large rivers and therefore need the greatest amount of fat reserves. They run in the spring through the autumn with the spring and summer runs being the most prolific. They are commercially caught from central California to northwest Alaska. You may have heard of "Ivory" salmon. Ivory salmon are a white-fleshed King salmon native to certain rivers of southeast Alaska and Canada. Most salmon get their color from carotene in the food they eat while white or Ivory Kings are genetically predisposed with an extra enzyme to process that carotene rather than collect it in their flesh. Ivory salmon is acclaimed for its milder, silkier and more buttery flavor.

Coho or "Silver" salmon are slightly smaller and have a lower fat content than King salmon. They are autumn spawners with peak runs in July and August. They are often present in small neighborhood streams and rivers like the Rogue River in southern Oregon.

Sockeye or "Red" salmon are unique, as they must spend their juvenile years in a lake. They are called "red" because their skin turns red when they spawn. The name sockeye means "fish of fishes" in the native Salish language. Whole fish rarely exceed four or five pounds, but we believe they are they the most flavorful of the wild salmon. We have a hard time buying sockeye because they are so highly prized in Japan they're often sold before the boat docks.

Pink (Humpback) and Chum (Keta or Dog) salmon are the bargain-basement salmon and we don't recommend using either for dinner. They are the smallest of the salmon and have very low fat contents. These salmon are mostly canned or smoked.

In the US, the Atlantic salmon on the retail market is always farm-raised, since wild Atlantic salmon are extremely rare and there is no longer a commercial fishery. Many of the East Coast's native Atlantic salmon populations are extinct, while remaining wild Atlantic salmon stocks in Maine and parts of eastern Canada are listed as an endangered species.

Steelhead trout, like Atlantic salmon, survive after spawning. They are a sea-going trout that have a medium fat content. While there are no major physical differences between rainbow and steelhead trout, the nature of their differing lifestyles has resulted in subtle distinctions in color, shape and flavor. Oregon does not allow commercial fisheries to fish for Steelhead and the British Columbian stocks are almost depleted. Sport and Native American fishermen are the only ones allowed to keep these prized fish. ❧

Olive Oil Poached Albacore Tuna
with Artichoke Salad and Lemon Vinaigrette

This dish is appealing for the home cook because it is simple, versatile and flavorful. The idea behind poaching in olive oil is to impart the delicate flavor of the oil to the fish without deep frying. The key is to keep the temperature of the oil below 200°F, so you should have an instant-read thermometer for this recipe. Leftover poaching oil can be strained and stored in an airtight container in the refrigerator and used again to make a flavorful base for salad dressings.

Albacore tuna (*Thunnus alalunga*), also called Tombo tuna, is a medium-size tuna found in temperate, subtropical and tropical oceans. Albacore tuna live longer and grow more slowly than other tunas. Most Albacore is sold as high-priced "white meat" canned tuna on supermarket shelves. Fresh Albacore has whitish-pink flesh, fairly soft texture and a mild, leaner flavor compared to other tuna species. We do not recommend Atlantic Albacore because it has been substantially overfished, but Albacore populations have remained abundant and sustainable in the Pacific.

OLIVE OIL POACHING LIQUID

1 quart extra virgin olive oil
5 sprigs thyme
5 sprigs rosemary
2 bay leaves
4 cloves garlic, peeled and crushed

TUNA

4 5-ounce Albacore tuna medallions
kosher salt and cracked black pepper
juice of 1 lemon

ARTICHOKE SALAD WITH LEMON VINAIGRETTE

8 red cherry or small pear tomatoes
8 yellow cherry or small pear tomatoes
1 large red onion, cut in half and thinly sliced
8 basil leaves, thinly sliced
12 canned artichokes bottoms packed in water, drained, rinsed and cut in half
2 ounces lemon juice
6 ounces extra virgin olive oil or oil from tuna poaching liquid
kosher salt and cracked black pepper
4 basil sprigs for garnish

TO PREPARE THE OLIVE OIL POACHING LIQUID: Combine the olive oil, thyme, rosemary, bay leaf and garlic in a saucepot small enough so the fish fits snugly, but large enough so the medallions do not touch each other and the oil will not spill over the sides. Place pan with oil over medium heat and heat until an instant-read thermometer inserted into the oil reaches 190°F.

TO PREPARE THE TUNA: Rub tuna with lemon juice and season with salt and pepper. Submerge the tuna in the olive oil mixture and cook approximately 5 minutes or until tuna is still pink in the center. Be sure to keep the oil temperature at 190°F. NOTE: this may require adjusting the intensity of the heat during the cooking process.

TO PREPARE THE ARTICHOKE SALAD WITH LEMON VINAIGRETTE: Combine tomatoes, red onion, basil and artichokes in a stainless steel or glass bowl. Combine lemon juice, olive oil, salt and pepper and pour over tomato-artichoke mixture.

TO SERVE: Divide artichoke salad among 4 room-temperature plates. Cut tuna medallions in half and place on top of salad. Drizzle warm olive oil poaching liquid on and around fish. Garnish with extra basil sprigs.

ADVANCE PREPARATION: The amount of oil varies depending on size of fish and the cooking vessel. Measure the quantity you need by arranging the fish in saucepot and pouring cold water over fish until they are covered. The pot should be large enough so that the liquid reaches only halfway up the sides. Remove fish from the pan and pour the water into a measuring pitcher to determine the amount of olive oil you'll need. Pat fish dry before cooking.

SUBSTITUTIONS AND OPTIONS: An alternative to stovetop poaching is to poach the fish in the oven. Place the tuna in a casserole or non-reactive ovenproof dish. Heat the olive oil, thyme, rosemary and garlic in a saucepan on top of the stove. When the oil mixture reaches 190°F, ladle the oil, thyme, rosemary and garlic over fish to completely submerge medallions. Transfer the dish to a pre-heated 250°F oven and continue cooking, uncovered, for 8 to 10 minutes or until the tuna is still pink in the center. Do not let the oil boil.

Our favorite red cherry tomato varieties are Tommy Toe or Tiny Tim, while our favorite yellow varieties are Olivette Jaune or Isis Candy.

Leftover fish can be completely submerged in the cool oil, covered and refrigerated. Use within 2 to 3 days.

WINE NOTES: For this dish, as with much of life itself, there are two paths you can travel. A dry white wine that coats the palate will broaden the ocean-like taste of the tuna, while a soft, delicate, slightly smoky, herbal- and garlic-scented red wine will bring out the earthy richness of the fish and match the flavored olive oil. Recommended: 2001 Signorello, *Seta*, Sémillon-Sauvignon Blanc, Napa Valley, California is the perfect ABC (anything but Chardonnay) wine; or 2000 Mirassou, Pinot Noir, Monterey, California.

Makes 4 entrée servings

Fennel-Crusted Halibut
with Roasted Tomato Broth

"Hippo of the Sea" is how the halibut's Latin family name *Hippoglossus* can be translated. "Holy flatfish" is the English derivation, with *hali* for holy and *but* for flat, hailing from the halibut's legacy as a special fish for holy days (or holidays) in medieval England. Halibut is the largest member of the right-eye flounder family. Alaskan and Canadian fisheries cooperate across the border to manage wild Pacific halibut stocks for long-term sustainability. Both countries operate under an Individual Transferable Quota (ITQ) system, under which fishermen "own" their quota and can fish anytime from March 15th to November 15th to fulfill their allocation.

We do not recommend purchasing Atlantic halibut, due to poor fishery management; most flounder and sole populations in the Atlantic, including Atlantic halibut, are seriously depleted. Since most Atlantic flatfish are caught with bottom trawls, bycatch of other species is a considerable problem, as is the harmful effect of trawling on ocean habitat. (See page 116 for a more thorough explanation.)

ROASTED TOMATO BROTH

1 pound large red heirloom tomatoes
1 tablespoon extra virgin olive oil

kosher salt and black pepper, to taste

4 tablespoons extra virgin olive oil
1 small yellow onion, roughly chopped
1 small fennel bulb, roughly chopped (save
 fennel fronds for garnish)
1 carrot, roughly chopped
2 cloves garlic, roughly chopped
¼ cup orange juice

¼ cup white wine
pinch saffron threads (optional)
roasted heirloom tomatoes, approximately 1 cup
4 cups fish stock, clam juice, vegetable stock,
 light chicken broth or water
kosher salt and black pepper, to taste

FENNEL CRUST AND HALIBUT

1 teaspoon kosher salt
1 teaspoon white pepper
1 teaspoon Italian parsley leaves
1 tablespoon fennel seed, toasted

½ loaf French bread, stale, cubed (about 2 cups)
4 5-ounce Pacific halibut fillets, trimmed,
 skin off
kosher salt and white pepper, to taste

TO PREPARE THE ROASTED TOMATO BROTH: Preheat the oven to 225°F.

Cut the tomatoes in half and squeeze out the seeds. Place tomatoes in a medium-size bowl, drizzle tomatoes with oil and season with salt and pepper. Place tomatoes, cut-side down on a parchment-lined baking sheet. Place baking sheet in oven and roast for 2 to 3 hours or until the tomatoes are very soft and slightly dry. Remove from oven and set aside.

NOTE: The roasted tomatoes may be stored in a sealed container in the refrigerator for up to 2 weeks.

In a large saucepan over medium heat, add the oil, onions, fennel, carrots and garlic. Cook, stirring often, until the vegetables are soft but not colored, about 10 to 15 minutes. Add the orange juice, wine and saffron. Bring to boil, reduce to a simmer and simmer until liquid is reduced by half, about 3 to 5 minutes. Add the roasted tomatoes, fish stock, salt and pepper. Bring to boil, reduce to a simmer and simmer until liquid is reduced by half, about 15 to 20 minutes. Strain sauce through a fine mesh strainer, taste and adjust seasoning. Keep warm.

TO PREPARE THE FENNEL CRUST AND THE HALIBUT: Preheat oven to 450°F.

To make the crust, place salt, pepper, parsley, fennel seed and bread in a blender or food processor and blend until fine crumbs are formed.

Place the fennel coating on a plate. Press the halibut fillets firmly into the coating so they are covered evenly. Turn to coat both sides. Place the halibut fillets on a large ovenproof sauté pan or baking sheet. Place fish in oven and roast for 8 to 10 minutes, or until the crust is crisp and the fish is just cooked through.

TO SERVE: Divide tomato broth among 4 warm bowls. Place halibut in the center of the bowl and garnish with fennel fronds.

ADVANCE PREPARATION: Both the tomato broth and the fennel crust may be prepared several days in advance. Store the broth in a sealed container in the refrigerator. Store the fennel crust in a sealed container in dry place, but do not refrigerate.

SUBSTITUTIONS AND OPTIONS: Other spices or combinations of spices, such as mustard seed, coriander or cumin, can be substituted in the crust mixture for the toasted fennel seed. Wild salmon, Pacific cod or Petrale sole can be used in place of the halibut.

You can also serve the crusted halibut on top of summer vegetable slaw, or with sliced heirloom tomatoes simply dressed with extra virgin olive oil, salt and cracked black pepper.

WINE NOTES: The anise flavor of the fennel crust will benefit from anise notes in a Sangiovese-based red wine. Recommended: 1999 Castellare di Castellina, Chianti Classico Riserva, Tuscany, Italy; or for something a little oaky try the 2000 Columbia, Red Willow Vineyard David Lake Signature Series, Sangiovese, Yakima Valley, Washington.

Makes 4 entrée servings

White Sturgeon
with Couscous and Spicy Eggplant

White sturgeon are the largest freshwater fish in North America and can weigh over 1,500 pounds, reach 20 feet in length and live for more than 100 years. Instead of scales, sturgeon are protected by a heavy sandpaper-like skin and five rows of bony plates, called scutes, that serve as an armorlike covering. They are a primitive, bottom-dwelling, slow-growing, late-maturing anadromous fish. White sturgeon spawn in the large rivers of the Pacific Northwest in the spring and summer months and remain in freshwater while young. They have extremely firm flesh with a rich, earthy flavor.

The bad news is that many wild sturgeon runs in the Pacific Northwest are on the endangered species list. We feel most fish farms actually promote ecological destruction and further protein loss. Since there must be an exception to every rule, we do recommend farm-raised white sturgeon from Stolt Sea Farm in Elverta, California. They raise white sturgeon in an ecologically and economically sustainable environment.

COUSCOUS

2 cups vegetable stock, chicken stock or water
½ tablespoon paprika, (we prefer smoked paprika)
kosher salt and white pepper, to taste
¼ cup extra virgin olive oil
1 small yellow onion, cut into small dice
1 small red pepper, seeds removed and cut into small dice
8 ounces couscous
½ cup green onions, roughly chopped

SPICY EGGPLANT

2 large globe eggplants, peeled and cut into 1-inch by 1-inch by 2-inch strips
kosher salt
⅓ cup vegetable oil
1 teaspoon fresh ginger, peeled and finely chopped
1 teaspoon garlic, finely chopped
1 small hot red chili, seeds removed and finely chopped
2 teaspoons chili oil or to taste
1 tablespoon granulated sugar
¼ cup rice wine vinegar
2 tablespoons orange juice
¼ cup vegetable stock or water
¼ cup soy sauce

STURGEON

4 5-ounce sturgeon fillets, skin off
kosher salt and white pepper, to taste
2 tablespoons vegetable oil
2 tablespoons butter

TO PREPARE THE COUSCOUS: In a medium-size saucepan over medium heat, add the vegetable stock, paprika, salt and pepper. Bring to a boil. Taste and adjust seasoning. Reduce heat to low and allow liquid to simmer.

In a large sauté pan over medium heat, add the oil. When oil is hot, add the onion and red pepper and cook until the vegetables are soft but not colored, approximately 8 to 10 minutes. Add the couscous and stir to coat the grains with oil.

Remove pan from heat. Add the simmering liquid to the couscous and stir to distribute the liquid evenly. Cover the pan and allow the couscous to steam for 5 minutes, or until all of the liquid is absorbed and the couscous is soft. Add green onions and "fluff" couscous with a fork. Keep warm.

TO PREPARE THE SPICY EGGPLANT: Place eggplant in a large colander placed over a large bowl. Sprinkle salt over eggplant. Allow eggplant to sit and release its moisture for 45 minutes to an hour.

Wash salt off of the eggplant and pat dry with a towel. Place a large sauté pan or wok over high heat. Add vegetable oil. When oil is hot, add eggplant and sauté until caramelized on the outside. Add the ginger, garlic and chili and cook 1 minute, until aromatics are just starting to turn golden brown. Add chili oil. Quickly add sugar, vinegar, orange juice, vegetable stock or water and soy sauce. Bring to a boil. Cook until the eggplant is soft and the liquid is thick enough to coat the back of a spoon.

TO PREPARE THE STURGEON: Place a sauté pan, large enough to hold all the fish, over medium heat. Season the sturgeon with salt and pepper. Add the oil and butter to the hot pan. When butter begins to foam, slip the fish into the pan. Sear the flesh for 4 to 5 minutes, or until a crust is formed. Turn the fish over and cook an additional 4 to 5 minutes, or until the flesh is opaque but still moist. Keep fish warm in a low-temperature oven.

TO SERVE: Divide couscous among 4 warm plates. Place spicy eggplant in the center of the couscous and place sturgeon on top of eggplant.

ADVANCE PREPARATION: The couscous and the eggplant may be prepared a day in advance and reheated prior to serving. Add a touch of vegetable stock or water to the pan while reheating.

SUBSTITUTIONS AND OPTIONS: Steamed rice makes a fantastic substitution for the couscous. Other firm vegetables, such as broccoli or cauliflower, will work in tandem or in place of the eggplant.

WINE NOTES: A dry Gewürztraminer with hints of orange and spice will hold up to the spicy heat of the eggplant and the richness of the fish. Recommended: 2001 Alderbrook, Gewürztraminer, Russian River Valley, California; or 2000 Covey Run, Gewürztraminer, Washington.

Makes 4 entrée servings

Fishing Methods

"There is nothing more powerful than an idea whose time has come." — Victor Hugo

There are increasing efforts internationally to balance human activity with protection of the marine environment. We often think of fish species in isolation, but each species is part of a complex ocean ecosystem; there are interactions between fish, plankton, nutrients, water and air, and if we don't understand how these interactions work, we can upset the relationships between species or between species and their habitat. Sustainable fisheries are sustainable because they are very focused fisheries, catching the target species and little else. They are generally active, not passive fisheries. Waste and bycatch is minimal.

Finfish Harvesting Methods

TROLLING: Trollers use hooks and lines with different lures to catch specific species of fish. The types of lures and the way they are arranged on the line enable trollers to target only desired species. Of all of the commercial fishing methods, trolling is the most desirable, due to low bycatch and minimal habitat damage.

LONGLINING: Longlines are used to fish large, open-water fish species. Longlining, as the name implies, involves the use of a long line with a series of baited hooks spread along the ocean floor, with the main line attached to floats. Longlines are notorious for having a high bycatch mortality rate, and may be responsible for some species of seabirds being listed as endangered species. In addition, this fishing method does not allow fishermen to select the size of the fish, so that undersized fish are often caught. Finally, if a longline is lost at sea, it continues to catch and kill fish until it sinks or there are no more hooks available.

TRAWLING: Trawling involves one or two fishing vessels towing a large funnel-shaped net between them. Nets of both bottom and mid-water trawlers are held open by two "doors," which act as paravanes, or underwater kites. Since trawling is a non-selective method of fishing, it causes a high mortality rate for many bycatch species.

DANISH SEINING: Danish seining is used to encircle, herd and finally trap the fish. A long, weighted rope fixed to each end of the seine net operates a net bag similar in shape to a trawl bag. The two ropes are used to encircle the fish and also to haul the net in. They are usually operated on the ocean bottom.

PURSE SEINING: Seining boats use large pear-shaped nets to encircle the fish. The net is then drawn together into a "purse" so the fish cannot escape. Purse seines gained public notoriety during the "dolphin-safe tuna" campaign of the 1980s; since dolphins would often follow tuna schools, when the purse seine fishers surrounded the school of tuna, dolphins would become trapped in the net and drown.

GILLNETTING: Gillnets are walls of netting set in straight lines and equipped with weights at the bottom of the net and floats at the top. The netting is usually anchored at each end. Fish swim through the virtually invisible netting and are entangled when their gills are caught in the webbing, hence the name "gillnetting." If allowed to drift freely, the method is referred to as driftnetting. The way the nets are suspended and the choice of mesh size allow gillnets to try to selectively target certain species and sizes of fish.

Shellfish Harvesting Methods

DIVING: Divers harvest shellfish by hand, one by one. Diving is highly selective with no bycatch. However, divers can damage habitat by trampling the ocean floor.

TRAPPING: Trapping uses devices such as cages or baskets to trap fish in a confined environment. Traps are often designed and baited to catch a particular species, as in a crab pot or lobster pot. A pot is a form of trap that usually rests on the bottom of the ocean, with or without bait, singly or in rows. The pots are connected by ropes to buoys on the surface marking their position. There is little bycatch associated with traps but some can occur from lost pots.

RAKING: Rakes and tongs are used to harvest clams, oysters and seaweed. The simple rakes, called scratch rakes or clam rakes, are like heavy garden rakes, but with longer, sharper teeth that are often curved upward toward the inside of the rake. Basket rakes are equipped with wire mesh baskets to hold the catch, and bull rakes have very long, often telescoping handles for operation from a skiff.

DREDGING: Dredges employ a heavy mesh "sock" to indiscriminately "suck up" everything from the sea floor. The gear is dragged along the bottom, behind the fishing boat, and the shellfish are held in a bag or sieve that allows the water, sand or mud to run out. Boat dredges are of varying weight and size but are generally fairly heavy, so their destructive impact on bottom habitats is significant. ∾

Steamed Pacific Cod
with a Stew of Mussels and Clams

Have you noticed that fish tend to lie? Chilean seabass is not a bass but actually Patagonian toothfish, California white seabass is a member of the croaker family, halibut is just an oversized flounder and Pacific lingcod is really a member of the Greenling family, not a true cod. That said, we suggest using a true Pacific cod, (a member of the *Gadidae* family), or lingcod or black cod, but not Atlantic cod, for this recipe.

Braising, poaching and steaming are closely related. Braising and poaching involve cooking in direct contact with liquid, while steaming involves suspending fish above a boiling liquid so the fish is cooked with the heat from the moist air, not directly by the hot liquid.

This steaming method has been adapted from Richard Olney and yields both a perfectly cooked moist fish and a sauce. Plates of fish are arranged on trays, sauce ingredients are added and the trays are stacked over a boiling flavorful liquid. We prefer a Chinese bamboo steamer for this recipe.

4 5-ounce Pacific true cod or lingcod fillets, skin off
kosher salt and white pepper, to taste

1 clove garlic, finely chopped
1 shallot, finely chopped
1 tablespoon fresh parsley, finely chopped
1 tablespoon fresh tarragon, finely chopped
¼ pound sun-dried tomato halves, dry, not stored in oil
1 rib celery, finely chopped

½ cup white wine
1 clove garlic, peeled

10-12 large spinach leaves, stems and spines removed

1 leek, cut into ¼-inch rounds
¼ cup Sauvignon Blanc or other dry, herbaceous white wine
2 tablespoons butter
12 Manila clams or littleneck clams
12 Pacific Mediterranean mussels or Prince Edward Island Atlantic blue mussels

1 shallot, finely chopped
water or fish stock

Season the cod fillets on both sides with salt and pepper. Wrap each fillet with spinach leaves. Place fillets, garlic, shallot, parsley, tarragon, sun-dried tomatoes, celery, leek, white wine, butter, clams and mussels on a plate deep enough to hold the liquid. Place the plate in a Chinese steamer and cover with lid.

In the bottom of a wok or a large skillet, place the wine, garlic, shallot and enough water or fish stock to cover the bottom with 1½ to 2 inches of liquid. Place Chinese steamer in wok or skillet. Place wok or skillet over medium heat and steam fish and shellfish until fish is just cooked all the way through and the shellfish opens, approximately 8 to 10 minutes. Discard any shellfish that does not open.

NOTE: Allow 8 to 10 minutes cooking time per each inch of thickness of the fish fillet.

TO SERVE: Divide vegetables and fish among 4 warm bowls. Place shellfish around fish and pour the sauce over.

ADVANCE PREPARATION: Cut all of the vegetables in advance, but assemble and cook the dish at the last minute.

SUBSTITUTIONS AND OPTIONS: California white seabass or sablefish (black cod) are excellent substitutes for the lingcod. On the West Coast, there are Manila clams, while on the east coast there are different varieties and sizes of hard shell and soft shell clams. There are Mediterranean mussels from Washington State on the West Coast and blue mussels from either Maine (the most common mussel grown in North America) or Prince Edward Island (the leading producer in Canada) on the East Coast.

Live clams and mussels, like live oysters, will remain alive for 7 to 10 days when stored in the refrigerator at 35°F to 40°F. Store covered with a damp towel. Live shellfish need to breathe, so never store them in an airtight container and never cover them with fresh water.

WINE NOTES: Fresh and light is the key. A crisp white wine with a structured mouthfeel, cream flavors and a dry citrus finish will balance the briny shellfish stew. Recommended: 2002 Paschal, Southern Oregon, Pinot Gris, Rogue Valley, Oregon; or 2000 Woodward Canyon, Charbonneau Blanc (Sémillon-Sauvignon Blanc blend), Walla Walla County, Washington.

Makes 4 entrée servings

Huge quantities of Atlantic cod are harvested by trawlers, which fillet and freeze the fish within hours of capture. Cod reproduce prolifically and should be able to sustain heavy fishing, but irresponsible, long-term overfishing and the destruction of their seafloor habitat by bottom trawlers have sent Atlantic cod (including US, Canadian, Icelandic and European stocks) into drastic declines. Although new management regulations are in place, it will take decades for Atlantic cod to recover. As an alternative, look for hook-and-line caught East Coast cod, along with their cousin the Pacific cod. Both are delicious and eco-friendly choices.

Game, Meat and Poultry Entrées:
Natural Meat Dishes from Forests and Farms

"Cooking is really not that difficult. In fact, it's more about
love and touch and caring than about special techniques or magical recipes.
It is about caring for and loving the foodstuffs your working with and
caring for and loving the people you are cooking for."

— CHARLIE TROTTER

GAME WAS ONCE CONSIDERED EXOTIC and only for special occasions or for that special meal at a fancy restaurant. We believe that game, meat and poultry are for everyday. They provide a complete palate of flavors and infinite flexibility. Our goal is to show that meat can be healthful, nutritious, sustainable and flavorful while demystifying the preparation.

Spring

HERB ROASTED WHOLE CHICKEN WITH COCOA VINAIGRETTE
SPLIT ROASTED CHICKEN WITH WILD RICE AND SWISS CHARD
SAGE RUBBED LEG OF PORK WITH APPLE-FENNEL PAN SAUCE

Summer

CRISP SKIN BREAST OF DUCK WITH WATERCRESS AND OLIVE-ORANGE SALSA
GRILLED RIB-EYE OF BEEF WITH BALSAMIC GLAZED ONIONS AND GRILLED SUMMER VEGETABLES

Autumn

GAME HEN EN COCOTTE WITH SWEET POTATO BREAD
PINOT NOIR MARINATED FLANK STEAK WITH BLUE CHEESE BUTTER

Winter

LAVENDER HONEY GLAZED VENISON ROAST WITH CAULIFLOWER-POTATO PURÉE
SEARED FALLOW DEER VENISON MEDALLIONS WITH POMEGRANATE-WALNUT SAUCE
BRAISED BEEF SHORT RIBS WITH CABERNET-ANCHOVY SAUCE
LAMB SHOULDER RAVIOLI WITH BLACK MISSION OLIVES

Why Pasture-Raised Meat?

Don't go changing that steak on the grill for a slab of tofu just yet. Beef can be healthy, and environmentally responsible, too.

Isn't all beef grass-fed? This may surprise you but the answer is "no." Until about 50 years ago all beef was grass-fed beef, but post-World War II farm subsidies resulted in a surplus of grain, primarily corn, that found its way into animal feed. The combination of this corn surplus, a powerful agricultural lobby and federal subsidies still drives today's beef industry.

In North America, the majority of cattle are weaned off grass while very young and raised in confinement with hundreds of other steers in feedlot pens, where they're fed a grain-based diet. Typically, the animals are also treated with hormones, feed additives and low-level antibiotics to boost their productivity and minimize the health problems derived from eating a high-starch diet and living in stressful, crowded conditions. Why are beef cattle raised this way? It's faster and more profitable than raising them on pasture, and fast growth is the mantra of the cattle industry.

Animals that are pasture-raised live dramatically different lives. They graze on natural grasses or stored forage from birth to market, never leaving the farm. They live such stress-free lives that they are rarely sick and never require the use of pharmaceutical drugs. As in nature, their heredity, health and the quality of the forage — not hormones or growth-promoting additives — determine their rate of growth.

Raising animals on pasture is not only better for the animals, it's also healthier for consumers. In particular, animals that graze on grass produce meat, and dairy products that have several times more health-promoting omega-3 fatty acids (the good fatty acids), vitamin E and beta carotene, but less total fat and less saturated fat than animals raised exclusively in a feedlot.

Raising animals on pasture is also better for the environment than raising them in confinement. In a feedlot operation, cattle deposit large amounts of manure in a small amount of space. The manure must be collected and transported away from the area. It costs money to transport the manure, so it is deposited as close to the feedlot as possible, risking overloading the surrounding soil with nutrients and contributing to ground and surface water contamination. On pasture-based farms, the animals deposit their manure over a relatively large tract of land, making the manure a valuable source of natural fertilizer — not a pollution problem.

Finally, because grazing animals "harvest" their own food, ranchers have little need for gas-guzzling farm equipment. Typically, such a farmer will have a tractor, a pick-up truck and haying equipment. Feedlot operations require a long list of heavy equipment, including tillers, planters, crop dusters, harvesters, grain grinders, commercial trucks, feed mixers and conveyer belts. It takes as much as ten times more fuel oil to raise cattle on grain than on grass.

One important thing to remember is that "grass-fed" does not mean organic, and organic does not necessarily mean grass-fed. Check to see how the meat is labeled and watch for these labels:

GRASS-FED: Animals are free-range or pasture- raised and not raised or finished on grain.

ALL NATURAL: The meat is minimally processed and contains no artificial ingredients, no hormones and no antibiotics.

ORGANIC: The animals are raised without hormones, antibiotics or chemical additives and processed according to USDA organic standards. The animal's feed must be 100 percent organic (no synthetic fertilizers, pesticides or herbicides). The animals may be fed grain and may or may not be free-range.

VEGETARIAN DIET: The animals are not fed any animal byproducts.

Fire up the grill and invite your cardiologist for dinner. ◠

Herb Roasted Whole Chicken
with Cocoa Vinaigrette

The smell, taste and flavor of a simple roasted chicken reminds us why we got into the cooking business in the first place. This chicken is extremely moist due to the quick brine that opens its pores and the "self basting" herb butter stuffing under the bird's skin. All you need is a glass of wine, potato purée, a green salad and a fire in the fireplace to make the perfect meal.

Brining is an age-old process of food preservation where meat is placed in a salt-water mixture before cooking to add flavor and tenderness while reducing the cooking time. By immersing meat in a liquid with a higher concentration of salt (1 cup of kosher salt to 1 gallon of water), the liquid will be absorbed into the meat. Because the meat is now loaded with extra moisture it will stay that way longer while it cooks.

The cocoa vinaigrette is reminiscent of a red *mole* from the Puebla and Oaxaca regions of central Mexico. Traditionally, *mole* is a smooth sauce made from a blend of onion, garlic, several varieties of chilies, ground seeds and often, a small amount of chocolate.

FOR BRINE
½ cup kosher salt
½ gallon cold water, or more

3½-4 pounds whole chicken, with giblets

HERB BUTTER STUFFING
1 tablespoon butter
½ medium yellow onion, finely chopped
3 cloves garlic, roughly chopped
reserved chicken livers, cut into small dice

¼ pound butter, softened
2 tablespoons chopped savory herbs (parsley, thyme, oregano and sage)
kosher salt and white pepper, to taste

COCOA VINAIGRETTE
¼ cup reserved, strained fat/pan juices
   from the roasted chicken
¼ cup vegetable oil
3 tablespoons white wine vinegar
½ teaspoon cocoa powder

⅛ teaspoon ground coriander seed
⅛ teaspoon ground fennel seed
⅛ teaspoon ground cinnamon
kosher salt and white pepper, to taste

TO BRINE THE CHICKEN: Wash the chicken, reserve the giblets and place the chicken and kosher salt in a large bowl. Add enough cold water to completely cover the chicken. Refrigerate at least 1 hour.

TO PREPARE THE HERB STUFFING: In a medium-size sauté pan over medium heat, melt the 1 tablespoon of butter. Add the onions and garlic and cook until the onions are is translucent but not colored. Add the livers and season with salt and pepper. Cook until slightly brown on the outside but still pink on the inside, about 3 to 4 minutes. Allow the liver/onion mixture to cool.

Combine the liver/onion mixture with the butter and savory herbs and the ¼ pound of soft butter in the bowl of an electric mixer. Mix until thoroughly combined. Refrigerate until just firm but not hard.

TO ROAST THE CHICKEN: Preheat oven to 450°F.

Remove chicken from brine. Rinse chicken under cold water and pat dry.

Using your fingers, gently separate and loosen the skin of the chicken from both the breast meat and leg meat. Press the herb butter under the skin and into the flesh. You will have about one quarter of the butter left over.

Truss the chicken by tucking the wing tips behind and under themselves (a chicken full nelson in wrestling terms), and by crossing the legs and tying them together with cotton kitchen string. Season the chicken with salt and pepper.

Place the chicken on a rack in a roasting pan and place the pan in the middle of the pre-heated oven. Roast the chicken for 20 minutes. Turn the oven down to 350°F and baste with the remaining herb butter and the pan drippings every 15 to 20 minutes. The chicken will take a total roasting time of approximately 45 minutes to 1 hour.

Remove the chicken from the oven and allow to rest 15 minutes before carving. Strain and reserve ½ cup of fat/pan juices for the cocoa vinaigrette.

TO PREPARE THE VINAIGRETTE: Place all ingredients in a blender and blend until smooth.

TO SERVE: Carve the chicken into 6 to 8 pieces and serve with the cocoa vinaigrette.

ADVANCE PREPARATION: The herb butter stuffing may be made several days in advance and refrigerated. Allow it to come to room temperature before stuffing under the skin of the bird.

SUBSTITUTIONS AND OPTIONS: The technique and stuffing will work for other poultry such as turkey, guinea hen, pheasant or even quail. The larger the bird, the longer the time in the brine. Twenty pound turkeys can be left in the brine for 8 to 12 hours or overnight.

We recommend serving this chicken with a potato purée or roasted potatoes, a blanched seasonal vegetable and a simple mixed green salad.

WINE NOTES: The dish needs either a crisp white wine with enough backbone and earthy elements to hold up to the cocoa and spices in the vinaigrette and the roasted flavors of the bird, or a young, ripe red wine with dark berry, cocoa and licorice notes. Recommended: 2000 Le Corti, Chianti Classico Don Tommaso, Tuscany, Italy; or 2001 Brick House, "organically grown" Gamay Noir, Willamette Valley, Oregon. Doug Tunnell, owner of Brick House, has pioneered organic grape growing and winemaking in the Pacific Northwest.

Makes 4 entrée servings.

Split Roasted Chicken
with Wild Rice and Swiss Chard

This is our favorite way to roast a bird. Split roasting allows the bird to lie flat and cook evenly. You will need strong kitchen scissors or shears to cut though the bird's backbone. A chef's trick is to season the bird just before it goes into the oven, and season it again after it comes out while it is resting. This final seasoning allows the salt and pepper to be absorbed by the skin, giving the bird a more "finished" flavor.

SPLIT CHICKEN

3½-4 pounds whole chicken, washed, giblets removed

kosher salt and cracked black pepper

WILD RICE WITH SWISS CHARD

1 cup wild rice

5 cups water

2 tablespoons olive oil

1 tablespoon garlic, finely chopped

2 shallots, finely chopped (or substitute 1 small red onion)

8 large Swiss chard, stems removed and leaves roughly chopped

kosher salt, to taste

1 tablespoon fresh summer savory leaves, roughly chopped

kosher salt and cracked black pepper, to taste

TO PREPARE THE CHICKEN: Place the chicken breast-side down on a cutting board. Using poultry or kitchen shears, cut off the wing tips. Cut along the entire length of the backbone, as near as possible to the center of the bone. Turn the bird over so the breast-side is facing up. Using the heel of your hand, strike or press down firmly on the breast. Do not be gentle, as the object is to crack the breastbone. The final step is to make a small slit with the point of a knife between the thigh and the end of the breast on both sides of the bird. Tuck the ends of the legs through the slit so the leg bones will be held in place.

 Preheat the oven to 450°F. Season the chicken with salt and pepper. Place chicken on a rack in a roasting pan. Place pan in oven and cook for 15 minutes. Baste the chicken with any juices that accumulate in the bottom of the pan. Reduce oven temperature to 375°F and continue basting every 10 to 15 minutes. The chicken will take 1 to 1¼ hours of total roasting time, depending on the size of the bird.

 The chicken is finished when a skewer is inserted into the largest part of the thigh and the juices run clear. Remove the bird from the pan and place on a plate. Season the skin of the bird again with salt and pepper, cover with aluminum foil and allow to rest 10 minutes before serving.

TO PREPARE THE WILD RICE: Rinse rice thoroughly in a strainer. Place the wild rice and water in a large saucepan over high heat. Bring to boil. Reduce heat and simmer for 30 minutes. Add salt. Continue cooking an additional 20 to 30 minutes or until rice has puffed. Remove from heat. Drain off any excess water. Reserve.

Place oil in a medium-size sauté pan heat over medium heat. Add garlic and shallots and sauté until soft but not colored, about 4 to 5 minutes. Add the chard, summer savory, salt and pepper. Continue cooking 2 to 3 minutes or until the chard has wilted. Add the wild rice and toss until heated through.

TO SERVE: Cut chicken into eight parts, (two legs, two thighs and each breast cut in half). Divide wild rice mixture evenly among four warm plates. Place two chicken pieces on top of rice.

ADVANCE PREPARATION: The wild rice mixture can be prepared a day ahead and warmed in a sauté pan with a little olive oil just before serving.

The wild rice mixture makes a wonderful chilled rice salad. Add diced dried fruit, such as dried cherries, dried apricots or raisins, additional herbs and either the white balsamic dressing (see page 68) or the basic vinaigrette (see page 20).

SUBSTITUTIONS AND OPTIONS: This recipe work perfectly well with cut up chicken instead of split. Split roasting is a very easy technique and is worth the effort and the monetary savings by buying a whole chicken and preparing it yourself.

In place of the summer savory you can substitute its Mediterranean cousins, fresh thyme, oregano or sage. Summer savory has a mild peppery flavor, sharper than thyme, not as hot as sage and earthier than oregano.

WINE NOTES: Try an off-dry white wine with refreshing, juicy acidity and enough intensity to stand up the grassiness of the wild rice and still whet the appetite for food. Recommended: 2000 Washington Hills, Dry Riesling, Columbia Valley, Washington; or 2001 Chateau Ste. Michelle-Dr. Loosen, Eroica, Riesling Columbia Valley, Washington. This wine is named to honor Beethoven's Third Symphony, and is a collaboration between Ernst Loosen of Dr. Loosen in Germany's Mosel region and Chateau Ste. Michelle's winemaker Erik Olsen.

Makes 4 entrée servings

Sage Rubbed Leg of Pork
with Apple-Fennel Pan Sauce

On a spring day several years ago, we received a phone call out of the blue from Paul Atkinson of Laughing Stock Farm. My friend John Neumiester, who sells us lamb from his Cattail Creek Farm, asked Paul to give us a call. He wanted to know of we would be interested in taking one or two of his organic, whole suckling pigs. Stu, being the butcher of our team, jumped at the chance, exclaiming, "I thought Paul only sold to restaurants in California like Chez Panisse and The French Laundry."

Since we buy only whole pigs, we often use several cuts of meat on a single plate. This recipe is an easier version using an underutilized cut of meat. Paul's pigs are, by far, THE BEST pork we have ever tasted. This means a lot coming from Stu, a man who grew up in Chicago.

1-6 pound leg of suckling pig (approximately 9 pounds with bone-in), trimmed of fat, boneless, with shank left in (substitute boneless leg of pork)
¼ cup Dijon mustard
¼ cup apple marmalade or apple jam
kosher salt and cracked black pepper, to taste
3 tablespoons garlic, finely chopped
¼ cup sage, finely chopped
¼ cup Italian parsley, finely chopped
fennel fronds from 1 bulb of fennel, finely chopped

2 tablespoons olive oil
1 carrot, cut into medium dice
2 stalks celery, cut into medium dice
1 medium onion, cut into medium dice
1 fennel bulb, cut into medium dice
1 Granny Smith apple or other tart apple variety, cut into medium dice
¼ cup apple cider vinegar or red wine vinegar
¼ cup dry, fruity red wine
1½ quarts brown veal stock, chicken stock or water

Preheat oven to 350°F.

Butterfly leg. Using a knife, make several slits in the outside and inside of meat, about 2 inches long and 1/8-inch deep, so seasoning can penetrate meat. Brush inside of leg with the mustard and apple jam. Season inside with salt and pepper, garlic, sage, parsley and fennel fronds. Roll meat to enclose herb mixture and tie with cotton kitchen string.

Heat oil in a large skillet or roasting pan. Season outside of suckling pig with salt and pepper, and brown on all sides. Remove leg from pan. Add carrot, celery, onion, chopped fennel bulb and apple to pan. Place suckling pig leg on top of vegetables. Place pan in oven and roast, turning and basting meat every 15 minutes for approximately 1 to 1½ hours, or until a meat thermometer inserted into the center reads 150°F-155°F.

Remove leg from oven and allow it to rest 10 to 15 minutes before removing string. Remove grease from pan. Place roasting pan over medium heat and add apple cider vinegar and red wine.

Allow wine to reduce until almost dry. Add stock and continue cooking until liquid is reduced by one-third of the volume. Season pan sauce with salt and pepper and strain. Keep warm.

TO SERVE: Slice leg into thin slices and pour sauce around. Serve with parsnip-potato rösti (see page 59).

ADVANCE PREPARATION: The leg can be prepared one day in advance of serving, but do not season the outside of the leg or roast it until ready to use. If there are any leftovers, serve the cold roasted pork with a salad of spicy greens, shaved fennel and julienned sour apples.

SUBSTITUTIONS AND OPTIONS: If you are not lucky enough to find a suckling pig, use a small leg of pork or a leg of lamb. If using lamb, we suggest eliminating the apple and the apple cider vinegar and adding 1 tablespoon of tomato paste to vegetables before the leg is placed on top.

WINE NOTES: Try a Rhône-style red wine with soft tannins and a bit of black fruit and spice. Recommended: 2001 Novy, Page-Nord Vineyard, Syrah, Napa Valley, California, owned by Adam & Dianna Lee of Siduri Wines; or 2001 Clos du Caillou, Bouquet des Garrigues, Côte de Rhône, France.

Makes 20 entrée servings

A Passion for Pigs:

Paul Atkinson of Laughing Stock Farm

Walk the pastures with Paul Atkinson and his young son Ansel, and you'll stride alongside a man who's been farming since he was 19. He knows every part of his 250-acre parcel of hills, forests and bottomland due east of Eugene, Oregon, land left by his father to him and his brother.

In 1986, Paul and a neighbor made goat cheese. Searching for a use for the whey left over from cheesemaking, he started raising pigs. They adored the nutritious milk byproduct. One thing led to another, and he was soon selling suckling pigs, those weighing five to six pounds. A visit from Chez Panisse's forager researching Northwest purveyors inspired his restaurant market.

"And if Alice Waters is buying from you," Paul says, "it's not long before you get a phone call from Charlie Trotter or Boulet in New York." He now raises and sells 125 pigs a year, making a profit, in part, he notes because his land is paid off.

"I've been urged to increase production," he says. "But I don't believe changing the scale would be appropriate for the size of this farm. It works as well right now to be sustainable. For me, the balance between the amount of land, its harvest, the number of animals and the cost/expense ratio is essential. Part of that balance is selling as locally as I can. If you sell locally, people have to think about who's getting their money for food."

In the barn, four plump sows are stretched out, all snoozing languorously. Nearby in a large pen 38 little piggies of varying sizes snuffle contently in clean hay. The sows have litters four times a year. The challenge, Paul notes, is to get the animals to a reputable slaughterhouse and on to the chefs who've ordered them. That's not easy. Where once there were five small slaughterhouses in the area, Paul now drives 100 miles to the nearest one. But he has established trucking connections to take the meat to his restaurant accounts. "All I have is my good name and the consistency of my product," he says. "I have to trust my suppliers to uphold my faith."

Paul says he appreciates The Peerless Restaurant's efforts in creating a menu from locally produced, seasonal produce and meats. "It's about education. If you can get one person eating at a restaurant to notice where their food comes from, there's a chance they'll remember when they get home and seek it out. That would be a big victory for local farmers everywhere." ～

Crisp Skin Breast of Duck
with Watercress and Olive-Orange Salsa

We have adapted Jacques Pepin's method for cooking duck breast. It draws out the most amount of fat from the skin, allowing the skin to get very crisp, while keeping the flesh moist. The key is to not discard any of the rendered duck fat while the breast is cooking.

We recommend using magret duck breasts for their superior flavor and lean meat. Magret means the breast of any duck that has been fattened for the production of foie gras. The word magret is from the French *maigre*, meaning lean: although the duck breast is covered in a thick layer of fat, the meat itself contains only 5 percent fat.

4 magret duck breasts
kosher salt and cracked black pepper, to taste
1 head garlic, cloves separated but not peeled
1 shallot, roughly chopped
1 sprig fresh thyme

1 bay leaf
2 cups watercress
½ cup red wine
1 cup brown chicken, game stock or water
1 cup Olive-Orange Salsa (see page 200)

Place a large, cast iron or other heavy-bottomed pan over medium heat. Score the duck breasts by cutting through the skin in a criss-cross pattern without cutting the meat. Season the breasts with salt and pepper. Place duck breasts, skin-side down in the hot pan. Cook the breasts until the fat begins to render and the skin starts to brown, about 10 to 15 minutes. Do not drain the fat as it comes out of the skin. Make sure the skin is not burning; lower the heat if necessary. Continue cooking the duck breast until the skin is golden brown and crisp, about an additional 20 minutes.

Turn the heat down to low. Leave the duck breasts, skin-side down partially submerged in the fat. Add the garlic, shallot, thyme and bay leaf and cover. Cook covered for about 10 minutes, or until the breasts are warm and pink in the center. Check occasionally to make sure the duck is steaming, not frying, in the oil.

Remove the duck from the pan and place on paper towels. Drain the duck fat from the pan, leaving the vegetables, and save the fat. Allow the duck breasts to rest for 5 minutes before serving.

NOTE: The reserved duck fat can be used to make Potato-Onion Tart Tatin (see page 54).

Return the pan with the vegetables to the heat. Add the watercress and cook until just wilted, about 3 to 5 minutes. Remove watercress from pan. Add the red wine and bring liquid to a boil, scraping the caramelized pieces on the bottom of the pan. Allow wine to reduce until almost dry. Add the stock or water and bring to a boil. Allow liquid to reduce by half its volume. Taste sauce and adjust seasoning. Strain sauce.

TO SERVE: Place wilted watercress in the center of the plate. Place duck breast on top of watercress. Pour sauce over duck and serve with salsa.

ADVANCE PREPARATION: The salsa can be prepared several days in advance and refrigerated. Cook the duck breasts and assemble the dish just prior to serving.

SUBSTITUTIONS AND OPTIONS: You may substitute Pekin duck breasts for the magret duck breasts. Pekin duck breasts have less overall fat, will shrink more and are lighter in flavor than Muscovy or Moulard ducks. The cooking time will be cut by at least half.

WINE NOTES: The best bet here is a red wine with soft tannins and bright citrus notes. Remember, a red Burgundy does not have to be expensive. Recommended: 2000 Vincent Girardin, Cuvée St. Vincent, Burgundy, France; or 2000 Au Bon Climat, Isabelle, Pinot Noir, Santa Barbara, California. The latter comes from an American winery created to produce high-quality handcrafted wine from traditional Burgundian varietals.

Makes 4 entrée servings

Grilled Rib-Eye of Beef
with Balsamic Glazed Onions and Grilled Summer Vegetables

As we mentioned, grass-fed beef is better for you, but it is the taste that matters to us. It has been our experience that you will have a passionate response: either love it or hate it. Grass-fed is leaner, gamier and will be tougher if cooked all the way through. The fat in grass-fed beef tastes lighter and does not coat your mouth like that of corn-fed beef; you will not get that heavy feeling after eating.

Grass-fed beef requires a few cooking tips. In general, grass-fed beef will cook more quickly than other beef. When grilling, first sear the meat over high heat, then move it to a cooler part of the grill to finish cooking. Be careful not to pierce the meat when turning or moving it, or the beef will lose some moisture.

BEEF AND VEGETABLES
- 1 cup extra virgin olive oil
- 2 tablespoons garlic, finely chopped
- 1 large eggplant, cut in half and then cut into ¼-inch thick slices
- 1 medium green zucchini, cut into ¼-inch thick slices
- 1 medium yellow squash, cut into ¼-inch thick slices
- 1 red pepper
- 1 yellow pepper
- kosher salt and cracked black pepper, to taste
- 4 10-ounce beef rib-eye steaks, trimmed of excess fat
- kosher salt and cracked black pepper, to taste

BALSAMIC ONIONS
- 2 medium yellow onions, thinly sliced
- 1 tablespoon butter
- 4 tablespoons balsamic vinegar

TO PREPARE THE RIB-EYE: Preheat grill to medium-high heat. Combine oil and garlic. Set half of the oil mixture aside for the steaks and half for the vegetables.

Place eggplant in a large colander set over large bowl. Sprinkle salt over eggplant. Allow eggplant to sit and give off moisture for 45 minutes to an hour. Wash salt off of eggplant and pat dry with a towel.

In a large bowl, toss all the vegetables with half of the oil mixture. Season with salt and pepper. Arrange eggplant, zucchini, squash and peppers on the grill at a 45 degree angle. Cook 3 to 4 minutes and then turn vegetables 90 degrees to create crosshatching marks. After 3 to 4 minutes, flip to other side and repeat process. Make sure the peppers are charred evenly on all sides.

Remove the vegetables from the grill and set aside. Place peppers in a paper bag, close the top and let them steam for 10 minutes to loosen their skins, then scrape the charred skin from the roasted peppers. Slice peppers in half. Remove the seeds and cut into ½-inch wide strips.

Brush remaining oil mixture on steaks with a basting brush. Sprinkle steaks with cracked black peppercorns and salt. Lay steaks on grill at a 45 degree angle. Cook 3 to 4 minutes and then turn 90 degrees to create crosshatching. After 3 to 4 minutes, flip steaks to other side, and repeat process. Grill until desired doneness.

TO PREPARE THE BALSAMIC ONIONS: In a medium-size sauté pan over low to medium heat melt butter. Add sliced onions and sauté, stirring occasionally, until onions are soft and golden brown, approximately 20 minutes. Add vinegar. Bring to a boil and cook until the volume is reduced by one third. Season with salt and pepper. Remove from heat and reserve.

TO SERVE: Arrange the grilled vegetables on a warm plate. Place steaks next to vegetables and top with balsamic onions.

ADVANCE PREPARATION: The onions can be made a day head and reheated in a sauté pan. The vegetables can be grilled a day ahead and reheated in a 350°F oven just prior to serving.

SUBSTITUTIONS AND OPTIONS: Mix and match whichever seasonal vegetables are the best and suit your taste. The balsamic onion mixture is also a wonderful accompaniment for stronger game meats such as grilled venison or buffalo.

WINE NOTES: A well-balanced, not over the top, not overly fruity red wine will work with the slightly sweeter and gamier flavor of the grass-fed beef and the reduced balsamic vinegar. Recommended: 2000 Troon Vineyard, Druid Fluid, Applegate Valley, Oregon; or 1999 Jade Mountain, La Provencal, California. The Applegate Valley is a sub-appellation within the Rogue Valley in southern Oregon, and is home to the most unusual acre of Zinfandel grapes named the "Druid Fluid Factory" in honor of winemaker Dick Troon's Scottish heritage.

Makes 4 entrée servings

Game Hen en Cocotte
with Sweet Potato Bread

As Julia Child said, "Whole chicken roasted in a covered casserole, in a buttery steam of herbs and aromatic vegetables, has a very special tenderness and flavor. Hot, served simply with the juices it has produced in its casserole, or cold on the buffet table or picnic, poulet en cocotte is one of the great French contributions to the art of chicken cookery. Except for the browning of the chicken on top of the stove before roasting, which is for the sake of appearances, this is a practically effortless cooking method."

This is a cooking method that actually benefits from using a slightly older, slightly gamier bird. The game hen we are referring to is a naturally raised Guinea hen or Guinea fowl, also known as a pintade or African pheasant. A mature Guinea fowl has a fifty-fifty ratio between meat and carcass. These birds are moist, meaty and substantially leaner than chicken. Do not use a Rock Cornish hen or Rock Cornish game hen because they are a cross between the Cornish and White Rock breeds of chicken and are very young, small and somewhat flavorless.

¼ pound all-natural sliced bacon cut into 1½-inch by ½-inch rectangles

4 cloves garlic, peeled

1 lemon, cut into quarters

1 stalk celery

1 sprig fresh thyme

1 bay leaf

3½-4 pounds whole guinea hen, washed, giblets removed

kosher salt and cracked black pepper, to taste

¼ pound button mushrooms or shiitake mushrooms, stems removed but left whole

24 baby carrots, peeled or 1 large carrot, peeled and cut into ½-inch by ½-inch by 2-inch julienne strips

1 small turnip, peeled and cut into wedges

2 small Yukon gold or other waxy potatoes, cut into wedges

4 ounces brown chicken or game stock or water

4 slices sweet potato bread, cut ½-inch thick and toasted (see page 204)

Preheat oven to 450°F.

Place an ovenproof casserole dish over medium heat and add the bacon. Cook, stirring frequently, about 12 to 15 minutes, or until bacon is crisp. Remove bacon and drain on paper towels but do not remove the bacon fat from the casserole.

Place the garlic, lemon, celery, thyme and bay leaf inside the guinea hen. Season the bird with salt and pepper. Place the guinea hen in the casserole dish and place the dish in oven. Cook uncovered for 15 minutes. Remove casserole from oven and pour off any fat accumulating on the bottom of the casserole. Reduce oven temperature to 350°F.

Surround the guinea hen with the rendered bacon, mushrooms, carrots, turnips and potatoes. Add the stock or water, cover the casserole dish and place in oven. Cook for about 1 hour, or until the juices run clear when a skewer is inserted into the largest part of the thigh.

TO SERVE: Remove the herbs, celery, lemon and vegetables from the inside cavity of the hen and discard. Place guinea hen on a serving platter. Surround the bird with the vegetables and spoon the juices from the casserole over the top. When cut into individual servings, serve the bird on top of sweet potato bread.

ADVANCE PREPARATION: The guinea hen may be cooked earlier in the day. When ready to serve, place the bird, vegetables and juice back into the casserole dish and place in a 350°F oven until warm.

SUBSTITUTIONS AND OPTIONS: Instead of a guinea hen, you can substitute a free-range, certified organic or natural chicken, a pheasant, or even a goose that has been cut into parts in order to fit into a casserole dish.

WINE NOTES: This dish needs a wine with vibrant fruit, a hint of spice and soft tannins to match with the "pumpkin pie" flavors in the sweet potato bread. Try a true Cru Beaujolais (not a lifeless Nouveau). Recommended: 2000 Jean Foillard, Première, Beaujolais, France; or 2000 Signal Hill, Stellenbosch, Gamay Noir, South Africa; or 2001 Brick House, "organically grown" Gamay Noir, Willamette Valley, Oregon, one of only a few Gamay Noir producers in the United States.

Makes 4 entrée servings

Pinot Noir Marinated Flank Steak
with Blue Cheese Butter

The flank section is found on the underside of the cow right below the loin and sirloin sections. The flank is the only steak in the carcass containing an entire large muscle. Other steaks are cut across the muscle fibers, while the flank steak fibers run the full length of the steak. Since the flank steak is one of the less tender but extremely flavorful steaks, we recommend marinating it with an acidic liquid, like the wine in this recipe, to help tenderize the meat.

Our favorite substitute for flank steak is hanger steak, also known as a hanging tender, butcher's steak (because butchers traditionally saved this full-flavored but somewhat unattractive cut of beef for themselves), butcher's tenderloin or onglet. It came to be called "hanger steak" because it is part of the diaphragm that literally hangs between the last rib and the loin. This cut is covered with a thin membrane and has a central vein that runs through the length of the cut; both should be removed (preferably by your butcher) before cooking.

MARINADE
¾ cup Pinot Noir or other fruity red wine

juice and zest of one orange

¼ cup red wine vinegar

½ cup honey

1 ounce soy sauce

1 tablespoon extra virgin olive oil

1 teaspoon garlic, finely chopped

1 teaspoon Dijon mustard

1 green onion, roughly chopped

1 dried hot chili *(optional)*

½ teaspoon ground cumin

½ teaspoon ground coriander

1 teaspoon cracked black pepper

FLANK STEAKS
2 2-pound beef flank steaks, trimmed
  of excess fat

kosher salt, to taste

BLUE CHEESE BUTTER
¼ pound soft butter

¼ pound blue cheese, preferably domestic

1 tablespoon parsley, finely chopped

1 tablespoon lemon juice

kosher salt and white pepper, to taste

TO PREPARE THE MARINADE: Combine all ingredients in a shallow stainless steel, ceramic or glass non-reactive dish. Stir well to make sure the honey, mustard and dried spices are dissolved.

TO PREPARE THE FLANK STEAKS: Add the flank steaks to the marinade and turn several times to make sure the meat is well coated. Cover and refrigerate 4 to 6 hours or overnight.

When ready to cook the steaks, remove the meat from the marinade. Place the marinade in a medium-size saucepan and bring to a boil. Reduce to a simmer and continue to cook until the liquid is reduced by three-quarters or it is thick enough to coat the back of a spoon. Keep warm.

Season the flank steaks with salt. Grill, broil or sauté steaks over medium heat, 5 to 8 minutes on each side for medium-rare. Allow the meat to rest on a plate for 5 minutes before slicing.

TO PREPARE THE BLUE CHEESE BUTTER: Combine all ingredients in the bowl of an electric mixer or food processor. Mix until well combined.

The butter can be either placed in a sealed container or rolled into a log using parchment paper or plastic wrap. Refrigerate or freeze until ready to use.

TO SERVE: Cut the steaks at a 45-degree angle across the grain of the meat. Serve with reserved, reduced marinade and small, thin pats of blue cheese butter.

ADVANCE PREPARATION: The marinade can be made several days in advance. Do not leave the flank steaks in the marinade for more than 12 hours or the acid from the wine and mustard will "cook" the meat too much. The blue cheese butter will keep 2 to 3 days in the refrigerator or can be frozen for up to a month.

SUBSTITUTIONS AND OPTIONS: As we mentioned, other less tender cuts of beef like the hanger steak, skirt steak or even a round of beef will benefit from the marinade. Additionally, flank steaks from buffalo, elk, venison or other "furred" game will work well.

The blue cheese butter is just one version of a *beurre composé* or classic compound butter. Almost any seasonings or flavoring can be incorporated into softened butter. The melted compound butter makes a wonderful sauce by itself or can be incorporated into another sauce to add an additional level of flavorings and richness.

WINE NOTES: Follow the "cook with it and drink with it" rule — one of our favorite guidelines. This recipe calls for a "big fella" Pinot Noir bursting with fruit and a good tannic backbone. Recommended: 2000 Hamacher, Pinot Noir, Willamette Valley, Oregon is a beauty with a touch of the beast; or 2000 Beaux Frères, Beaux Frères Vineyard, Pinot Noir, Willamette Valley, Oregon.

Makes 8 to 12 entrée servings

Cooperative Winemaking Goes Green:

Eric Hamacher and Ned Lumpkin
of Carlton Winemakers Studio

If you build a cooperative winemaking facility, they will come.

Prophetic words in Oregon's winemaking circles. The only thing lacking was someone with the vision and drive to make it happen. Enter Eric Hamacher and Ned Lumpkin. In 2000, the winemakers opened Carlton Winemakers Studio in Carlton, Oregon, a sleepy farming town in Yamhill County, southwest of Portland.

The Dundee Hills of Yamhill County resemble the Burgundy region of France like no other place on the planet. A farming region for more than a century, about 30 years ago someone recognized the similarity, and Yamhill County started its slow rejuvenation from agricultural hard times to vintners' paradise. Rolling hills, rich volcanic soil, and a balance of sun and rain created an ideal microclimate for temperamental Pinot Noir grapes.

Hamacher, an oenologist who studied at UC Davis, researched options carefully before breaking ground for the environmentally aware facility. Built alongside a railroad track in a former grass seed field, the building resembles one of the big rambling barns traditional to the area. It's the first winery in America to earn the Leadership in Energy and Environmental Design (LEED) certification. It's also registered with and certified by the US Green Building Council (USGBC).

To qualify, the winery features state-of-the-art equipment in a gravity-driven building, along with natural light, passive solar heat, natural air flow and a variety of recycled materials. Recycling practices are followed in the production process. Each winemaker using the shared facility operates independently with separate cellars and his or her own staff, but all enjoy the benefits of state-of-the-art equipment.

Hamacher confesses he had a mission. "I wanted others to be inspired by the design of the building and consider the idea for themselves," he says. "We have a stunning winery that happens to be green, and it's a terrific, cost-effective place to work and make remarkable wines."

Many of the West's master winemakers agree. Tony Soter, an early master of California's Pinot Noir, believed in the project from the start and used the facility to make his first Oregon-crafted Pinot Noirs and Chardonnays. Other luminaries of Oregon's winemaking world followed, including Jack Bagdade, Andrew Rich and Lynn Penner-Ash.

"This is truly an artist's studio for winemakers, a place for vintners to experiment and share, and it's all done with the environment in mind," says Hamacher.

Here at The Peerless we'll raise a glass to that. ❧

Lavender Honey Glazed Venison Roast with Cauliflower-Potato Purée

Fallow deer originated in the Mediterranean region of the world, and today can be found throughout Europe, New Zealand and the United States. While most commercially available farm-raised venison comes from red deer, we prefer fallow deer meat because it's extremely lean and tender. We have converted many game-wary customers with the mild, almost beef-like taste of fallow deer.

For the accompanying vegetable purée, we cook, purée and rice the cauliflower and potatoes separately. This will result in a smoother, dryer purée, allowing you to add more butter and cream. More butter and cream. Need we say more?

GLAZE/SAUCE

¼ cup lavender honey

1 teaspoon cracked black peppercorns

1 teaspoon fresh lavender leaves, finely chopped (or substitute ½ teaspoon dry lavender leaves)

2 allspice berries, crushed

3 juniper berries, crushed

¾ cup apple brandy

1½ cups apple cider

¾ cup white wine vinegar

TO FINISH THE SAUCE

2 tablespoons butter

VENISON RACK ROAST

2 fallow deer venison racks, bones frenched, fat trimmed

kosher salt and cracked black pepper, to taste

vegetable oil

CAULIFLOWER-POTATO PURÉE

4 large russet potatoes, peeled and cut into cubes

½ head cauliflower, florets trimmed

2 tablespoons soft butter

2 ounces heavy cream, warm

kosher salt and white pepper, to taste

TO PREPARE THE GLAZE: In a medium-size stainless steel saucepan, over medium heat, combine all of the ingredients except butter and whisk well. Bring the mixture to a simmer and cook for 5 minutes or until volume is reduced by one-third. (Approximately 2 cups of liquid should remain.) Reserve 1 cup for glaze and 1 cup for sauce.

TO PREPARE THE VENISON: Preheat oven to 450°F.

Season the venison racks with salt and pepper. In an ovenproof sauté pan over medium heat, add just enough oil to cover the bottom of the pan. Sear the venison on one side until lightly brown. Rotate the venison and brown other sides.

Brush glaze on meat. Place pan in oven and roast venison 15-20 minutes, basting with glaze every 5 minutes, until meat is medium-rare (approximately 125°F internal temperature on a meat thermometer). Remove the venison and let it rest for 10-15 minutes.

TO PREPARE THE CAULIFLOWER-POTATO PURÉE: In separate saucepans, cover potatoes and cauliflower with salted cold water. Bring each to a boil and cook until completely tender, about 10-15 minutes. Combine the butter and cream in a small saucepan and place over medium heat until warm.

Drain potatoes and cauliflower. Pass potatoes through a food mill or potato ricer. Purée cauliflower in a food processor until smooth. Combine potatoes and cauliflower in a bowl. Slowly add cream/butter and mix by hand until a smooth purée is formed. Season with salt and pepper.

TO SERVE: To finish the sauce, bring the sauce to a boil over high heat. Remove from heat and swirl in the butter, 1 tablespoon at a time until the sauce is shiny and smooth. Place purée in center of plate. Slice venison rack into individual chops and place 3-4 chops next to purée. Pour sauce over the venison.

ADVANCE PREPARATION: The glaze can be made ahead and stored in the refrigerator for up to a month. Honey, like wine, has its own *terroir* and sense of place. Seek out local honeys and small producers.

SUBSTITUTIONS AND OPTIONS: Venison leg, loin or tender can also be used or even a pork rack will make a great substitute. The glaze/sauce also works well as a barbecue glaze for beef or salmon. Regulate the heat of the grill carefully because the honey in the glaze will burn easily.

Steamed or blanched seasonal vegetables, lightly tossed in melted butter, makes a great finishing touch to the dish. We recommend root vegetables such as turnips, rutabagas, celery root and parsnips.

WINE NOTES: The honey and the allspice in the glaze require a wine with some spice but balanced with toasty oak and ripe berry flavors. Recommended: 2000 Conde de Haza, Ribera del Duero, Spain; or 2000 Abacela, Tempranillo, Umpqua Valley, Oregon. Earl and Hilda Jones of Abacela have pursued their passion for making fine Spanish-style wine in America.

Makes 4 entrée servings

Seared Fallow Deer Venison Medallions with Pomegranate-Walnut Sauce

Pomegranates, derived from the French words, *pomme garneté* (seeded apple), is one of the world's oldest cultivated fruit. They are usually allowed to ripen on the tree before being picked. Ripe pomegranates often have black spots on the outer skin and don't always look like the perfect, blushing fruit. Not to worry: the blemishes do not affect the arils, the edible juice sacs, or the delicious, crunchy seeds.

Pomegranate concentrate is a tart, brownish syrup that is sometimes labeled pomegranate molasses and is made from reduced and concentrated pomegranate juice. A staple in Middle Eastern cuisines, pomegranate concentrate has an exotic sweet-tart flavor and is used in meat marinades and *fesenjoon*, a dip or meat condiment. Our pomegranate sauce is a warm version of *fesenjoon* and is used as a pan sauce for the venison.

POMEGRANATE SAUCE
Makes 1½ cups

1 tablespoon olive oil
2 cloves garlic, peeled and finely chopped
1 cup walnut pieces, removed from the shell
¼ cup pomegranate concentrate or pomegranate molasses

2 cups water
kosher salt, to taste

VENISON

4 5-ounce fallow deer venison medallions, cut from the loin

kosher salt and cracked black pepper, to taste
2 tablespoons vegetable oil

TO PREPARE THE POMEGRANATE SAUCE: Place the oil in a large sauté pan over medium heat. Add the garlic and sauté until lightly browned and soft, about 2 to 3 minutes. Remove the garlic and oil from pan and reserve. Return the pan to the heat and add the walnuts. Dry roast the nuts in the pan, stirring occasionally, until toasted, about 6 minutes. Remove nuts from the pan. In a blender or food processor, purée the garlic, walnuts, pomegranate concentrate and water. Add salt to taste.

TO PREPARE THE VENISON: Season venison with salt and pepper. Place a large cast iron or heavy sauté pan over high heat. Add the oil, and heat until it just begins to smoke. Carefully add the venison medallions. Sear the venison on all sides until the meat caramelizes and is golden brown, about 4 to 5 minutes on each side.

Remove venison and any fat left in the pan. Return pan to the heat and add the pomegranate sauce. Cook the sauce until half of the liquid remains. Keep warm.

TO SERVE: Place medallions of venison on warm plates. Pour sauce over them and serve with onion marmalade (see page 203) and roasted root vegetables (see page 56).

ADVANCE PREPARATION: The pomegranate sauce can be made several days in advance and stored in a covered container in the refrigerator.

SUBSTITUTIONS AND OPTIONS: A filet of beef or even a New York beef strip steak will make an excellent substitute for the venison.

Reduce the water to 1 cup and the pomegranate sauce will make a wonderful spread or dip for chilled meats.

WINE NOTES: The rich flavor of venison likes to be matched with something sweet in the same way that ham does. A smoky, black cherry, plumy Syrah will both hold its own with the pomegranates and make the venison happy. Recommended: 2001 Soléna, Del Rio Vineyard, Syrah, Rogue Valley, Oregon; or 2001 d'Arenberg, "The Footbolt," Shiraz, McLaren Vale, Australia. Francis "d'Arry" d'Arenberg Osborn (grandson of the founder, teetotaller and lay preacher, John Osborn) has almost single-handedly established the McLaren Vale region as an indispensable part of the Australian winemaking landscape and propelled his wines to almost cult status.

Makes 4 entrée servings

Braised Beef Short Ribs
with Cabernet-Anchovy Sauce

This is one of our favorite recipes for several reasons. First, by using a cut of meat not normally used, you promote economic and environmental sustainability by making use of all the beef. The concept goes back to our practical European training where chefs "use everything from an animal." The short rib of beef is cut from the beef back ribs consisting of seven ribs from the rib section, including the meat between the rib bones.

Second, this is a perfect dish for winter — curl up around a fire, sip a glass of red wine, and savor succulent braised meat so tender it literally falls off the bone.

Last, we like to think this recipe playfully illustrates that the concept of "surf & turf" can go beyond lobster and filet. The saltiness of the anchovy rounds out the rich beef flavors and takes this simple dish from ordinary to sublime.

BRAISED BEEF SHORT RIBS

2 pounds natural beef short ribs, cut 1½-inch thick and trimmed,
kosher salt and cracked black pepper, to taste
vegetable oil, as needed
1 medium onion, peeled and roughly chopped
1 carrot, peeled and roughly chopped
2 ribs celery, roughly chopped
3 cloves garlic, peeled, roughly chopped
1 tablespoon whole black peppercorns

1 bay leaf
4 sprigs fresh thyme
½ cup port wine
1 cup Cabernet Sauvignon wine or other (substitute a relatively non-fruity, dry red wine)
2-3 cups chicken stock, veal stock, beef stock or water
1-2 oil-packed anchovy fillets, rinsed

Preheat oven to 350°F. Season ribs with salt and pepper and set aside.

Place a large ovenproof braising pan over medium-high heat. Add enough oil to coat the bottom of the pan. Add the ribs and brown all sides. Remove meat and most of the fat from the pan. Add the onion, carrot, celery and garlic to the pan. Sauté the vegetables until they begin to brown. Add the peppercorns, bay leaf and thyme. Add both wines to the pan and simmer until the liquid is reduced by half. Return the ribs to the pan and add enough stock to just cover the meat. Bring stock to a boil and then reduce to a simmer.

Cover and place pan in oven. Braise 3 to 4 hours or until meat is tender and just begins to fall off the bone.

Remove meat from pan and keep warm. Strain the cooking liquid into a saucepan. Simmer until liquid is reduced by half. Add the anchovies. Using a blender, purée until smooth. Taste and adjust seasoning. Keep warm.

TO SERVE: Serve with sautéed greens and caramelized root vegetables (see page 56) or potato purée.

ADVANCE PREPARATION: The beef can be made several days ahead of serving. We actually feel the flavors are better and more complex if the beef is allowed to cool and then is reheated in the sauce and served the following day.

SUBSTITUTIONS AND OPTIONS: Any leftover meat can be shredded and made into a luxurious ravioli filling or pasta sauce.

   If you choose not to make your own stock, purchase an organic, natural stock with no added salt (see Sources and Information section).

WINE NOTES: The wine reduction in the braising liquid (later turned into the sauce for the dish) ties the food to the wine. The salty flavor of the anchovies will cut through both the fattiness of the ribs and balance the sweetness of the fruit in a young Cabernet Sauvignon or Merlot. Recommended: 2000 Walla Walla Vintners, Cabernet Sauvignon, Walla Walla Valley, Washington; or 2000 Leonetti, Merlot, Columbia Valley, Washington.

Makes 4 entrée servings

Lamb Shoulder Ravioli
with Black Mission Olives

Lamb shoulder is another underutilized cut of meat. I promised my lamb supplier, John Neumiester of Cattail Creek Farm, that if he sold us the regular "restaurant" cuts of lamb, such as racks, loins and legs, that we would make sure we also used the "off-cuts" like the shoulder.

This recipe is not only flavorful, but any extra lamb-olive filling makes a wonderful second meal. Toss leftover filling with pasta noodles or, if time is of the essence, simply make a sandwich with the filling and a little Dijon mustard.

LAMB SHOULDER

1 lamb shoulder, boneless, trimmed of
   excess fat
kosher salt and black pepper, to taste
vegetable oil, as needed
1 medium onion, roughly chopped
1 carrot, roughly chopped
2 ribs celery, roughly chopped
3 cloves garlic, roughly chopped
1 tablespoon tomato paste

1 tablespoon black peppercorns
1 bay leaf
2 sprigs fresh thyme
2 sprigs Italian parsley
2 sprigs fresh rosemary
½ cup red wine vinegar
½ cup white wine
2-3 cups chicken stock, veal stock, beef stock
   or water

RAVIOLI FILLING

braised lamb shoulder
1 tablespoon fresh mint, finely chopped
2 ounces Black Mission olives, pits removed,
   roughly chopped

ground black pepper, to taste
1-2 tablespoons lamb sauce
1 recipe egg pasta dough, rolled out to thin
   sheets (see page 17)

TO PREPARE THE LAMB SHOULDER: Preheat oven to 350°F. Cut the lamb shoulder into 1-inch cubes. Season with salt and pepper.

In a large ovenproof braising pan over medium-high heat, add enough oil to coat the bottom of the pan. Add lamb and sauté, stirring occasionally, until the meat is golden brown on all sides. Remove lamb from pan. Place pan back on heat and add the onion, carrot, celery, garlic and tomato paste. Sauté until the paste begins to brown. Add the peppercorns, bay leaf, thyme, parsley and rosemary. Add the vinegar and wine to the pan and reduce the liquid until half of the volume remains. Return the lamb back to the pan and enough stock to just cover the meat. Bring stock to a boil and then reduce to a simmer.

Cover and place pan in oven. Braise 1 to 1½ hours or until meat is tender.

Remove meat from pan. Strain the cooking liquid into a saucepan. Simmer until liquid is reduced by half. Taste and adjust seasoning.

TO PREPARE THE RAVIOLI: With two forks, shred the lamb meat as finely as possible, discarding any fat. In a medium-sized bowl, combine the lamb, mint, olives and pepper. Moisten the filling with a tablespoon or two of the sauce. It should be moist but not saucy. Gently stir well to mix. Taste and adjust seasoning.

Cut the pasta sheets into 4-inch by 8-inch rectangles. Place one tablespoon of the lamb-olive mixture on half of each rectangle. Lightly wet two edges of the pasta around the filling with water. Fold over the pasta, like a book, to make a 4-inch by 4-inch square. Press down the edges and around the filling of each ravioli to seal and to squeeze out any air bubbles.

Bring a large pot of salted water to a boil.

TO SERVE: Add the ravioli to the boiling water and cook until the pasta is tender, about 4 to 6 minutes. Drain the ravioli. Bring the reserved lamb sauce to a boil. Place four ravioli in each of four warm soup bowls and pour the sauce over the pasta.

ADVANCE PREPARATION: The lamb shoulder can be braised several days in advance but it is easier to shred the meat when it is still warm.

The raviolis can be made up to a day in advance and kept refrigerated or placed on a sheet pan between pieces of parchment paper and frozen. Once frozen, carefully place the raviolis in a sealed bag and store them in the freezer for up to a week. When ready to serve, take them from the freezer directly to the boiling water. Do not thaw them out ahead of time or they will become soggy.

SUBSTITUTIONS AND OPTIONS: You can substitute leg of lamb, lamb shank or lamb neck for the lamb shoulder. Additionally, almost any other braised or cooked meat or game will work in place of the lamb.

You may substitute egg roll, wonton and gyoza (pot sticker) wrappers for the pasta dough. The texture of the final dish will be slightly more "chewy" but will still yield a wonderful result.

A lovely first course is to roll up excess filling in plastic wrap, like a sushi roll, and chill for several hours. Slice the chilled lamb mixture and serve with a salad and toasted French baguette slices.

WINE NOTES: Even though we use white wine in the braising liquid we suggest serving a young Cabernet. Make sure the filling and the sauce are not under-seasoned, as salt and vinegar tend to soften the tannins in a young red wine. Recommended: 1999 Sequoia Grove, Cabernet Sauvignon, Napa Valley, California; or 2000 Château Les Ormes de Pez, St. Estèphe, Bordeaux, France.

Makes 6 entrée servings, about 30, 4-inch-square ravioli

The Lamb Man:

John Neumeister of Cattail Creek Farm

"It's entirely grass-fed, organic, and it's simply the best lamb anyone's ever eaten," says Stu. "It tastes like lamb is supposed to, that wonderful rich taste, the sweetness, tenderness and deep flavor. We couldn't wait to put it on our menu."

John Neumeister is the man behind this superb lamb. He has a farmer's genes and an entrepreneur's instincts. In the 1970s, enticed by the year-round lush grasses of Oregon's Willamette River valley and its hippie-era idealist communes, he moved west from his family's Ohio sheep farm.

When farming is in your bones, you can't run away from it. And when you're raising lamb and selling to the best restaurants, you don't compromise on the quality or on land management practices that yield a stellar product. In 1983, John bought his own ranch and named it Cattail Creek Farm. With open bottomland along the river and small pastures, it's rich and fertile with grasses — rye, alfalfa, clover — that sheep adore.

"We've chosen a different path," he says. "Our pastures are dedicated to sheep production. We use our own land or rent land from small farms, about 20 acres or so, using small fields of 5 to 10 acres for sheep grazing; there's an efficiency of scale there. Quality is our most important ingredient." Dotted with white Romneys, some Dorsets and a few Navajo Churros lazily grazing emerald hills, the pastures in view are a serene sight, and a testament to hard work.

Slowly and steadily over 20 years, John developed a niche market for his organic lamb among the West Coast's top restaurants. "We've only gotten to where we are in the past year and with a team effort, but I do this because it's fun. I love restaurant people," he says, "with all their quirks and demands and volatility." He does most restaurant deliveries and direct marketing himself, something few farmers do, while a partner now tends to the day-to-day chores of raising their 400 ewes.

"It's a seasonal product, so that puts a spin on marketing efforts, too. Relationships are the key, along with taste, of course." Along with lamb that truly tastes like lamb. ∽

Vegetarian Entrées:
The Bounty of Fields and Gardens

"Let the monopolies tremble at a green revolution.
We have nothing to lose but the burger chains. We have a world
to win. Veggies of world, Unite!"

— NEVILLE HEATH FOWLER

WE ARE NOT VEGETARIANS, but we do love vegetables. We do not approach vegetable cookery as an afterthought or as an exercise in eating healthy or even handle vegetables the same way we handle proteins. We prefer to approach vegetable-based dishes as a celebration of the ingredients. Our job as chefs is to enhance their extraordinary shapes, colors, textures and flavors. We encourage you to seek out your own network of local purveyors and farmers. Find out what's in season and then buy it. Don't be afraid to take it home and roast it, sauté it, blanch it, braise it or steam it. Concentrate on the flavor components of a dish, use extremely fresh seasonal produce, and the nutritional aspects of the cuisine will fall into place.

Spring
GOAT CHEESE-RICOTTA GNOCCHI
BEGGAR'S PURSE FILLED WITH SPRING VEGETABLES

Summer
ROASTED WHOLE CANDY SWEET ONIONS
HEIRLOOM TOMATO AND SUMMER SQUASH TORTE

Autumn
ROOT VEGETABLE AND ONION MARMALADE PAVÉ
MARINATED TOFU "PICCATA"

Winter
SQUASH GNOCCHI WITH TOASTED PUMPKIN SEEDS AND BROWN BUTTER SAUCE
WILD MUSHROOM CRÊPES WITH RED WINE REDUCTION

Goat Cheese-Ricotta Gnocchi

Because of her skill in making these little pillows of love, Mary has been given the nickname, the "Diva of Dumplings." Gnocchi are simple dumplings to which almost any flavor can be added. They have their culinary roots in Italy, but similar dumplings are also found in other European cultures. This is one of the easiest gnocchi to make. The secret is to dry the wet ingredients as much as you can before using them. Drain the ricotta of excess water by placing it in a strainer over a bowl and leaving it in the refrigerator for at least 30 minutes before using,

GNOCCHI
½ cup ricotta cheese, drained
½ cup chèvre-style, soft goat cheese
   (approximately ¼ pound)
1 large egg

1 teaspoon kosher salt
¼ teaspoon white pepper
1 to 1½ cups all-purpose flour

CREAM SAUCE
2 tablespoons butter
1 small yellow onion, finely chopped
1 cup dry white wine

2 cups heavy whipping cream
¼ teaspoon grated nutmeg
1 teaspoon lemon juice
kosher salt and white pepper, to taste

TO PREPARE THE GNOCCHI: In a bowl, place the drained ricotta, goat cheese, egg, salt and pepper. Add 1 cup of the flour and mix. Knead until just combined and the dough is smooth but not sticky. You may or may not need the remaining ½ cup of flour. DO NOT OVERMIX. Allow dough to rest 10-15 minutes.

Divide the dough in four portions. Roll each portion of dough into a thin strip, about the diameter of your thumb, and cut strip into ¼-inch to ½-inch-long pieces.

TO PREPARE THE CREAM SAUCE: In a large sauté pan, melt butter over medium heat. Add the onions and cook, stirring often, until soft but with no color, approximately 10 to 12 minutes. Add the wine and cook until one quarter of the liquid remains. Add the cream and cook until half of the volume remains. Add the nutmeg, lemon juice, salt and pepper. Keep warm.

TO SERVE: Bring a large pot of salted water to a boil. Place the gnocchi in the boiling water and cook until the gnocchi begin to float to the surface. Drain well. Add gnocchi to the cream sauce, toss and serve in a warm bowl.

ADVANCE PREPARATION: The gnocchi dough will keep in the refrigerator for 1 to 2 days, or may be frozen for up to 3 weeks.

SUBSTITUTIONS AND OPTIONS: The sauce can easily be turned into a blue cheese or parmesan cheese cream sauce by adding 2 ounces of crumbled or shredded cheese after the cream has reduced. You can also add 2 tablespoons of finely chopped fresh savory herbs such as parsley, thyme, rosemary, oregano, summer savory or marjoram to the gnocchi dough.

If making this dish for that special someone, add 1 tablespoon of white truffle oil to the gnocchi dough and sprinkle shaved truffles (Oregon white truffles, of course) over the top of the finished dish.

WINE NOTES: The creamy, rich flavors of the gnocchi will soften the acid of a crisp, acidic white wine, making the wine seem softer and suppler. With a softer acid, more full-bodied white, the wine's flavor will match with the dish's starchiness, creating sweetness and length of flavor. Recommended: For a wine that is the essence of Italian Pinot Grigio, try 2002 Livio Felluga, "Esperto" Pinot Grigio, Friuli-Venezia-Giulia, Italy. Or for a domestic Pinot Grigio with more body, try 2002 WillaKenzie, Pinot Gris, Willamette Valley, Oregon.

Makes 4 entrée servings

Beggar's Purse filled with Spring Vegetable

A beggar's purse was originally the name for an appetizer consisting of a mini crêpe topped by a teaspoon of caviar and then a dab of crème fraîche. It was made popular at the New York restaurant, The Quilted Giraffe. Our beggar's purse consists of a filled phyllo dough pouch tied and baked to resemble a draw-string purse.

FILLING

4 tablespoons vegetable oil

4 ramps (wild leeks) or 1 large cultivated leek, cut into small dice

4 stalks asparagus, ends trimmed, cut into small dice

1 rib celery, cut into small dice

1 carrot, peeled and cut into small dice

2 spring onions or 1 small yellow onion, cut into small dice

¼ pound fava beans or French green beans, cut into small dice

¼ pound morel mushrooms or shiitake mushrooms, cleaned and cut into quarters

2 cloves garlic, finely chopped

kosher salt and cracked black pepper

½ cup dry white wine

BEGGAR'S PURSES

8 sheets phyllo dough

vegetable oil, as needed

2 tablespoons fresh parsley, finely chopped

1 teaspoon fresh thyme, finely chopped

kosher salt and cracked black pepper, to taste

TO PREPARE THE FILLING: Place the oil in a large sauté pan over low to medium heat. Add the ramps, asparagus, celery, carrots, onions, beans, mushrooms, garlic, salt and pepper. Sauté, stirring often, until vegetables are soft but with no color, approximately 15 to 20 minutes. Add wine and cook until the liquid is almost dry. Taste and adjust seasoning. Allow the vegetables to cool.

TO PREPARE THE BEGGAR'S PURSES: Preheat oven to 375°F.

Cut each phyllo dough sheet in half to form a total of 16 squares. Cover the phyllo with plastic wrap and a damp towel while working, so it does not dry out.

Place one sheet of phyllo on your work surface. Brush a little oil all over the sheet, especially the edges of the phyllo. Place a second sheet on top in the opposite direction to make a cross. Brush oil on top of the second sheet as before. Sprinkle a little of the chopped herbs, salt and pepper over the entire surface. Place two more sheets in an X pattern on top of the previous cross pattern. Brush each sheet with oil before placing the next sheet on top. You will now have a stack of four squares.

In the middle of the top sheet of phyllo, place one quarter of the cooled filling. Pull all the sides up towards the center to make a purse. Tie the top with cotton string. Brush the outside of each purse with oil and season with salt and pepper. Continue the same procedure to make a total of four purses.

Place the purses on a baking tray brushed with vegetable oil. Bake for 15 to 20 minutes or until phyllo purses become a light golden brown.

TO SERVE: Cut the string from the phyllo purses, place in a shallow soup bowl, and serve with seasoned vegetable stock (see page 19).

ADVANCE PREPARATION: The filling can be made a day or two ahead but only fill and bake the purses when you are ready to serve them. The phyllo dough will get soggy if the purses are filled in advance and not baked immediately. The completed purses may be made several weeks in advance, placed in a sealed container and frozen. Take them directly from the freezer to the oven when ready to bake.

SUBSTITUTIONS AND OPTIONS: Just as with the Spring Vegetable Soup recipe, change the vegetables based on what looks best and has the best flavor in your market or garden. Use summer squash, corn, bell peppers and basil in the summer months, or use autumn mushrooms and roots during the autumn months.

Add the filling to your favorite pasta to make a wonderful chilled vegetable pasta salad or a light vegetable pasta entrée.

Our favorite substitute for phyllo dough is *Feuille de Brik,* a thin, savoury crêpe-like dough made without eggs. Use only one sheet per beggar's purse.

WINE NOTES: You could drink a white wine with this dish, especially a Chardonnay with some richness and a touch of oak character, a quality that pairs well with the morel mushrooms in the filling. For a racier choice, choose a Zinfandel with a wild-berry character. The dish makes the wine classier, enabling the fruit flavors to shine. Recommended: 2001 Mission Hill Family Estate, Reserve Chardonnay, Okanagan Valley, British Columbia; or 2001 Green & Red, Chiles Mill Vineyard, Zinfandel, Napa Valley, California.

Makes 4 entrée servings

Roasted Whole Candy Sweet Onions with Toasted Barley and Sweet Pepper Filling, Summer Beans with Savory Herb Sauce

A Candy Sweet onion is a storage variety of sweet onion that grows especially well in the volcanic soil of the Cascade mountain range of southern Oregon. Other sweet onions such as Walla Walla, Vidalia, Maui or Texas 1015 Supersweets may be substituted in this recipe, but we're partial to the flavor of Candy Sweets and think the flavor will not be quite the same. Roasting the onion caramelizes the sugars and turns its flavor into an irresistible nutty sweetness. The onion purée, taken from the center of the roasted onions, rounds out the earthiness of the barley filling.

ROASTED WHOLE ONIONS:

4 Candy or other sweet onion variety, peeled but left whole

kosher salt and cracked black pepper, to taste

3 cups barley and sweet pepper filling

SAVORY HERB SAUCE

reserved roasted onion rings

¼ cup white wine

1 cup vegetable stock or water (see recipe in the Basics section)

2 tablespoons savory fresh herbs,

kosher salt and white pepper, to taste

BARLEY AND SWEET PEPPER FILLING

3 cups toasted barley, cooked

1 red pepper, roasted, seeds removed and diced

1 yellow pepper, roasted, seeds removed and diced

1 green pepper, roasted, seeds removed and diced

2 tablespoons savory herbs, chopped

kosher salt and white pepper, to taste

SUMMER BEANS

2 cups mixed summer beans (haricot vert, yellow wax beans, cranberry beans, fava beans, fresh edamame beans, etc.) cleaned and blanched

2 tablespoons olive oil

TO ROAST THE ONIONS: Preheat oven to 375°F.

Place onions in a roasting pan; add enough water to cover the onions halfway up their sides. Bake in oven, turning every hour, for 3 to 3½ hours or until onions are tender. Remove onions from their liquid and allow to cool. Remove the inner rings of the onions, leaving the two outer layers intact. Reserve inner rings for sauce. Fill each onion with some of the barley filling. Heat onions in oven for 10-15 minutes, until hot in the center.

TO PREPARE THE SAVORY HERB SAUCE: In a sauté pan, combine reserved inner onion rings and wine. Cook over medium heat and reduce wine until pan is almost dry. Add stock or water and bring to a boil. Remove from heat. Purée the sauce in a blender until smooth. Add herbs, salt and pepper. Keep warm.

TO PREPARE THE BARLEY AND SWEET PEPPER FILLING: Combine all ingredients in a medium-sized stainless steel bowl. Toss and season with salt and pepper.

TO PREPARE THE SUMMER BEANS: In a sauté pan over medium heat, heat the olive oil. Add the beans and toss until warmed all the way through.

TO SERVE: Place some of the mixed summer beans in the center of a plate, place a warm onion on top of beans and drizzle some sauce over and around it.

ADVANCE PREPARATION: The roasted onions, the sauce and the barley and pepper filling may be made several days ahead, but keep them separate. Fill the onions the day you will serve them.

SUBSTITUTIONS AND OPTIONS: As we mentioned, any sweet onion variety may be substituted for the Candy Sweet onion. The barley and sweet pepper filling makes a wonderful side dish on its own. Any combination of savory herbs including parsley, thyme, rosemary, oregano, summer savory and marjoram will work in this recipe.

WINE NOTES: A smooth, caramelized, toasty and slightly spicy Chardonnay or sparkling wine is needed to balance the both the earthiness of the barley and the natural sweetness of the onion and the roasted peppers. Recommended: 2001 Eola Hills, "Mystery Block" Reserve Chardonnay, Applegate Valley, Oregon; or 1999 Argyle, Brut, Willamette Valley, Oregon.

Makes 4 entrée servings

Inspired by Onions:

*Vince and Mary Alionis of
Whistling Duck Farm*

Vince Alionis knows southern Oregon's
geology as intimately as any geologist. He
can explain how the ancient volcanic soil or
Old Caldera overlay gives his property five
different soil types, scientifically described as
"chaotic." The result is tremendous biological
diversity, plus rich, black earth that nourishes
a range of vegetables from Candy Sweet and
Walla Walla onions to kale, rainbow chard,
leeks, chicory, arugula and spinach. Two green-
houses on the farm offer protective shelter for
heirloom tomato seedlings and tender veggies.

Vince and his equally knowledgeable wife
Mary, who runs the business side of the farm,
have been farming in the Rogue Valley and
Cascade Mountains of southern Oregon for
more than ten years. For them it's not just
about organic, for-profit farming. It's about a
lifestyle, stewardship of the land, an integra-

tion of community-based farming in CSAs
(Community Supported Agriculture), educational opportunities like the Eco-Farming
Internship Program, and permaculture land
use, a systems approach to farming.

Mary Alionis says, "The CSA program
that gives us cash in January and February
changed everything in how we manage our
business." Seventy-five full-share members in
Whistling Duck's CSA program account for
about one-third of the farm's income. Members
of Oregon Tilth, they follow stringent standards for both cultivation and harvesting the
farm's produce. Along with their CSA program,
Vince and Mary sell to area restaurateurs and
retail outlets. Any produce not sold to these
customers goes to regional growers' markets.

The onions Vince and Mary deliver from
Whistling Duck Farm would make most chefs
swoon, and we say that having made the
acquaintance of many varieties of sweet onions;
Stu worked in Georgia where he used Vidalias
extensively, and Mary went to school in Walla
Walla, Washington, where she picked her share
of the world-famous Walla Walla Sweets. We
have both visited the Hawaiian Islands and
tasted Maui Sweets right at the source. When
Vince first brought us a just-picked Candy
Sweet, it tasted sweeter than some apples.

"Let's roast the onion to mellow out the
sweetness a little and balance it with the earthiness of a grain. Hey, Mary, do we still have
barley? You know what, Stu, fold in some of
those summer beans Vince and Mary brought
us. Save the centers of the roasted onions and I
can make a wonderful coulis with a nice white
wine reduction." Thus another Peerless recipe
is born. ◠

Other American Sweet Onions

"I crawled into the vegetable bin, settled on a giant onion and ate it, skin and all. It must have marked me for life for I have never ceased to love the hearty flavor of onions." — JAMES BEARD

Sweet onions contain no more sugar than regular storage onions, but taste sweeter because they are much lower in sulfuric acid (the mysterious thing that makes you cry), and are grown in low sulfur, mineral-rich soil. No onion will taste as sweet as a ripe peach or a juicy strawberry, but a sweet onion's low acid content takes the harsh bite out of a regular onion's distinctive flavor and allows the onion to achieve a milder, sweeter blend of flavors. Onion type, soil conditions and amount of daylight during the growing season can all affect the final flavor and resulting sweetness.

Springsweets and 1015 Supersweets onions (named for the suggested planting date of October 15th) are from Texas, and are usually the first sweet onions available in the spring.

Vidalia onions are named for a town in Georgia, and are grown in 20 specific counties as mandated by a Federal Marketing Order. They first appeared in 1931 when Georgia farmer Mose Coleman discovered that the onions he planted were not hot, as he expected, but actually sweet in flavor. They are available in late spring through early summer.

Sweet Imperial onions are grown in the rich, loamy, desert soil of southern California's Imperial Valley. They are globe-shaped and available spring through early summer.

Walla Walla onions are grown in Walla Walla County in southeastern Washington and a portion of Umatilla County in northeastern Oregon. Their seeds originated in Italy and then were transplanted to the Mediterranean island of Corsica. These sweet onions are available throughout the summer.

AmeriSweet onions hail from the low-sulfur soils around the Grand Rapids area of Michigan. These onions have a thicker, deeper-colored skin than spring/summer sweet onions. They are available throughout the autumn.

Maui onions from Hawaii are grown in volcanic soil. Like Vidalias, they are a Yellow Granex-type hybrid, originating from varieties developed in Texas. They are available late spring through early winter.

Heirloom Tomato and Summer Squash Torte

Is it a cake, a pie, or a wrongdoing? A torte — not to be confused with a legal tort — is a sweet, rich cream cake covered with nuts or fruits that originated in Austria. Our savory version resembles a vegetable pie. We use the best of summer's bounty, layer it with fresh mozzarella and enclose it in pastry. The flavorful roasted red pepper sauce adds a touch of sweetness and color.

For this recipe, use fresh, high-moisture cow's milk mozzarella that contains more than 52 percent moisture, or Capriella (half goat's milk, half cow's milk mozzarella) from the Mozzarella Company in Dallas, Texas. Paula Lambert founded the business in 1982, using the same exacting methods for handcrafting fresh mozzarella that she witnessed while living in Italy.

TORTE SHELL AND FILLING

- double recipe savory tart dough (see page 18)
- 1 tablespoon olive oil
- 3 to 4 large heirloom tomatoes, such as Brandywine, Green Zebra or Yellow Taxi
- 2 small green zucchini
- 2 small yellow squash
- 1 cup fresh basil leaves, approximately 1 ounce
- 2 medium yellow onions, cut in half and thinly sliced
- ½ pound fresh mozzarella, high moisture if available
- kosher salt and cracked black pepper, to taste
- 1 teaspoon Dijon mustard

RED PEPPER SAUCE

- 4 red peppers
- 2 tablespoons olive oil
- 1 medium yellow onion, roughly chopped
- 1 carrot, peeled and roughly chopped
- 1 teaspoon hot paprika
- 1 cup white wine
- 4 cups vegetable stock or water
- kosher salt and white pepper, to taste

TO PREPARE THE TORTE SHELL: Preheat oven to 400°F.

Lightly flour a table or cutting board and a rolling pin. Cut the dough in half and place it on the board. Using a rolling pin, roll each piece of dough out from the center until it forms a circle about ⅛-inch thick and 12-inches in diameter. Prick the entire surface of the dough with a fork. Press one dough circle into a 12-inch tart pan and trim off the excess pastry. Place the remaining circle on parchment paper on a baking pan and refrigerate both for 30 minutes.

Blind bake the tart shell by placing the tart pan on a baking sheet. Line the dough with foil or parchment and fill it with dried beans or pie weights. Bake for 10 minutes. Remove beans and bake 10 minutes or until the bottom is a light golden brown. Remove from oven and cool tart shell on a rack for 30 minutes before filling.

TO PREPARE THE FILLING: In a medium-sized sauté pan over medium heat, add the oil. Add the onions and season with salt and pepper. Sauté until tender but not colored, about 8 to 10 minutes. Remove onions and allow them to cool completely.

Remove the core from the tomatoes and cut into ¼-inch thick slices. Cut the ends off of the zucchini and squash and cut lengthwise into ¼-inch thick slices. Cut the mozzarella balls into ¼-inch slices.

Brush the bottom of the pre-baked shell with mustard. Line the bottom with the cooled onions. Arrange half of the tomato slices in a spiral pattern on top of the onions. Season with salt and pepper. Arrange the zucchini and squash slices on top of the tomatoes and season with salt and pepper. Arrange the basil leaves and the remaining half of the tomatoes on top of the squash. Season with salt and pepper. Arrange the sliced mozzarella on top of tomatoes. Lay the other circle of dough on top of the torte shell and crimp the edges to seal. Using a pastry brush, lightly coat the top of the torte with olive oil. Cut two small vent holes in the top crust to let steam escape.

Place torte on a baking sheet. Bake in 375°F oven for 35 to 45 minutes or until top is golden brown and vegetable filling is soft. To test for doneness, insert a skewer into the center of the torte. If it encounters no resistance, the torte is done cooking. Remove torte from oven and place on a cooling rack to cool.

TO PREPARE THE RED PEPPER SAUCE: Preheat oven to 375°F.

Place peppers on a baking sheet and place in oven. Roast 15 minutes, turning once or twice, or until the skin of the peppers are slightly charred. Place peppers in a paper bag, seal the top and allow them to steam 10 to 15 minutes. When peppers are cool, remove the skin, stems and seeds. Roughly chop the peppers.

In a medium-size saucepan over medium heat, add the oil. Add the peppers, onions, celery, carrot, salt and pepper. Sauté until the vegetables are soft but not colored. Add paprika and wine, and simmer until the volume is reduced by half. Add the vegetable stock or water and simmer until the liquid is reduced by half. Using a blender, purée until sauce is smooth. Taste and adjust seasoning.

TO SERVE: Remove torte from pan. Cut torte into 4 to 6 wedges and serve with red pepper sauce.

ADVANCE PREPARATION: The torte can be made a day ahead, refrigerated and reheated in a 250°F oven for 20 to 30 minutes or until warm.

SUBSTITUTIONS AND OPTIONS: You can substitute puff pastry, usually available in the freezer section of your market, for the tart dough. Allow the frozen puff pastry to come to room temperature, prick the pastry, roll it out and bake per the tart dough instructions.

WINE NOTES: A Sangiovese-based red wine with a long, spicy, herbal finish will work perfectly with the tomatoes and peppers in this dish. Recommended: 2000 Atlas Peak, Sangiovese, Napa Valley, California; or 2000 Podere La Brancaia, Chianti Classico, Tuscany, Italy.

Makes one 12-inch torte, 4 to 6 entrée servings or 8 to 10 appetizer servings

Root Vegetable and Onion Marmalade Pavé

A pavé — named because it resembles a paver or brick — is a cross between a pasta-less lasagna and a dairy-free gratin. The pavé is extremely low in fat and high in flavor. It is one of those dishes that must be made ahead of time but is very easy to make.

2 russet potatoes, peeled and sliced lengthwise into thin slices

1 celery root, peeled and sliced lengthwise into thin slices

2 butternut squash, peeled and sliced lengthwise into thin slices

2 turnips, peeled and sliced lengthwise into thin slices

2 rutabaga, peeled and sliced lengthwise into thin slices

½ cup onion marmalade (see page 203)

kosher salt and white pepper, to taste

Preheat oven to 350°F.

Line an 8-inch by 8-inch square baking pan with aluminum foil. Spray the foil with nonstick cooking spray. Starting and ending with potatoes, form layers of sliced vegetables, slightly overlapping each over. Season each layer with salt and pepper. Continue alternating vegetables and onion marmalade until you reach the top of the pan.

Spray an additional sheet of aluminum foil with nonstick spray and cover the vegetables. Place a weighted pan on top of the dish and bake in oven until vegetables are tender, approximately 2 to 2½ hours.

Allow pavé to cool in the refrigerator, with the weighted pan on top, at least 4 hours or overnight.

TO SERVE: Invert the pan and remove the pavé from the pan. Cut into 2-inch by 2-inch squares. Sauté the pavé in a nonstick pan until both sides are brown and place in 350°F oven until warm in the center.

ADVANCE PREPARATION: The pavé should be made at least one day and up to 3 days in advance. Allow the pavé to rest, weighted, in the refrigerator, at least 4 hours or preferably overnight.

SUBSTITUTIONS AND OPTIONS: Any low-moisture vegetable (including summer squash, roasted peppers or other root vegetables) can be substituted. For a richer dish, add grated cheese and/or cream between the layers.

WINE NOTES: If you are serving this pavé as an entrée by itself, the earthy root vegetables require an aromatic, lightly oaky, dry white Rhône-style wine. Recommended: 2000 Griffin Creek, Viognier, Rogue Valley, Oregon; or 1999 Chateau La Nerthe, Chateauneuf-du-Pape Blanc, Southern Rhône, France.

Makes 4 entrée servings or 10 to 12 side dish servings

Marinated Tofu "Piccata"

According to *The Food Lover's Companion* by Sharon Tyler Herbst, "piccata" consists of a seasoned and floured escalope of veal, or sometimes chicken, that is quickly sautéed and served with a sauce made from the pan drippings, lemon juice and chopped parsley. This vegetarian twist on the Italian classic typifies what *The Sustainable Kitchen* is all about: use a few fresh ingredients, prepare them in a simple manner and use a little technique to achieve a dish bursting with flavor.

At The Peerless we used to make our own tofu just to see if we could. The additional soy milk that was left over was an added benefit to accompany our house-made granola. Instead of going through this laborious process, we recommend you buy a good brand of organic extra-firm tofu.

MARINATED TOFU

1 clove garlic, finely chopped
½ teaspoon fresh rosemary, finely chopped
½ teaspoon fresh oregano, finely chopped
½ teaspoon Italian parsley, finely chopped
½ cup extra virgin olive oil

¼ cup white wine
¼ cup lemon juice
16 ounces organic extra firm tofu, sliced into ¼-inch thick squares

PICCATA

marinated tofu
kosher salt and white pepper, to taste
½ cup all-purpose flour
2 tablespoons olive oil
2 tablespoons butter
juice of 1 lemon

¾ cup white wine
2 tablespoons nonpareille capers, drained and roughly chopped
2 tablespoons Italian parsley, finely chopped
1 tablespoon butter
dried red chili flakes, to taste (optional)

TO PREPARE THE MARINATED TOFU: Combine the garlic, rosemary, oregano, parsley olive oil, wine and lemon juice. Place the tofu in a shallow stainless steel or glass bowl. Pour marinade over tofu, making sure marinade complete covers the tofu. Cover and refrigerate 2 hours or overnight.

TO PREPARE THE PICCATA: Remove the tofu from the marinade and pat dry. Season the tofu with salt and pepper. Lightly dust the tofu slices with the flour, patting off any excess flour.

In a large sauté pan over medium heat, add the olive oil and butter. When the butter begins to foam, add the tofu. Sauté the tofu on one side until golden brown. Turn tofu over and continue cooking until other side has browned. Remove tofu from pan.

In the same pan over medium heat, add the lemon juice and white wine. Cook until the liquid has reduced in volume and has just begun to thicken. Remove pan from heat and stir in capers, parsley, butter and chili flakes.

TO SERVE: Pour sauce over tofu to coat.

ADVANCE PREPARATION: Marinate the tofu several hours before or overnight. Do not flour or cook the tofu until ready to serve or the coating will become soggy.

SUBSTITUTIONS AND OPTIONS: The marinade and technique will produce a wonderful chicken piccata. Do not leave the chicken in the marinade for more than 30 minutes or the acid in the lemon juice and wine will "cook" the protein.

Serve the piccata with sautéed autumn wild mushrooms, such as chanterelles, lobster mushrooms or matsutakes. We prefer to use matsutake mushrooms because they have a meatiness and slight spicy pungency that will hold up to both the acid in the sauce and the texture of the tofu. If you can not find matsutakes, substitute small portabello mushrooms.

WINE NOTES: Two choices spring to mind for this dish. A serious big Italian or Napa Valley white that is barrel-fermented in the Burgundian tradition or a Sonoma County Sauvignon Blanc with a crisp dry finish. Recommended: 2000 Pahlmeyer, Chardonnay, Napa Valley, California a "big-fella" California-style Chardonnay at its best; or try 2000 Matanzas Creek, Sauvignon Blanc, Sonoma County, California.

Makes 4 entrée servings

Roasted Squash Gnocchi
with Toasted Pumpkin Seeds and Brown Butter Sauce

After spending our first autumn in the Rogue Valley, we were inspired to give the classic Italian potato recipe our own twist by adding roasted squash along with the roasted potatoes. The key to making gnocchi is to make sure that the dough isn't too sticky and that you don't over mix or over knead the dough.

SQUASH GNOCCHI

1 small butternut squash (approximately
   1 to 2 pounds)
kosher salt and white pepper, to taste
1 pound baking potatoes (approximately
   2 large potatoes)
1 egg yolks
1 whole egg

1½-2 cups all-purpose flour
1 teaspoon kosher salt
⅛ teaspoon ground nutmeg
⅛ teaspoon ground cinnamon
¼ teaspoon ground allspice
½ teaspoon ground white pepper

BROWN BUTTER SAUCE

4 tablespoons butter
juice of one lemon

kosher salt and white pepper, to taste
toasted pumpkin seeds (as a garnish)

TO PREPARE THE SQUASH GNOCCHI: Preheat oven to 375°F. Cut squash in half lengthwise and remove the stem and the seeds. Season the cut-side of the squash with salt and pepper. Place squash, cut-side down on a baking sheet with the whole potatoes, and roast them until soft, about 45 minutes. Allow to cool slightly.

Scrape squash flesh from their skins. Purée squash flesh in a food processor until smooth. Retain ¾ cup of purée. (Extra purée can be frozen for another use.) Scrape potato flesh from their skins and then pass flesh through a food mill/ricer.

In a large bowl, combine squash purée, potato purée, egg yolk and whole egg. In a separate bowl, combine 1½ cups of flour, salt, nutmeg, cinnamon, allspice and white pepper. Slowly add dry ingredients to egg mixture. Knead until the mixture is just combined and smooth, but not sticky. You may or may not need the remaining ½ cup of flour. DO NOT OVERMIX. Allow dough to rest 10-15 minutes.

Divide the dough in four portions. Roll dough into thin strips and cut into ¼-inch to ½-inch pieces.

TO PREPARE THE BROWN BUTTER SAUCE: In a large sauté pan over medium heat, melt the butter. Cook the butter until it begins to foam and turn slightly golden brown. Remove from the heat, add the lemon juice, salt and pepper. The butter will continue to cook and will develop a nutty smell and taste.

TO SERVE: Bring a large pot of salted water to a boil. Place the gnocchi in the boiling water and cook until the gnocchi begin to float to the surface. Drain well and add to pan with the brown butter sauce. Serve with toasted pumpkin seeds.

ADVANCE PREPARATION: The gnocchi dough will keep in the refrigerator for 1 to 2 days or may be frozen for up to 3 weeks.

SUBSTITUTIONS AND OPTIONS: Sugar pumpkin or sweet potatoes will also work in place of the squash. Additionally, you may use all potato in place of the squash and use more potato to make simple potato gnocchi. You may add fresh chopped herbs to the brown butter sauce once the butter has browned. Sage is our favorite, but almost any herb will work. You will need some acid component in the butter sauce. White wine vinegar or other citrus juice will work in place of the lemon juice. Cooked cabbage (bok choy or savoy cabbage) makes a good addition to the gnocchi if you wish to make a complete meal. A broth made from the leftover squash purée can be used as a lighter substitute for the brown butter sauce.

WINE NOTES: The richness of the butter sauce and the earthiness and caramelized flavors of the roasted squash need a crisp, dry Alsatian-style Riesling. Recommended: 2001 Domaine Zind Humbrecht, Clos Häuserer, Alsace, France; or 2002 Leeuwin Estate, Art Series, Reisling, Margaret River, Australia.

Makes 4 entrée servings

Winter Squash

In Alexander Dumas's distinguished *Grand Dictionary de Cuisine*, he includes directions on how to cook an elephant. For many people, elephant cookery is less daunting than dealing with the large category of winter squash. Winter squashes come in a plethora of varieties, shapes, sizes and colors. Despite their outward differences, winter squashes, with few exceptions, are all handled alike for cooking purposes.

Winter squash can be baked whole, peeled for purées and soups, cut in half and stuffed or sautéed.

Winter squashes are in season from September through March and can be stored in a cool, dry place for up to two months. Make sure that you select firm, thick-shelled squash that feel heavy for their size. Wrap cut squash in plastic and store in the refrigerator up to one week.

ACORN SQUASH: These are popular because of their small size — one squash can be cut in half and baked to make two servings. The biggest drawback to this variety is that the rind is quite hard and therefore difficult to cut. Select acorn squash with as much green on the rind as possible. Substitutes: Buttercup squash (drier) or Hubbard squash (much larger).

BANANA SQUASH: This variety is so large that grocers usually cut it into smaller chunks before putting it out. It's tasty, but its biggest virtue is the beautiful golden color of its flesh. Substitutes: Butternut squash (drier with nuttier, sweeter flavor) or Sugar Pumpkin (sweeter).

BUTTERCUP SQUASH: This is a sweet squash with a creamy orange flesh. The biggest shortcoming of this variety is that it tends to be a bit dry. Substitutes: Butternut squash (nuttier, sweeter flavor; easier to peel when raw), Acorn squash (less flavorful, moister) or Delicata squash (more flavorful and creamier).

BUTTERNUT SQUASH: This squash is very easy to use. It's small enough to serve a four-person family without leftovers, and the rind is thin enough to peel off with a vegetable peeler. The flavor is sweet, moist and slightly nutty. Substitutes: Buttercup squash (not as sweet and moist; harder to peel when raw), Acorn squash (not as sweet; harder to peel when raw) or Delicata squash (creamier).

CINDERELLA PUMPKIN: This squash, called *Rouge Vif D'Etampes* in French, received its name because it resembles Cinderella's fairy-tale coach. They have a very thick but sweet-tasting bright orange flesh. They are also used for carving and decorations. Substitutes: Sugar Pumpkin, Butternut squash or Hubbard squash.

DELICATA SQUASH: This is one of the tastier winter squashes with creamy pulp that tastes a bit like sweet potatoes. Substitutes: Butternut squash, Buttercup squash or sweet potato.

HUBBARD SQUASH: Hubbards and the heirloom variety called "Sweet Meat" have tasty flesh, but are very large and not easy to handle because their rind is hard to cut through. Substitutes: Sugar Pumpkin, Buttercup squash (easier to peel when raw, but with a drier, sweet flavor) or Banana squash.

KABOCHA SQUASH: This orange-fleshed winter squash has a striated green rind. It's sweeter, drier and less fibrous than other winter squash, and it tastes a bit like sweet potatoes. In Japan, Kabocha squash symbolizes good health and luck. Substitutes: Butternut squash, Acorn squash or Turban squash.

SUGAR PUMPKIN: Also known as a pie pumpkin. Do not use the larger jack o'lantern pumpkin variety, as its flesh is too watery and not as sweet as that of the sugar pumpkin. Substitutes: Canned pumpkin purée is convenient and a good substitute for the fresh. Substitutes: Hubbard squash (especially in pies), Butternut squash (also good in pies) or sweet potatoes.

SPAGHETTI SQUASH: After it's cooked, you can dig a fork into the flesh of a spaghetti squash and pull out long yellow strands that resemble spaghetti. Though they taste like squash, the "noodles" can serve as a low-calorie substitute for pasta. Substitutes: Butternut squash, Banana squash or Sweet Dumpling squash will taste similar, but no other squash will form strands when cooked.

SWEET DUMPLING SQUASH: This is a fairly small squash, so it can be cut in half, baked and served as an individual portion. The flesh is sweeter and drier than that of other winter squash and the peel is soft enough to be eaten when cooked. Substitutes: Butternut squash, Kabocha squash or Acorn squash.

TURBAN SQUASH: This squash has a gorgeous rind, but the flesh is not very flavorful. It makes a terrific autumn centerpiece or you can hollow it out and use it as a serving vessel. Substitutes: Butternut squash or Acorn squash. ❧

Wild Mushroom Crêpes with Red Wine Reduction

The mention of the word crêpe brings images of a flambéed dessert with orange sauce or a thin pancake full of ham and cheese. Our crêpe is actually a version of a *banh xeo*. *Banh xeo* is a cross between a crisp eggless crêpe, a vegetable wrap and a fluffy omelet, and actually predates the French colonial era in Vietnam.

The filling consists of the bounty of wild mushrooms available during the winter in the Pacific Northwest. The general rule when cooking wild mushrooms is to bring out their natural flavors by sprinkling the mushrooms with the "holy trinity" of salt, soy sauce and a pinch of sugar. After all, you don't have to try too hard to bring out the flavor of a food that isn't the least bit timid.

WILD MUSHROOM FILLING

2 tablespoons vegetable oil
1 shallot or small red onion, finely diced
¼ pound chanterelle mushrooms, cleaned and cut into ¼-inch pieces
¼ pound lobster mushrooms, cleaned and cut into ¼-inch pieces
¼ pound porcini mushrooms, cleaned and cut into ¼-inch pieces
2 teaspoons soy sauce
¼ teaspoon granulated sugar
kosher salt and ground black pepper, to taste

PINOT NOIR REDUCTION

1 shallot, finely chopped
1 cup Pinot Noir
10 tablespoons butter, diced and kept cold
kosher salt and ground black pepper, to taste

CRÊPES

1 cup rice flour
½ cup all purpose flour
1 teaspoon kosher salt
1 teaspoon granulated sugar
½ teaspoon curry powder, Vietnamese or Indian Madras-style

4 tablespoons vegetable oil

4 green onions, thinly sliced (white and green parts)
½ cup coconut milk
1½ cups water

¼ pound radish sprouts

TO PREPARE THE WILD MUSHROOM FILLING: In a large sauté pan over medium heat, add the oil. Add the shallot and season with salt and pepper. Sauté until tender but not colored, about 4 to 5 minutes. Add all of the mushrooms and sauté until golden brown and tender, about 10 to 12 minutes. Add the soy sauce and sugar and continue cooking until the soy sauce is almost completely reduced. Taste and adjust seasoning.

TO PREPARE THE PINOT NOIR REDUCTION: In a medium saucepan over medium-high heat, combine the shallot and the wine. Cook until the liquid is reduced to a syrup. Reduce the heat to low. Add the butter, a few pieces at a time, whisking to incorporate each addition before adding more. Work the pan on and off the heat to regulate the temperature so that it does not become too hot. Keep warm.

TO PREPARE THE CRÊPES: In a large bowl, whisk together the rice flour, all-purpose flour, kosher salt, granulated sugar, curry powder, green onions, coconut milk and water.

For each crêpe, heat 1 tablespoon of oil in an 8-inch, nonstick pan over medium heat. Add ¼ of the cooked mushroom filling. Without removing the mushrooms, pour in ¼ of the batter, between ½ cup and ¾ cup of crêpe batter. Quickly tilt the pan in all directions to allow the batter to completely cover the bottom of the pan. Cover and cook for 3 to 5 minutes.

Uncover and check for doneness. The crêpe should pull away from the sides of the pan, be well-browned and lacy on the bottom, and look a bit dry on the top. Place ¼ of the radish sprouts on top and fold the crêpe over and keep warm.

Repeat three more times with remaining crêpe mix and filling.

TO SERVE: Place crêpe on warm plates and serve with Pinot Noir reduction.

ADVANCE PREPARATION: The mushroom filling can be made a day ahead and refrigerated.

SUBSTITUTIONS AND OPTIONS: This can become a "one pan" meal by using the same 14-inch non-stick pan to both sauté the mushroom filling and make one large crêpe. Dried mushrooms may be substituted for the fresh mushrooms. Soak the dried mushrooms for 30 minutes in the same wine used in the pinot noir reduction.

WINE NOTES: Recipes with wild mushrooms are perfect for showing off a good Burgundy-style wine. Pinot Noir is a grape variety that inspires strong emotions; it's all about sex. There's just no other way to describe the elusive appeal of the combination of a great Pinot Noir and wild mushrooms. The aromas arouse the senses, stimulate pheromones and generally appeal to the sensual side of our nature. Recommended: 2001 Bergström, Cumberland Reserve, Pinot Noir, Willamette Valley, Oregon; or 2001 By Farr, Pinot Noir, Geelong, Australia.

Makes 4 entrée servings

Desserts: To Complete Your Experience

"Life is uncertain. Eat dessert first."
— ERNESTINE ULMER

MAKING DESSERTS AND PASTRIES IS EXACTING, methodical and requires patience — qualities Mary seems to possess and Stu does not. There are always seasonal inspirations for Mary's endeavors — the first rhubarb in springtime; bush and cane berries, cherries, and peaches arriving as summer days heat up; pears, pumpkins and apples heralding autumn; citrus bringing their own form of sunshine in winter; and then, of course, there's always chocolate. Mary's the first to agree that once you learn the foundations and pay attention to seasonal flavors, a whole world of delectable creations will open up for you.

Even those who cannot commit to an extravagant chocolate creation or a rich fruit dessert will find solace in the satisfying sweetness and texture of a simple cookie. Here are some simple and some more complex desserts. The key to all of the recipes is the depth and intensity of flavor you will achieve.

Chocolate
TRIPLE CHOCOLATE-HAZELNUT CRUNCH BAR
WHITE CHOCOLATE CHEESECAKE WITH BLUEBERRY CARAMEL SAUCE ❦ CHOCOLATE PEPPERMINT BROWNIE

Spring
CHILLED SYRAH POACHED RHUBARB SOUP ❦ PEERLESS CRÈME BRÛLÉE

Summer
PEACH UPSIDE-DOWN POLENTA CAKE WITH PEACH SYRUP ❦ PINOT NOIR GRANITÉ WITH FRESH BERRIES

Autumn
SPICED SUGAR PUMPKIN CAKE

Winter
WARM APPLE PIE WITH APPLE BRANDY SAUCE
HONEY TANGERINE MERINGUE TARTLET WITH GRAND MARNIER PASTRY CREAM AND BERRY COULIS

Cookies
PISTACHIO-ORANGE BISCOTTI ❦ SUN-DRIED CHERRY BISCOTTI
MACADAMIA NUT BUTTER AND WHITE CHOCOLATE CHIP COOKIES
HONEY ALMOND MACAROONS ❦ ESPRESSO SHORTBREAD ❦ SISKIYOU MOUNTAIN COOKIES

Triple Chocolate-Hazelnut Crunch Bar

A small confession: One of Mary's favorite treats is Ben & Jerry's Toffee Heath Bar Crunch Ice Cream. Sometimes she shares and sometimes she doesn't. This recipe fuses classic flavors with a slight Northwest twist by adding hazelnuts. The various chocolate layers are spread into a pan, glazed with more chocolate and then cut into long bars.

MILK CHOCOLATE-HAZELNUT LAYER
7 ounces milk chocolate, coarsely chopped
6 ounces hazelnut butter, crunchy
2 tablespoons vegetable oil

2 ounces hazelnuts, toasted and
   coarsely chopped

DARK CHOCOLATE MOUSSE
5 ounces bittersweet chocolate,
   coarsely chopped

1¼ cups heavy cream

WHITE CHOCOLATE GLAZE
6 ounces white chocolate, coarsely chopped
2 teaspoons butter

½ cup heavy cream

TO PREPARE THE MILK CHOCOLATE-HAZELNUT LAYER: Line an 8-inch-square pan with plastic wrap.

Melt milk chocolate in a double boiler and whisk until smooth. In a mixing bowl, mix hazelnut butter and oil until smooth. Stir in the melted chocolate. Mix in the hazelnuts. Spread the mixture into plastic-lined pan. Refrigerate until firm, approximately two hours.

TO PREPARE THE DARK CHOCOLATE MOUSSE: Melt bittersweet chocolate in a double boiler and whisk until smooth. Remove chocolate from the double boiler and let chocolate come to room temperature. Whip cream into soft peaks. Fold half of cream into melted chocolate then fold in remaining cream. Pour mixture over chilled milk chocolate layer. Refrigerate until firm.

TO PREPARE THE WHITE CHOCOLATE GLAZE: In a saucepan, bring cream and butter to a boil. Pour over white chocolate and whisk until smooth. Lift chocolate layers from the pan and remove the plastic wrap from the bottom. Place the chocolate layers on a rack. Pour white chocolate glaze over the chocolate layers and refrigerate until firm.

TO SERVE: Cut the square into 1-inch wide by 4-inch long bars. Serve with crème anglaise (see page 15) and white chocolate ice cream.

ADVANCE PREPARATION: The entire dessert or individual layers can be made several days in advance, covered with plastic wrap and refrigerated. Serve the bars within a day or two of being cut.

SUBSTITUTIONS AND OPTIONS: You may easily substitute creamy peanut butter and peanuts for the hazelnut butter and the hazelnuts.

WINE NOTES: Chocolate's extreme sweetness and mouth-coating texture smothers many wines and quite often needs an older fortified wine to compete, although it does have some affinity with Muscat. These wines give nutty toasted nuances that mirror the nut flavors in the dessert. Recommended: Taylor Fladgate, 20-year-old Tawny Port; or NV(non-vintage), Yalumba, Museum, Muscat.

Makes 4 to 6 dessert servings

White Chocolate Cheesecake with Blueberry Caramel Sauce

Cheesecake and white chocolate — the flavor is worth the extra calories! Although a seemingly odd pairing, the slight acidity of the blueberries adds the necessary balance to the almost overly sweet caramel sauce. Underneath it all is a dreamy cheesecake with its creamy white chocolate essence that makes this one of our more complex-flavored desserts.

CHOCOLATE CRUST
10 ounces chocolate cookie crumbs
½ cup granulated sugar
1 teaspoon ground cinnamon

1 tablespoon all-purpose flour
½ cup butter, melted

WHITE CHOCOLATE GANACHE
4 ounces white chocolate, coarsely chopped
1 tablespoon butter

½ cup heavy cream

CHEESECAKE FILLING
1½ pounds cream cheese, room temperature
1 cup granulated sugar
1 tablespoon all-purpose flour

1 teaspoon vanilla extract
4 eggs
white chocolate ganache, from above

2 tablespoons cocoa powder, to dust top of cake

BLUEBERRY CARAMEL SAUCE
1 cup granulated sugar
¼ cup water
¼ teaspoon lemon juice
¼ teaspoon lemon juice

1 cup fresh blueberries (or use ½ cup dried blueberries soaked in ½ cup of Cassis or white wine)
1 cup heavy cream

TO PREPARE THE CRUST: In a bowl of a food processor, place the chocolate cookie crumbs (chocolate cookies placed in a food processor and processed into fine crumbs), sugar, cinnamon and flour. Process until smooth. Slowly add the melted butter and continue mixing until combined. Press the cookie crumb crust evenly over the bottom of a 9-inch springform pan. Refrigerate the crust until ready to use.

TO PREPARE THE GANACHE: Place the chocolate in a small bowl. In a saucepan, bring cream and butter to a boil. Pour over white chocolate and whisk until smooth. Keep at room temperature until ready to use.

TO PREPARE THE FILLING: Preheat oven to 325°F.

Place the cream cheese in the large bowl of an electric mixer. With the mixer on low speed, using a paddle, beat the cream cheese until soft and creamy, about 5 minutes. Scrape down the sides of the bowl. Increase speed to medium and gradually add the sugar. Continue mixing and add the flour and vanilla extract. Add the eggs one at a time until well combined. Reduce speed to low and pour in the reserved white chocolate ganache.

Pour the filling into prepared spring form pan. Bake for 1 to 1½ hours or until top is slightly puffed and the center is firm. Turn off the oven, prop open the oven door and allow the cheesecake to cool in the oven for an additional hour. Place the cake on a wire rack to cool completely. Refrigerate the cake 4 to 6 hours or overnight.

TO PREPARE THE BLUEBERRY CARAMEL SAUCE: In a heavy-bottomed, medium-sized saucepan, combine sugar, water and lemon juice. Place over medium heat and cook until the sugar mixture turns a light caramel color. Remove from heat. Add the blueberries (add any remaining Cassis if using dried blueberries) and cream. Return the sauce mixture to the heat and simmer until the sauce is thick enough to coat the back of a spoon. Allow sauce to cool slightly and the purée in a blender.

TO SERVE: Dust the top of the cake with cocoa powder. Unmold the cake and cut into 12 pieces. Serve with blueberry caramel sauce and fresh berries.

ADVANCE PREPARATION: The crust and the ganache can be made several days ahead and refrigerated. Warm the ganache before adding it to the filling by placing the container with the ganache in a saucepan half full of hot water.

SUBSTITUTIONS AND OPTIONS: To make a White Chocolate-Cappuccino filling, add a coffee-cream mixture (1 tablespoon of instant coffee boiled together with ¼ cup of heavy cream) to the filling mixture after adding the white chocolate ganache. Use fresh blueberries or other fresh berries if available or dried berries soaked in liquor in the off season.

You can substitute graham cracker crumbs, vanilla wafer crumbs or ground nuts for the chocolate cookie crumbs.

WINE NOTES: The rich and decadent flavor of the cheesecake needs a wine with enough richness to hold up to the caramel's sweetness and some crisp acidity to balance it. Recommended: 1999 Cave Spring, Niagara Peninsula, Icewine Riesling, Canada; or 2001 Lava Cap, Muscat Canelli, Sierra Foothills, California.

Makes one 9-inch cake, or 12 servings

Chocolate Peppermint Brownie

Brownies — especially chocolate brownies — ice cream and milk may be the ultimate "had-a-hard-day" comfort foods. Since we cannot leave anything alone for long, we tinkered with the classic and added peppermint extract to our moist "cake-like" brownie recipe and serve it with a rich, decadent chocolate sauce.

PEPPERMINT BROWNIE

1 cup soft butter

2 cups granulated sugar

4 eggs

1 teaspoon vanilla extract

1 teaspoon peppermint extract

1½ cups all-purpose flour

⅔ cup cocoa powder

½ teaspoon iodized salt

CHOCOLATE SAUCE

4 ounces bittersweet chocolate, cut into small pieces

2 tablespoons butter

3 tablespoons heavy cream

TO PREPARE THE PEPPERMINT BROWNIE: Preheat the oven to 350°F. Grease and flour a 9-by-13-inch pan.

Sift together the flour, cocoa powder and salt. Reserve. In a bowl of an electric mixer fitted with a paddle, on low speed mix together the butter and sugar until creamy. Add the eggs, one at a time and beat until smooth. Add the vanilla extract and peppermint extract. Slowly add the flour, cocoa and salt and continue mixing until just combined. Pour the brownie mixture into the prepared pan and bake for 30 minutes or until a skewer inserted in the middle comes out clean.

Let brownie cool for 15 to 20 minutes before cutting.

TO PREPARE THE CHOCOLATE SAUCE: Place the chocolate, butter and cream in a stainless steel bowl and wrap the top of the bowl with plastic film. Place the bowl over a *bain-marie* — a large saucepan one-quarter filled with water and placed over medium heat. When the chocolate has melted, stir until mixture is smooth.

TO SERVE: Cut brownie into large, 2½-inch by 2½-inch, squares. Place squares on plate, drizzle chocolate sauce over each brownie, and serve with ice cream and peppermint sprigs.

ADVANCE PREPARATION: There are few things better than a rich chocolate brownie right out of the oven. However, both the brownie and the chocolate sauce may be made a day ahead and stored tightly wrapped in the refrigerator. Let the brownies come to room temperature before serving and reheat the chocolate sauce over a *bain-marie*.

SUBSTITUTIONS AND OPTIONS: One cup of chopped white or dark chocolate or chopped nuts can be added to the brownie mixture after you add the flour. For a flavored chocolate sauce, add 1 ounce of flavored alcohol such as triple sec, pear or apple brandy, Chambord or Frangelico.

WINE NOTES: There is nothing subtle in this dessert nor should there be in the wine you drink with it. Some say the ONLY wine to drink with chocolate is a chilled Banyuls. Banyuls is an appellation from Languedoc-Roussillon in the south of France. This fortified wine must have at least a 15 percent alcohol content and must be made from a minimum of 50 percent Grenache grape. If it is a Grand Cru Banyuls, it must be made from at least 75 percent Grenache and aged in wood for a minimum of 30 months. The unique thing about this wine is that it is purposely oxidized by placing small barrels of it in the sun during the summertime to create a style of wine called "Rancio." Recommended: 2001 Domaine de La Rectorie, Banyuls, France.

Makes one 9x13-inch pan, or approximately 20 squares

Chilled Syrah Poached Rhubarb Soup

Rhubarb is a perennial plant that forms long, thick and tasty stalks in the spring. Never eat the leaves or roots because they can cause the tongue and throat to swell, preventing breathing. The deeper the red, the more flavorful the stalks are likely to be. Small to medium-sized stalks are generally more tender than large ones, which may be stringy. To store, first trim and discard the leaves and keep the stalks, unwashed and wrapped tightly in plastic, in the refrigerator for up to three weeks.

The sweetness of strawberries is most often used to balance the sourness of rhubarb. In this recipe, we use the lush berry and black pepper flavors of Syrah grapes and the spiciness of fresh ginger to complement the rhubarb's tartness.

1½ cups Syrah wine or other red wine with sweet berry overtones
1 cup granulated sugar
1 teaspoon fresh ginger root, peeled and finely chopped

1 star anise
1 cinnamon stick
1¾ pounds rhubarb stalks, roughly chopped
juice of 1 lemon
½ cup water

mint springs, for garnish

In a large stainless steel saucepan, combine all ingredients. Place pan over low to medium heat and simmer for 45 minutes or until rhubarb is tender. Remove star anise and cinnamon. Purée in a blender or food processor until smooth. Strain through a fine strainer. Refrigerate until chilled.

TO SERVE: Ladle soup into chilled bowls and serve with strawberry sorbet, sliced strawberries and fresh mint.

ADVANCE PREPARATION: The flavors will be better and more complex if the soup is made several days ahead and given a day of rest in the refrigerator.

SUBSTITUTIONS AND OPTIONS: A cup of heavy cream or plain yogurt can be stirred into the chilled soup for a richer dessert.

WINE NOTES: This dish was originally designed for a winemakers' dinner featuring the wines of Adam Lee of Siduri and Novy Wines. Recommended: 2000 Novy, Page-Nord Vineyard, Syrah, Napa Valley, California; or for something special and unusual, try the 2000 Castle Vineyards, Port of Syrah, Sonoma Valley, California.

Makes six 6-ounce servings

Chilled
Sweet Pea
Soup. Page 72

LEFT:
*Sweet Corn
and Shiitake
Mushroom
Custard,
page 33*

RIGHT:
*Sweet Corn
and Shiitake
Mushroom
Custard
(coming out
of oven)*

LEFT:
*Dungeness Crab
and Fuji Apple
Salad with Curry
Mayonnaise,
page 62*

RIGHT:
*Rogue Creamery
Blue Cheese Tart,
page 28*

Selection of Oysters on the Half Shell with Dipping Sauces, page 48

Cornmeal Fried Oysters with a Salad of Organic Greens and Lemon–Caper Aioli, page 50

Yellow Tomato Gazpacho with Avocado–Tomato Salsa, page 80

RIGHT:
Grilled Rib-Eye of Beef, page 133

LEFT:
Game Hen en Cocotte with Sweet Potato Bread, page 135

Spice-Rubbed Salmon with Savory Herb Sauce, page 104

RIGHT:
Fennel-Crusted Halibut with Roasted Tomato Broth, page 112

Lavender Honey Glazed Venison Roast with Cauliflower– Potato Purée, page 140

Sage Rubbed
Leg of Pork with
Apple–Fennel
Pan Sauce,
page 128

Heirloom Tomato and Summer Squash Torte, page 158

*Peach Upside-Down
Polenta Cake with
Peach Syrup, page* 179

*Pinor Noir
Granité,
page* 181

*Honey Tangerine
Meringue Tartlet
with Grand Marnier
Pastry Cream and
Berry Coulis, page* 186

Peerless Crème Brûlée

This classic crème brûlée is the bestselling dessert on our menu and the most requested recipe. We have made crème brûlée infused with everything from green tea to chocolate but our simple vanilla version is so rich and flavorful there is no need for additional ingredients.

The key to making crème brûlée is to make sure you have a smooth custard and a very thin caramel coating on top. We recommend going to your local hardware store and purchasing a propane torch to make the caramelized coating. You can also use your broiler if you cannot find a torch, but place the chilled, cooked molds in a pan of ice water to keep the custards cold while the tops are caramelizing.

½ cup egg yolks (approximately 8 large
   egg yolks)
½ cup vanilla sugar (see page 19)
3½ cups heavy cream

½ cup milk
1½ vanilla beans, cut in half lengthwise and
   seeds scraped from the inside
additional vanilla sugar for caramelizing the top

Preheat oven to 300°F. Place the yolks and sugar in a large stainless steel bowl. Whisk together to combine.

NOTE: Do not let the yolks and sugar sit together longer than 5 minutes or a chemical reaction will occur and the sugar will begin to "cook" the yolks.

In a large saucepan, combine the heavy cream, milk, vanilla pods and seeds. Bring to a boil. Watch carefully as the cream has a tendency to boil over.

Pour the cream mixture into the egg mixture, a little at a time, continually whisking until all of the cream mixture and sugar mixture has been incorporated. Pass the custard base through a fine strainer.

Place six 6-ounce ovenproof moulds in a large, flat ovenproof pan. Pour the custard evenly into the moulds and place the pan in the oven. Fill the large pan one-half full of hot water. Be careful not to splash any water onto the custards. Cover the large pan with aluminum foil and bake for 45 minutes to 1 hour. The custards are finished when, if gently shaken, they are just set.

Refrigerate the custard 2 to 4 hours or overnight.

TO SERVE: Preheat the broiler, making sure it is very hot. Coat the top of each custard with a thin layer of vanilla sugar. Place the custards in a large pan with ice water and place the large pan 2 to 3 inches from the broiler. Broil until the sugar has caramelized.

ADVANCE PREPARATION: The crème brûlée mixture can be made several days ahead and kept in the refrigerator until ready to bake. The cooked custards can be made, chilled, individually wrapped and refrigerated several days ahead of serving.

SUBSTITUTIONS AND OPTIONS: As we mentioned, you can infuse the cream mixture with tea, ginger, chocolate or almost anything you can imagine. Being purists to some degree, we still prefer the elegantly simple vanilla version.

WINE NOTES: The caramelized sugar top begs for a sherry with crisp acidity and a not-too-sweet burnt caramel finish. Recommended: 1975 Bodegas Toro Albal·, PX, Gran Reserva, Sherry, Spain; or NV Bodegas Dios Baco, Amontillado Jerez, Sherry, Spain.

Makes six 6-ounce servings

Peach Upside-Down Polenta Cake
with Peach Syrup

The peach is a member of the rose family, a cousin to apricots, cherries, plums and almonds. Peaches are usually classified as clingstone (the fruit of the peach clings to the stone or pit), semi-freestone (the fruit pulls away from the stone when the peach is fully ripened) and free-stone, the most popular, where the fruit of the peach readily pulls away from the stone.

July and August are peak months for fresh peaches. The fruit is extremely perishable, so buy only the amount you intend to use or eat within a few days. Choose peaches that are firm to the touch, but whose flesh yields with gentle pressure. The fruits should be free of bruises with a warm, fragrant aroma.

PEACH-POLENTA CAKE

½ cup blanched almonds, peeled
¼ cup granulated sugar
½ cup polenta or cornmeal

1 cup all-purpose flour
1 teaspoon kosher salt

8 tablespoons soft butter
½ cup granulated sugar
2 eggs

1 teaspoon pure vanilla extract
1 teaspoon peach schnapps *(optional)*

5 peaches, peeled, cut in half, (we recommend Red Haven or Suncrest varieties, both freestone varieties)

PEACH SYRUP

½ pound peaches, peeled, cut in half and roughly chopped, approximately 2 peaches
1 cup granulated sugar
½ cup dry white wine
½ cup water

1 tablespoon peach schnapps *(optional)*
1 vanilla bean, split lengthwise, seeds scraped

NOTE: To remove the skins, blanch the peaches in boiling water for one to two minutes and then immediately plunge fruit into ice water to cease the cooking process. The skin should easily slip off. Do not let the peaches soak in the water.

TO PREPARE THE PEACH-POLENTA CAKE: Preheat oven to 350°F.

Place the almonds and sugar in a food processor and pulse until they are finely ground. In a medium-sized bowl, combine the almond/sugar mixture, polenta, flour and salt.

Place the butter and sugar in a bowl of an electric mixer. Beat with a paddle using medium speed, until the butter is creamy and smooth. Add the eggs, one at a time, until fully incorporated. Add the vanilla extract and peach schnapps. Turn the mixer to low and add the dry ingredients a little at a time.

Cut the peach halves into ¼-inch wedges. In the bottom of a 9-inch springform pan, arrange the peaches in concentric circles, starting in the center of the pan, forming a spiral pattern. Spoon the batter over the peaches. Bake for 30 to 40 minutes or until the cake springs back when lightly pressed and a toothpick inserted in the center comes out clean. Remove the sides from the pan and allow the cake to cool on rack.

TO PREPARE THE PEACH SYRUP: In a small stainless steel saucepan, combine the peaches, sugar, wine, water and vanilla bean and seeds. Set over low to medium heat and simmer, stirring occasionally, until the mixture is slightly syrupy, about 6 to 8 minutes. Remove from heat. Allow syrup to cool to room temperature. Cover and refrigerate until cold, at least 2 hours or overnight.

Remove the vanilla bean pieces from the syrup. Place syrup in a blender or food processor and purée until smooth.

TO SERVE: Turn cake over onto a serving plate and remove the bottom of the pan. Cut into 6 to 8 wedges and serve with peach-vanilla syrup.

ADVANCE PREPARATION: The cake can be made several days ahead of time and refrigerated. Remove the cake from the refrigerator and allow it to come to room temperature before serving.

SUBSTITUTIONS AND OPTIONS: In place of the peaches, substitute other stone fruit such as plums or apricots, or substitute tree fruit such as apples, figs or pears. Make sure the fruit is thinly sliced so that it will be cooked through when the cake is baked.

WINE NOTES: A slightly sweet dessert wine with peach overtones will put you over the top. Recommended: 2001 Casta Diva, Alicante Muscat, Bodegas, Spain.

Makes one 9-inch cake or ten 3 ½-inch individual cakes

Pinot Noir Granité

Granité, if you are French, or *granita* if you are Italian, is a grainy, frozen mixture of sugar, water and a flavored liquid. A sorbet or sherbet, on the other hand, is prepared with a higher proportion of sugar to liquid and frozen in a conventional, beater-type ice-cream maker to make a creamy, smooth almost ice-cream-like consistency. Granités always have a distinct granular texture, as the name suggests.

This wine granité is light, easy to make and not as icy as traditional granités or as sweet as sorbet. It makes a wonderful base for those perfect late summer berries.

1 lemon, juice and zest finely chopped,
  separated
1 orange, juice and zest finely chopped,
  separated
1½ cups water
1½ cups sugar
2 whole cloves
2 whole star anise
2 whole allspice berries
5 whole black
  peppercorns
1½ cups Pinot Noir wine

Combine lemon zest, orange zest, water, sugar, cloves, star anise, allspice and black peppercorns in a stainless steel saucepan. Place pan over medium heat and simmer 5-10 minutes or until sugar is dissolved and the spices are infused into the syrup. Allow syrup to cool completely.

Mix the lemon juice, orange juice and Pinot Noir into the cooled syrup. Strain the mixture into a freezer-safe shallow glass or stainless steel dish. Cover the dish with plastic and place in the freezer.

With a fork, stir and scrap the granité every 30 minutes until ice crystals form and the mixture is firm, approximately 2 hours.

TO SERVE: Spoon the granité into individual bowls and top with a mixture of fresh berries. Serve immediately.

ADVANCE PREPARATION: The syrup can be made up to a week ahead and the granité can be made several days ahead and kept tightly covered in the freezer.

SUBSTITUTIONS AND OPTIONS: Almost any fruit-forward wine, red or white, will work in place of the Pinot Noir. To make a citrus-flavored granité, substitute 1½ cups of citrus juice for the wine.

WINE NOTES: A light and refreshing, not overly sweet sparkling wine or dessert wine will work well with the ice. Recommended: 2001 Silvan Ridge, Early Muscat, Semi-Sparkling, Oregon; or for a delightful rosé, try 1998 Hyatt, Black Muscat, Yakima Valley, Washington.

Makes 4 servings, approximately 5 cups

Spiced Sugar Pumpkin Cake

This cake has the texture of a quick bread and the autumn flavors of pumpkin and "pumpkin pie" spices. Pumpkin is one of those tastes that you either love or hate. We happen to love it. This cake is designed to leave no doubt that you are eating pumpkin.

½ cup dried black currants
¼ cup water, boiling
1 tablespoon hazelnut liquor or brandy
1 cup cake flour (substitute all-purpose flour)
¼ teaspoon kosher salt
1 teaspoon baking soda
¼ teaspoon ground cinnamon
⅛ teaspoon nutmeg, freshly grated
¼ teaspoon fresh ginger root, peeled and freshly grated

⅛ teaspoon ground cloves
⅛ teaspoon ground cardamom
⅛ teaspoon ground white pepper
2 eggs
½ cup honey
¾ cup vegetable oil
1 cup pumpkin purée (see Substitutions, below)
¼ cup hazelnuts, toasted, peeled and roughly crushed

Preheat oven to 325°F.

Place the currants in a bowl and pour boiling water and liquor or brandy over them. Set aside and allow them to plump 15 to 20 minutes. Drain and reserve any excess liquid.

Spray a 9-inch cake pan (either round or square) with nonstick spray. In a medium-sized bowl, mix together flour, salt, baking soda, cinnamon, nutmeg, ginger, cloves, cardamom and pepper. In a bowl of an electric mixer, beat together the eggs and honey until light and fluffy. With the mixer running, slowly beat in the oil. Beat in the dry ingredients, constantly scraping down the sides of the bowl. Add the pumpkin purée and beat until smooth. Stir in the nuts and currants.

Pour the batter into the prepared pan and bake until golden brown and a skewer inserted in the center comes out clean, about 35-40 minutes. Allow the cake to cool slightly, then unmold the cake, place on a cake rack and allow to cool completely.

TO SERVE: Cut the cake into 12 wedges (if using a round pan) or 3-inch squares (if using a square pan). Serve with vanilla ice cream and drizzle with any reserved soaking liquid.

ADVANCE PREPARATION: The cake may be made 1 to 2 days ahead and either served at room temperature or warmed in a 250°F oven.

SUBSTITUTIONS AND OPTIONS: We have used hazelnuts and currants in the recipe to give this cake a Northwestern flair. You can either omit both or substitute toasted walnuts, pine nuts or almonds for the hazelnuts and golden raisins for the currants. If you choose not to roast your own Sugar Pumpkins, canned pumpkin purée will work fine.

WINE NOTES: Choose a late-harvest Gewürztraminer with tastes of raisin, spice and intense honey, and a little acidity to match the pumpkin and balance the cake's sweetness. Recommended: 1998 Erath, Late Harvest Gewürztraminer, Willamette Valley, Oregon.

Makes one 10-inch cake, 12 servings

Warm Apple Pie
with Apple Brandy Sauce

In Mary's family, dessert is pie not cake. Pies are Julie's, Mary's mother's forté, partly thanks to the crust recipe handed down over two generations from her Midwest ancestors.

The only variation we have made to the original crust recipe is to use unsalted butter in place of the original lard. The key to making a light and flaky crust is to keep everything very cold, work on a marble surface if you have one, and do not overwork the dough.

CRUST

2 cups all-purpose flour

1 teaspoon kosher salt

¾ cup butter, chilled and cut into small pieces

¼ cup or more water, very cold

APPLE FILLING

6 cups Gravenstein, Braeburn or Granny Smith apples, peeled and thinly sliced

½ cup granulated sugar

2 tablespoons all-purpose flour

1 teaspoon ground cinnamon

pinch ground nutmeg

1 teaspoon lemon zest

1 tablespoon all-purpose flour

1 tablespoon butter, cut into small pieces

APPLE BRANDY SAUCE

1 tablespoon butter

1 tablespoon fresh ginger root, peeled and finely chopped (about a 2-inch piece)

6 Gravenstein, Braeburn or Granny Smith apples, peeled and coarsely chopped

1 cup dark brown sugar

1 teaspoon ground cinnamon

½ teaspoon iodized salt

1 cup apple brandy

TO PREPARE THE CRUST: On a table, mix together flour and salt. Add the butter and using a pastry cutter, fork or your fingertips, incorporate until the flour mixture resembles small peas. Add a small amount of cold water a little at a time until you are able to gather the dough into a ball. Wrap the dough in plastic wrap and refrigerate for at least 30 minutes.

NOTE: Do not knead or overmix the dough. When the dough comes together it should be dry enough to hold its shape but not be wet.

Divide dough in half. Roll each half into a circle approximately 12-inches in diameter. Line a 9-inch pie pan with one circle and place the lined pie pan and the remaining circle in the refrigerator with a cloth on top until ready to use.

TO PREPARE THE FILLING: In a large bowl, combine the sliced apples, sugar, flour, cinnamon, nutmeg and lemon zest.

TO COMPLETE THE PIE: Preheat oven to 400°F.

Dust the bottom of the pie shell with the additional tablespoon of flour. Add the pie filling. Dot the top of the filling with the additional tablespoon of butter. Cover the filling with the remaining circle of pie dough. Seal the edges with water and crimp. Vent the top by placing a few slits in the top. Place in middle rack of the oven and bake for 15 minutes. Reduce oven temperature to 350°F and bake an additional 25 to 30 minutes, or until the filling begins to bubble and the crust is golden brown.

TO PREPARE THE APPLE BRANDY SAUCE: In a medium-sized saucepan over medium heat, melt butter. Add ginger and sauté for 1 minute. Add apples, brown sugar, cinnamon, salt and apple brandy. Simmer, uncovered, until apples are very tender, about 45 minutes.

Purée in a blender until a smooth sauce consistency is formed. If sauce is too thick, add warm water and purée. Keep warm.

TO SERVE: Allow the pie to sit a room temperature 15 to 20 minutes. Cut the pie into 8 wedges and serve with apple brandy sauce.

ADVANCE PREPARATION: The pie may be made 1 to 2 days ahead and either served at room temperature or warmed in a 250°F oven.

SUBSTITUTIONS AND OPTIONS: Add dried or fresh cranberries or sun-dried cherries to the apples. In the spring substitute rhubarb; in the summer substitute stone fruit such as apricots, peaches or plums; and in the fall, substitute pears for the apples.

For an interesting twist and to add a complex layer of flavor, add ½ cup of fresh carrot juice to the apple brandy sauce before you purée the apple mixture. The combination of apples and carrots will both surprise you and convince you to think "outside of the box."

WINE NOTES: This sweet pie calls for a luscious, high-acid dessert wine that is delicate on the palate. Recommended: 2001 King Estate, Vin Glacé Pinot Gris, Oregon; or for something totally different, try a wine with a creamy tropical flavor that we believe honors our business partner Crissy — 2001 Tobin James Cellars, "Charisma," Late Harvest Zinfandel, Paso Robles, California.

Makes one 9-inch pie, 8 servings

Honey Tangerine-Meringue Tartlet with Grand Marnier Pastry Cream and Berry Coulis

Murcotts, also called Honey tangerines, are a late winter citrus variety usually available January through March in our neighborhood and always a treat on gray Northwest winter days. As the name suggests, these orange globes are honey sweet and easy to peel. They have a refreshing tartness and a strong, alluring scent that's especially seductive with the creamy, fluffiness of the meringue in this dessert.

To answer the perennial question of what to do with leftover egg whites, we created a version of a New Zealand/Australian Pavlova dessert — a meringue base with whipped cream and fresh fruit. The Pavlova was first created in the early 1930s in honor of the ballerina Anna Pavlova, a Russian ballerina who was the most celebrated dancer of her time.

MERINGUE TARTLET SHELLS
½ cup egg whites
¼ teaspoon cream of tartar
⅛ teaspoon iodized salt

½ cup granulated sugar
⅓ cup powdered sugar
½ tablespoon cornstarch

GRAND MARNIER PASTRY CREAM
2 cups milk
½ cup granulated sugar
3 tablespoons cornstarch
4 egg yolks

1½ ounces butter
½ tablespoon Grand Marnier or other orange-flavored liquor

BERRY COULIS
Makes approximately 3/4 cup
1½ cups fresh or frozen berries, strawberries, raspberries, blackberries, etc..

¼ cup powdered sugar
1 tablespoon lemon juice

TO ASSEMBLE TARTS
6-8 honey tangerines, peeled, pith removed, and segmented

powdered sugar for dusting
mint springs, for garnish

TO PREPARE THE MERINGUE TART SHELLS: Preheat oven to 250°. In a stainless steel or copper bowl, add the egg whites, cream of tartar and salt. Whip vigorously until foamy. Slowly add granulated sugar. NOTE: Make sure that you beat the egg whites well and that the sugar is fully dissolved before continuing on to the next step. Continue whipping until stiff peaks are formed (the mixture will triple in volume). Sift the powdered sugar and cornstarch. Gently fold into egg whites.

Draw six 5-inch circles on a piece of parchment paper the size of a baking sheet. Flip the paper over and place it on a baking sheet. Place the meringue mixture in a piping bag with a star tip. Beginning from the center of each circle, pipe the meringue in concentric circles until it fills the circle outlined on the parchment paper.

Place baking sheet pan in a 250°F oven for 1 hour. Reduce oven temperature to 200°F and continue baking another 2 hours or until the meringues are firm and dry. The shells should have little or no color. When cool, peel meringues off the paper.

TO PREPARE THE GRAND MARNIER PASTRY CREAM: In a stainless steel saucepan, combine milk and ¼ cup sugar. Bring to a boil and remove from heat. In a stainless steel bowl, combine remaining ¼ cup sugar with cornstarch and egg yolks. Mix until smooth. Add a little of the milk mixture to the egg mixture, stirring constantly. Continue adding remaining milk until it is fully incorporated. Return mixture to the saucepan and cook, stirring constantly, over medium heat until mixture is thick and coats the back of a spoon. Do not let the mixture boil.

Remove from heat and add butter and Grand Marnier. Refrigerate in a stainless steel or glass container, placing plastic wrap over the top to prevent a skin from forming.

TO PREPARE THE BERRY COULIS: Combine all ingredients in a blender. Purée until smooth. Strain and reserve.

TO SERVE: Spread pastry cream evenly on each tartlet shell. Arrange tangerine segments in a circular flower pattern on top of pastry cream. Dust each tartlet with powdered sugar and garnish with mint sprig. Serve with berry coulis.

ADVANCE PREPARATION: The meringue shells, pastry cream and berry coulis can be made several days ahead. Store the meringue shells in an airtight container. The berry coulis will store in the refrigerator for several days or the freezer for several months. We suggest using any extra coulis as a sauce for ice cream or sorbet.

SUBSTITUTIONS AND OPTIONS: Valencia oranges, Moro oranges (blood oranges), Meyer lemons or even grapefruit make good substitutions for the tangerines. In place of the pastry cream, substitute lemon curd or even Meyer lemon curd (see page 188).

WINE NOTES: Choose a sweet but delicate wine that has enough honey and citrus flavors to hold up to the sweetness of the tangerines and enough spice to cut through the richness of the pastry cream. Recommended: 2001 Andrew Rich, Les Vigneaux, Gewürztraminer, Willamette Valley, Oregon (made from frozen grapes).

Makes six 5-inch tartlets

Meyer Lemons

Meyer lemons are an excellent substitute for Honey tangerines. Frank Meyer, an employee of the US Agriculture Department, brought the first Meyer lemon tree to the US from China in 1908. It was used primarily as an ornamental shrub or container plant until the early 1980s, when the lemons caught the attention of a few Californian chefs. Believed to be a cross between an orange and a lemon, the Meyer lemon is particularly sweet compared with its tart cousins, the Eureka and Lisbon lemons, which are the varieties most commonly found in supermarkets.

The Meyer lemon also differs from other lemons in that the whole fruit can be used; the peel and pulp can be cooked or added raw to a salad. The fruits are delicate, so wrap them tightly in plastic and store them in the refrigerator for no more than a few days after purchase. ❧

MEYER LEMON CURD

4 egg yolks
2 whole eggs
½ cup granulated sugar
½ cup Meyer lemon juice

In a stainless steel bowl, combine egg yolks, whole eggs, granulated sugar and Meyer lemon juice. Place bowl over a saucepan of simmering water. Stir continuously with a rubber spatula until the curd starts to thicken. Change to a whisk and continue whisking until the mixture is thick, approximately 5 minutes.

Place in a glass or plastic container and cover the surface with plastic wrap to prevent a skin from forming. Refrigerate until needed.

Makes 1 cup, enough for six 5-inch tartlets

Pistachio-Orange Biscotti

In Italian, biscotti means "twice cooked." The word biscotto is derived from *bis* (twice) and *cotto* (cooked). Biscotti is also the generic term for cookies in Italian. The cookies are said to have originated during Columbus's time and are credited to an Italian baker who originally served them with Tuscan wines. The dough is formed into logs and baked until golden brown. The logs are then sliced and the individual biscotti are baked again to give them their characteristic dryness and nutty, toasted flavor.

3 cups all-purpose flour
1½ cups granulated sugar
¼ teaspoon iodized salt
1 teaspoon baking powder
2 teaspoons vanilla extract

3 eggs
3 egg yolks
juice and zest of one orange
1 cup pistachios, roughly chopped

Preheat oven to 375°F.

In a bowl, combine flour, sugar, salt and baking powder. In a separate bowl, whisk together vanilla extract, whole eggs, egg yolks, orange zest and orange juice. Pour the wet ingredients into the dry ingredients. Mix until completely incorporated. Add the pistachios and mix gently until evenly distributed.

On a surface dusted with flour, roll the dough into 3 logs about 1½ inches wide by 12 inches long. Place the logs on a baking sheet lined with parchment paper or on a nonstick mat. Bake at 375°F for about 25 to 30 minutes, until lightly brown. Let logs cool completely.

Lower the oven temperature to 300°F. Cut the logs on a diagonal, approximately ½-inch thick. Lay the biscotti cut-side down on a baking sheet and bake for 15 minutes or until golden brown and dry.

ADVANCE PREPARATION: The finished biscotti may be stored in an airtight container for a week or wrapped tightly and stored in the freezer for a month.

SUBSTITUTIONS AND OPTIONS: You can substitute almost any nut for the pistachios and almost any citrus fruit for the orange. An interesting twist to this recipe is to substitute 1 cup of coarsely ground cornmeal for the all-purpose flour. The cornmeal will add an interesting textural component and the corn flavor pairs well with the citrus.

WINE NOTES: Biscotti are traditionally dipped in coffee, espresso or in a glass of Beaumes-de-Venise. To match the orange flavor, we recommend an orange Muscat or an ice wine with orange flavors. Recommended: 1998 Woodward Canyon Winery, Orange Muscat, Columbia Valley, Washington; or 2000 Hyatt Vineyards, Black Muscat Ice Wine, Yakima Valley, Washington.

Makes approximately 2 dozen biscotti cookies

Sun-Dried Cherry Biscotti

Cherries are a favorite fruit in the Pacific Northwest. When the first dark red Bings arrive in the market, followed shortly by golden blushed Rainiers, we know summer is truly here. Using dried cherries in the biscotti gives you the sweet flavor of summer all year round and they're a wonderful surprise if you are used to the traditional almonds.

3 cups all-purpose flour
1½ cups granulated sugar
¼ teaspoon iodized salt
1 teaspoon baking powder
2 teaspoons vanilla extract

3 eggs
3 egg yolks
⅛ cup Kirsch or cherry liquor
1½ cups sun-dried cherries

Preheat oven to 375°F.

In a bowl, combine flour, sugar, salt and baking powder. In a separate bowl, whisk together vanilla extract, whole eggs, egg yolks and Kirsch.

Pour the wet ingredients into the dry ingredients. Mix until completely incorporated. Add the sun-dried cherries and mix gently until evenly distributed.

On a surface dusted with flour, roll the dough into 3 logs about 1½ inches wide by 12 inches long. Place the logs on a baking sheet lined with parchment paper or on a nonstick mat. Bake at 375°F for about 25 to 30 minutes, until lightly brown. Let logs cool completely.

Lower the oven temperature to 300°F. Cut the logs on a diagonal, approximately ½-inch thick. Lay the biscotti cut-side down on a baking sheet and bake for 15 minutes or until golden brown and dry.

ADVANCE PREPARATION: The finished biscotti may be stored in an airtight container for a week or wrapped tightly and stored in the freezer for a month.

SUBSTITUTIONS AND OPTIONS: You can substitute almost any dried fruit (such as dried blueberries) for the cherries and other flavored liquor (such as Cassis) for the Kirsch. You can also omit the fruit and add various spices or the zest and juice of various citrus fruits. Biscotti may also be dipped in melted dark or white chocolate.

WINE NOTES: Biscotti are traditionally dipped in coffee, espresso or in a glass of Beaumes-de-Venise. Try matching a berry liquor, such as Framboise, to bring out the fruit flavor of the cookie. Recommended: 2000 Jaboulet, Muscat de Beaumes-de-Venise, Rhône, France; or NV Bonny Doon, Framboise, Santa Cruz Mountains, California.

Makes approximately 2 dozen biscotti cookies

Macadamia Nut Butter and White Chocolate Chip Cookies

Can you say Reese's Peanut Butter Cup? The recipe for these cookies came from Tiffany Dodge, our long-time, long-suffering pantry cook. Her boyfriend at the time was working at Maranatha Natural Foods which produces all-natural nut and seed butters. He came home one day with a jar of organic macadamia nut butter and she let her creativity reign.

2 cups all-purpose flour
½ teaspoon baking soda
⅛ teaspoon salt
10 tablespoons butter
⅔ cup macadamia nut butter
⅔ cup dark brown sugar

1 cup granulated sugar
2 eggs
3 egg yolks
2 teaspoons vanilla extract
1 cup macadamia nuts, roughly chopped
6 ounces white chocolate chips

Preheat oven to 350°F.

In a medium-size bowl, combine flour, baking soda and salt. Set aside. In a bowl of an electric mixer, combine butter, macadamia nut butter, brown sugar and granulated sugar. Using a paddle with the mixer on medium speed, combine until mixture is creamy. Add the eggs and egg yolks one at a time until they are fully incorporated. Add vanilla extract. Turn to low speed and slowly add flour mixture until fully incorporated. Remove bowl from mixer. Using a wooden spoon, fold in the nuts and chocolate by hand.

Wrap the dough in plastic film and refrigerate until firm.

Break off chunks of dough and roll them into small 1-inch in diameter balls. Place the balls on a nonstick baking sheet or on a baking sheet lined with parchment paper. Leave plenty of space between the cookies as the dough will spread when baking. Bake for 8 to 10 minutes or until edges turn golden brown.

ADVANCE PREPARATION: The dough can be stored tightly wrapped in the refrigerator for a week or frozen for up to a month. Once baked, the cookies may be stored in an airtight container for a week or wrapped tightly and store in the freezer for a month.

SUBSTITUTIONS AND OPTIONS: You can easily substitute peanut butter and peanuts, or other nut butters and other nuts, for the macadamia nut butter and macadamia nuts. You can also replace the white chocolate chips with either bittersweet or semi-sweet chocolate chips. You may also leave the chocolate out of the recipe altogether, but Mary says why bother baking these cookies at all.

WINE NOTES: There is a natural affinity between Vin Santo wine and chocolate-nut desserts. Vin Santo is Italy's "holy wine" and is made from dried grapes in order to concentrate the sugar before being fermented, and aged in small barrels. Recommended: 1996 Capezzana, Vin Santo Del Carmignano Riserva, Tuscany, Italy.

Makes approximately 2 dozen cookies

Honey Almond Macaroons

A macaroon is a small meringue cookie, usually made with almonds or coconut, characterized by a crisp outer crust and a soft, moist interior. Cookie lore tells us these treats were first made in an Italian monastery around the late 1700s. Carmelite nuns baked these cookies to pay for their housing when they needed asylum during the French Revolution. The nuns followed the principle: "Almonds are good for girls who do not eat meat."

Honey is the world's original sweetener. Honey comes in over 300 varieties with various colors and flavors depending on the blossoms visited by the bees and the terrain around their hives. It has properties that attract and keep moisture, making it ideal for pastries that you want to prevent from drying out. Honey's high sugar content makes for what we call GBD (Golden, Brown and Delicious) baked goods.

2 egg whites
pinch iodized salt
¼ cup honey
1 teaspoon almond extract

8 ounces finely ground blanched almonds, (about 2 cups sliced, blanched almonds ground in a food processor)
24 whole almonds (optional)

Preheat oven to 300°F. Line 2 large baking sheets with parchment paper.

In a bowl of an electric mixer, beat the egg whites on low speed until foamy, about 2 to 3 minutes. Add the salt, increase the mixer speed to high and beat until soft peaks form, 3 to 4 minutes. Reduce mixer speed to low and gradually add the honey, a little at a time, pouring away from the beater. Continue beating until the whites are stiff and glossy, about 5 to 8 minutes. Stop beating and add the almond extract. Fold in the ground nuts.

Drop the mixture by tablespoonfuls, 1½ inches apart, onto the prepared baking sheets. If using whole almonds, press one almond into the center of each mound. Bake until firm and golden brown, about 20 minutes. Let cookies cool on the baking sheets for 2 minutes, then transfer them to a rack and let cool completely.

ADVANCE PREPARATION: Once baked, the macaroons may be stored in an airtight container for a week or wrapped tightly and stored in the freezer for up to a month.

SUBSTITUTIONS AND OPTIONS: You may substitute ⅔ cup granulated sugar for the honey. To make coconut macaroons, substitute 1 cup of sifted cake flour and 1 cup of shredded coconut for the ground almonds.

WINE NOTES: Macaroons call for a rich, not-too-sticky, dessert wine with honey, almond and floral aromas and flavors. Recommended: 2001 Hogue, Late Harvest White Riesling, Columbia Valley, Washington; or 1997 Tenuta di Riseccoli, Vin Santo del Chianti Classico, Tuscany, Italy.

Makes approximately 2 dozen cookies

Espresso Shortbread Cookies

These cookies personify the Norwegian proverb that says, "Cookies are made of butter and love." Shortbread cookies are Scottish in origin, and these tender-crisp, butter-rich cookies were once associated mainly with Christmas and Hogmanay (Scottish New Year's Eve). Even without the Scottish heritage, we love them year round and confess that this espresso-flavored variation is our favorite cookie for dunking in milk or crumbling over ice cream. If you are feeling whimsical, dip these rich cookies into a White Russian for a very grown-up version of "milk and cookies."

2 tablespoons dried instant coffee
2 tablespoons water
1 teaspoon coffee extract (optional)
8 ounces soft butter
1 cup granulated sugar
¼ teaspoon iodized salt

1 egg
1 egg yolk
1 teaspoon vanilla extract
2½ cups all-purpose flour
extra granulated sugar for dusting on top
    of cookies

Preheat oven to 350°F.

In a small bowl, combine the dried instant coffee, water and coffee extract, if using.

In a mixing bowl of an electric mixer, combine the butter and sugar. Mix on high speed until creamy and the butter is light and soft. Turn the mixer speed down to medium and slowly add the salt, egg and egg yolk. When the eggs have been fully incorporated, add the vanilla extract and the water/coffee mixture. Turn the mixer speed to slow and gradually mix in the all-purpose flour.

Using parchment or wax paper, roll the dough into 2 logs about 1½ inches wide by 12-inches long. Place the logs in the refrigerator for 3 to 4 hours until the dough is firm.

Unwrap cookie dough and slice into ¼-inch thick slices. Lay the cookies on a baking sheet. Sprinkle additional sugar over each cookie. Bake for 10 to 12 minutes or until golden brown.

ADVANCE PREPARATION: Shortbread cookie dough must be firm before baking or the cookie will spread and be very thin and flat. This dough can be made a day ahead and refrigerated before slicing. You can freeze the dough, well wrapped in plastic, for up to a month before slicing and baking. Once baked, the shortbread may be stored in an airtight container for a week or wrapped tightly and stored in the freezer for a month.

SUBSTITUTIONS AND OPTIONS: The coffee can be omitted and up to 4 tablespoons of citrus juice and zest may be substituted. Chopped nuts like pecans or almonds may be folded into the dough before the logs are formed.

WINE NOTES: Madeira is a fortified wine made by adding alcohol before the fermentation is complete. This stops the fermentation process and leaves residual sugar in the wine. Sercial is the driest style and tends to have toasted coffee overtones. Recommended: NV (non-vintage) Blandy's Sercial Madeira 5 year old, Portugal; or try a simple Kahlua and coffee.

Makes approximately 2 dozen cookies

Siskiyou Mountain Cookies

We currently live in southern Oregon where the Siskiyou Mountain range crosses the Cascade Mountain range. These chunky cookies remind us of looking around on our drive home and seeing the majestic volcanic mountain formations lining our valley.

2 cups all-purpose flour
1 teaspoon baking powder
1 teaspoon baking soda
1 teaspoon iodized salt
8 ounces soft butter
1 cup light brown sugar
2 eggs

2 tablespoons whole milk
2 teaspoons vanilla extract
1 cup oats
1 cup granola *(preferably natural, hemp granola)*
6 ounces semi-sweet chocolate chips
6 ounces white chocolate chips
1 cup walnuts

Preheat oven to 350°F.

In a small bowl, sift together the flour, baking powder, baking soda and salt. Set aside.

In the mixing bowl of an electric mixer, combine the butter and brown sugar. Mix on high speed until creamy and the butter is light and soft. Lower the mixer speed to medium and slowly add the eggs one at a time until fully incorporated. Add the milk and vanilla extract. Reduce mixer speed to low and slowly add flour mixture until fully incorporated. Remove bowl from mixer. Using a wooden spoon, fold in the oats, granola, chocolate and nuts.

Wrap the dough in plastic film and refrigerate until hard.

Break off chunks of dough and roll them into small 1-inch diameter balls. Place balls on a nonstick or parchment-lined baking sheet. Leave plenty of space between the cookies as the dough will spread when baking. Bake for about 8 to10 minutes or until golden brown on edges.

ADVANCE PREPARATION: The dough can be stored tightly wrapped in the refrigerator for a week or frozen for up to a month. Once baked, the cookies may be stored in an airtight container for a week or wrapped tightly and stored in the freezer for a month.

SUBSTITUTIONS AND OPTIONS: This is a "kitchen sink" cookie recipe. You name it and it's in there. Check your baking cupboard to see what's on hand; experiment and enjoy.

WINE NOTES: A wine with high residual sugar and alcohol and a hint of caramel and butterscotch will not only stand up to everything happening in this cookie but be its equal. Recommended: 2000 Lilly Pilly, Noble Blend, Australia.

Makes approximately 2 dozen cookies

Preserving the Harvest

B ACK IN THE DAYS BEFORE REFRIGERATION, freeze-drying, vacuum-pack processing, aseptic packaging and even canning, savvy cooks invented ways to store food for future use. Salting, smoking, pickling, confiting and drying were the most common methods of food preservation, especially on country farms. Root cellars for storing vegetables like potatoes, parsnips and carrots, and fruit like apples, were also common, and a necessity.

Today, in some sense, we've come full circle, seeking greater flavor and taste and control of what we eat and how it's raised, grown, processed and preserved. Happily, we can take advantage of the freezer — it really works now. Along with the revival of cooking with herbs, we're also rediscovering methods of preserving foods that were common over a century ago. Preserving the harvest dovetails perfectly with the concept of sustainable cooking, since it's all about using what is produced or raised locally, what's in season, and storing it so it can be used in the future. Here are some of our favorite ways of storing, preserving and eating seasonal foods.

Spring

PICKLED SHIITAKE MUSHROOMS
ONION MARMALADE

Summer

BASIL PURÉE
TOMATO-LAVENDER PIPÉRADE

Autumn

SWEET POTATO BREAD ❧ MEDJOOL DATE CHUTNEY
PEAR COMPOTE

Winter

OLIVE-ORANGE SALSA
JERUSALEM ARTICHOKE PICKLES

Pickled Shiitake Mushrooms

Pickling, which is a long-established method of preserving foods, is common to almost every type of world cuisine. In pickling, a preserving liquid, based on either a strong salt solution to make brine, or on vinegar to make an acid-based liquid, covers the food being pickled and acts to prevent enzymes and bacteria from breaking it down.

We suggest serving these mushrooms with the Corn and Shiitake Mushroom Custard (see page 33). Additionally, they make a wonderful accompaniment to grilled polenta or even the Parsnip-Potato Rösti (see page 59). The recipe can easily be double or tripled.

PICKLING LIQUID

½ cup water

½ cup red wine vinegar

¼ cup granulated sugar

2 teaspoons kosher salt

1 tablespoon whole black peppercorns

1 teaspoon yellow mustard seed

½ teaspoon crushed hot red chili flakes

1 teaspoon fresh ginger root, peeled and finely chopped

2 allspice berries

1 bay leaf

TO PREPARE THE PICKLING LIQUID: Combine water, vinegar, sugar, salt, peppercorns, mustard seed, chili flakes, ginger, allspice berries and bay leaf in a medium-sized stainless steel saucepan. Place saucepan over high heat and bring to a boil. Reduce heat and allow the pickling liquid to simmer for 10 minutes.

½ cup shiitake mushrooms, stems removed and thinly sliced

TO PREPARE THE PICKLED MUSHROOMS: Place the sliced shiitake mushrooms in a large stainless steel or glass bowl. Strain the hot liquid and pour over the shiitake mushrooms. Cover the bowl with plastic wrap and allow the mushrooms to cool to room temperature. Refrigerate mushrooms, covered in pickling liquid.

SUBSTITUTIONS AND OPTIONS: Almost any cultivated or wild mushroom will work in place of the shiitake mushrooms. The pickles can be kept refrigerated for several weeks.

Makes approximately ¼ cup

Basil Purée

Everyone goes mad for pesto each summer and can't get enough, but we think this simple version that's purely basil leaves blended with olive oil is even more versatile. Buy basil in bulk amounts at the farmers' market or, even better, grow your own basil in a sunny part of the garden. Use this version of pesto as a spread for sandwiches or a sauce for pasta or poultry.

1 cup basil leaves
½ cup extra virgin olive oil
kosher salt, to taste

Blanch the basi leaves by placing them in boiling salted water for 15 to 20 seconds, and then immediately plunging them into an ice-water bath. Remove leaves from the ice-water and pat dry.

Place basil leaves in the bowl of a food processor. Add salt. With the machine running, slowly drizzle in the oil until a smooth purée is formed. You may have to scrape the sides of the bowl several times in order to purée all of the leaves.

ADVANCE PREPARATION: The purée can be stored tightly wrapped in the refrigerator for 2 to 3 days. After that the bright green color will fade. Mix the purée well to incorporate the oil before serving. The pesto can be frozen in small, serving-size containers. To use, thaw it in the refrigerator. Microwave thawing tends to cook the pesto and dull the bright green color.

SUBSTITUTIONS AND OPTIONS: We prefer using Sweet Genovese basil because it is slower to bolt than other varieties and less likely to become bitter when used in sauces. Any herb or mix of herbs may be substituted for the basil. Make sure all stems have been removed before you purée the leaves. The bright green herb oil can be drained from the purée and used to flavor appetizers and entrées.

Makes approximately ½ cup

Olive-Orange Salsa

The only difference between green olives and black olives is ripeness. Unripe olives are green and fully ripe olives are black. We prefer the fully ripened flavor of black olives for this Mediterranean-inspired recipe because green olives have to be soaked in a lye solution before brining, while ripe black olives can proceed straight to brining.

The acidity of the citrus balances the both the saltiness of the olives and fresh herbs. This salsa makes a great crostini appetizer or a delicious condiment with grilled beef, lamb or duck.

2 navel oranges	¼ teaspoon sweet paprika
1 small red onion, cut into small dice	¼ teaspoon ground coriander seed
½ cup oil-cured black olives, pitted and roughly diced	¼ teaspoon ground cumin seed
3 tablespoons extra virgin olive oil	¼ teaspoon ground fennel seed
1 clove garlic, finely chopped	¼ teaspoon cracked black pepper
1 teaspoon nonpareilles capers, drained and roughly chopped	1 teaspoon fresh basil, roughly chopped
	1 teaspoon fresh oregano, roughly chopped

To make orange segments, use a paring knife, cut off the peel and the white pith of the orange. Working over a stainless steel bowl, cut between the membranes to release the segments. Some juice will accumulate in the bowl. Cut each segment into 4 pieces.

NOTE: Make sure you remove all of the white pith before you cut the orange into segments, otherwise the pith will add a bitter, tannic flavor to the salsa.

In the stainless bowl with the reserved juice, combine the orange segments and all of the remaining ingredients. Taste and adjust seasoning. Be careful of adding any additional salt as the olives are salty and will add the necessary salt component to this dish.

ADVANCE PREPARATION: Prepare the salsa and chill in the refrigerator at least 1 to 2 hours in advance to allow the flavors to blend. The salsa will keep several days in a sealed container in the refrigerator.

SUBSTITUTIONS AND OPTIONS: The following is a list of black olive varieties we like:

ASCOLANO: This is a Californian black olive with a light, even skin color, small pit, tender fruit and very little bitterness.

GAETA: This Italian dark-purple olive is dry-salt cured, then rubbed with oil. It has a wrinkled appearance, mild flavor, soft texture and is packed with rosemary and other herbs.

KALAMATA: This famous Greek black olive is harvested fully ripe and is brine-cured. It has a deep-purple color, almond shape and a rich, fruity flavor.

LIGURIA: The Liguria is a brine-cured Italian olive with a vibrant flavor. It is sometimes packed with stems still attached.

MANZANILLA: These large, rounded olives from California have a brilliant purple color that changes to deep blue-black when mature. The taste is slightly bitter but exceedingly rich. Manzanilla olives are used for 70% of the olive oil made in California.

MISSION: Originally cultivated on the Franciscan missions in California, Mission olives are medium sized and oval shaped with a jet-black color when ripe. The flesh is very bitter but firm, with a freestone pit.

NIÇOISE: This small French olive is harvested when fully ripe and has a rich, nutty and mellow flavor. Niçoise olives have a high pit-to-meat ratio and are often packed, stems intact, with herbs.

PONENTINE: This mild-flavored Italian black olive is brine-cured then packed in vinegar.

SEVILLANO: The largest-size commercial California olive variety, Sevillano olives are very large and have a bluish-black color when ripe. The pit is large and clings to the flesh. This variety has a low oil content and is generally used for making Sicilian-style brine-cured olives.

Makes approximately 2 cups

Tomato-Lavender Pipérade

Pipérade, a Basque specialty, is an open-faced omelet garnished with onions, peppers, tomatoes, and ham. Our recipe for the pipérade sauce is a simple pepper sauté with fresh lavender to play up the Mediterranean flavors. Use it as a bed for firm-fleshed fish, a simple chicken breast or, if you are in a traditional mood, as a filling for an omelet.

2 tablespoons extra virgin olive oil
1 large yellow onion, cut into half moons
2 large red heirloom tomatoes, peeled, seeds
   removed and cut into thin strips
2 large red bell peppers, cut in half, stem and
   seeds removed and cut into thin strips
2 cloves garlic, peeled and finely chopped
1 teaspoon smoky or sweet paprika
1 tablespoon fresh lavender leaves,
   finely chopped
kosher salt and ground black pepper

In a large sauté pan, heat the olive oil over medium heat. Add the onion and cook until soft, about 5 minutes. Add the tomatoes, peppers, garlic, paprika, lavender, salt and pepper. Cook until almost all of the liquid is absorbed. The pipérade can be kept refrigerated for 7 to 10 days.

Makes approximately ¼ cup

Onion Marmalade

What do you do when you have a plethora of onions? Here's a solution. We adopted the term marmalade (technically a fruit preserve with pieces of fruit suspended in a clear jelly) and applied it to this onion relish. Maybe it's because the sweetness of onions makes them a natural partner for meat and poultry, much like certain fruit sauces (think duck à l'orange). The sweet and sour flavor is reminiscent of a chutney without raisins.

4 medium yellow onions, sliced into thin
  half moons
1 cup white wine vinegar or sherry vinegar
2 cups dry white wine
1 cup water
3 tablespoons granulated sugar
1 tablespoon fresh thyme, finely chopped
kosher salt and white pepper, to taste

Combine the ingredients in a medium-sized, stainless steel saucepan. Place over high heat and bring to a boil. Reduce heat and simmer, approximately 35 to 45 minutes or until onions are soft and liquid is almost dry.

ADVANCE PREPARATIONS: Do not cut the onions until you are ready to use them. Because the vinegar and wine in this recipe act as preserving agents, this marmalade will keep up to one month in a sealed container in the refrigerator.

SUBSTITUTIONS AND OPTIONS: Almost any onion or member of the lily family will work in this recipe. You may also substitute any type of red wine and red wine vinegar or balsamic vinegar for the liquid. If using a sweet onion variety, reduce the sugar by half. Taste to see if the marmalade needs additional sugar, vinegar, salt or pepper.

Makes approximately 1 cup

Sweet Potato Bread

This is a savory bread rather than a sweet quick bread. It is a terrific alternative to potatoes if you are making roast chicken. When you soak up the juices with this bread, your taste buds will think "stuffing" and you will be transported to Thanksgiving Day.

1½ cups all-purpose flour
1 teaspoon baking powder
½ teaspoon baking soda
1 teaspoon iodized salt
2 tablespoons brown sugar
¼ teaspoon ground cinnamon
¼ teaspoon ground nutmeg
2 whole eggs

¼ cup vegetable oil
1 tablespoon lemon juice
2 tablespoons orange juice
1 teaspoon orange zest
¼ cup whole milk
2 cups sweet potatoes, peeled and shredded
　(approximately 1 large sweet potato)

Preheat oven to 350°F. Butter and flour one 9x5-inch loaf pan.

In a large mixing bowl, sift together the flour, baking powder, baking soda, salt, sugar, cinnamon and nutmeg. Set aside.

In another mixing bowl beat eggs. Stir in oil, lemon juice, orange juice, orange zest, milk and sweet potatoes. Add wet ingredients to dry ingredients and mix until all ingredients are just incorporated and smooth. Do not over mix.

Pour batter into prepared loaf pan. Place in oven and bake 45 minutes or until a skewer inserted in the center comes out clean. Cool in pan on a wire rack for 10 minutes, then remove bread from the pan and place on wire rack to cool completely.

TO FREEZE: When the bread has cooled, wrap it in paper towels and place it in freezer bags. The paper towels absorb any moisture and the bread won't get damp when it is defrosted.

Makes 1 loaf

Pear Compote

Pears are one of the delights of living in the Rogue Valley. The orchards bloom in a burst of white in March, then turn brilliant new green a month later, and by August are laden with a bonanza of pears — Bosc, Comice, Anjou, Bartlett and more. We eat as many as we can, then make this compote with the rest. It's a little like applesauce in texture, but the vanilla, lemon, ginger, black peppercorns and cardamom gives the compote a more complex flavor profile.

¼ cup dry white wine
¼ cup water
½ teaspoon granulated sugar
1 vanilla bean, split lengthwise, seeds scraped
1 teaspoon lemon zest, finely chopped
1 teaspoon lemon juice

1 teaspoon fresh ginger root, peeled and finely chopped
3 cardamom pods, crushed
6 whole black peppercorns, crushed
1½ cups Anjou or Bartlett pear peeled, core removed and cut into small dice

In a heavy, large saucepan, place wine, water, vanilla bean with seeds, ginger, lemon zest, cardamom pods, black peppercorns and pears. Place pan over medium heat and bring to boil. Reduce heat to low and simmer gently for 10 minutes or until the pears are soft but still hold their shape and the liquid is reduced to half its volume.

Serve at room temperature or slightly warm to release the full flavors of the fruit. Store, covered, in the refrigerator for up to two weeks. The compote can be canned and kept, unopened for several months.

Makes approximately 1 cup

Medjool Date Chutney

Dates are native to hot, dry desert regions of the world, particularly the Middle East and North Africa. In the United States, date palms grow abundantly in the area around Palm Springs, California. Prized for their high sugar content, the semi-dry varieties of dates grown in California are naturally dried and used most often for cooking and eating. Medjool dates are deep red with thick flesh, little fiber and a rich flavor. The concentration of the fruit provides just the right sweetness to balance the vinegar and curry in this chutney.

Chutneys add a depth of flavor when mixed with an assortment of grains or vegetables and make an ideal accompaniment when served over a rich-tasting fish or poultry.

2 tablespoons olive oil
1 medium yellow onion, peeled and finely chopped
2 cloves garlic, finely chopped
1 teaspoon fresh ginger root, peeled and finely chopped
1 teaspoon fresh hot red chili, finely chopped or crushed red pepper flakes (optional)

2 pints fresh Medjool dates, roughly chopped (substitute 2 cups dry dates)
½ curry powder
¼ cup golden raisins
1 ounce brown sugar
6 ounces red wine vinegar
2 ounces tawny port wine
kosher salt and cracked black pepper, to taste

Place a medium-sized, stainless steel saucepan over medium heat. Add oil and sauté onions until soft but not colored. Add garlic, ginger, and chili and continue cooking 2 minutes. Add dates, curry powder, raisins, sugar, vinegar and port wine and bring to a boil. Reduce heat and simmer, stirring often, approximately 20 minutes or until liquid is reduced to a syrup.

Serve at room temperature or slightly warm to release the full flavors of the fruit. Store, covered, in the refrigerator for up to two weeks. The chutney can also be canned and kept, unopened, for several months.

Makes approximately 2 cups

Jerusalem Artichoke Pickles

Neither from Jerusalem nor an artichoke, this small vegetable is actually an edible tuber related to the sunflower. As pickles, Jerusalem artichokes make a crisp, flavorful companion for fish, poultry or beef, or as a garnish for soup (see page 91).

2 cups pickling liquid (see page 198)
1 medium yellow onion, cut into thin half moons
1 pound Jerusalem artichokes, julienned

Scrub the Jerusalem artichokes carefully under cold running water. Place pickling liquid, onions and Jerusalem artichokes in a medium-size, stainless steel saucepan. Place over high heat and bring to a boil. Reduce heat and simmer, approximately 10 to 15 minutes until the onions and artichokes are tender. Allow to cool.

SUBSTITUTIONS AND OPTIONS: Almost any root vegetable (celery root, carrots, turnips, etc.) will work in place of the Jerusalem artichokes. The pickles can be kept refrigerated for several weeks.

Makes approximately 2 cups

Preserving Herbs

Drying herbs in brown paper bags is a tried and true, age-old method. Dehydrators work extremely well, but bag drying is simple and just as effective. Once you try this drying method, you'll have the process down pat and be able to repeat the steps anytime.

Rinse the herbs thoroughly and dry completely. Tie small bunches of herbs by their stems and place the herb bunches inside paper bags, leaves down, and tie the top of the bags closed with strings. Hang the bags in a warm, dry area with good air flow until the herbs are dry. Do not dry herbs in a microwave or an oven. Dried herbs are stronger than fresh herbs: 1 tablespoon of fresh herbs equals 1 teaspoon of dried herbs. ❧

Drying Mushrooms

Dried mushrooms are a useful addition to any kitchen cupboard.

Almost any mushroom can be dried, since over 90 percent of a mushroom's mass is water. Drying is a quick, easy and safe method of preservation. First, remove all visible dirt from the mushroom using a moist towel or brush. Do not rinse or soak the mushrooms in water. If the mushrooms are large, slice them into fairly thin slices. Either use a dehydrator or dry them in an oven.

To dry mushrooms in an oven, place them on a rack and make sure the mushrooms do not touch each other during drying. Place the rack in an oven set on the lowest setting: 110°F to 120°F. Leave the door open about two inches so fresh air can come in and moist air can flow out. The total drying time will be between 15 to 24 hours. When the mushrooms are dried, place them in plastic bags or sealed containers, where they will last up to a year, if kept dry. Mushrooms should be checked every month or so for evidence of bugs. Dried mushrooms can also be stored in the freezer, indefinitely.

Before they can be used, soak mushrooms for at least 30 minutes in warm water, stock or wine. The benefit of using dried mushrooms is that the soaking liquid can be part of the liquid called for in the recipe or, if reduced slightly, as a sauce on its own.

Matching Food and Wine

"Chefs don't create from recipes, we create from tastes."

— GRAY KUNZ

O nce upon a time it was considered easy to pair wine with food: great food and great wine used to only come from Europe. No longer. Now you need to understand how taste works, what its components are, how it can be layered and how it can be balanced.

The Basic Tastes

The most important thing to remember when matching wine and food is your tongue. It doesn't lie. It perceives the basic tastes in both food and wine: sourness, sweetness, bitterness, saltiness and umami. Umami is not perceived as a separate taste but helps to layer the other basic tastes.

SOURNESS: Acid in salad dressing can wreak havoc with some wines. If you serve an acidic wine with a mildly acidic salad dressing, the wine's sourness will be negated by the salad's sourness and you will be left with a pleasant, successful match. Acidic wines also are terrific for salty and smoky foods. Briny oysters are a fantastic match with a crisp, dry white wine such as Muscat or a sparkling wine, and cold-smoked salmon is Nirvana with a tart, refreshing white wine such as a dry Riesling.

SWEETNESS: Sweet food makes sweet wine taste less sweet. If you have a California Chardonnay that's a little sweet, the wine may taste overly sweet with a piece of grilled mackerel. Add a sweet tropical fruit or a sweet pepper, such as mango and red pepper salsa, and the wine will now taste dry and balanced. A mildly sweet wine can taste like lemon juice when drunk with very sweet dessert. But if you make sure the dessert wine is at least a little bit sweeter than the dessert itself (such as a Sauternes or a Canadian ice wine with a light pound cake), the wine will retain its sweetness.

BITTERNESS: Like-with-like is the key. Wines with a little bitterness make foods with a little bitterness taste less bitter. The tannins inherent in a young Cabernet from France or California balance the slight bitterness that grilling imparts to a steak.

SALTINESS: There are no salty wines, but there are plenty of wines that relieve the saltiness of salty food. Serve acidic, non-oaky, low-alcohol wines with salty food. The classic mate for saltwater fish is lemon. Salt brightens the flavors and facilitates a balance between sweetness and acidity by decreasing the sourness of acid and increasing the sweetness of sugar.

UMAMI (pronounced oo-MOM-ee): Umami, "delicious essence" in Japanese, has been labeled the fifth taste or what Brillat-Savarin called the "savory taste." Umami-rich foods are those high in natural glutamates and include things like seaweed, Parmigiano-Reggiano cheese, soy sauce, fish sauce, green tea, oily fish such as sardines and mackerel, fresh tomato juice, sun-dried tomatoes, peas, dried mushrooms and aged beef. Adding foods that are high in umami to other dishes will "pump up" the overall flavor of other tastes. Umami flavors tend to aggravate bitterness and tannins in wine. When matching these foods with wine, choose wines that are fruit-forward such as an Alsatian Pinot Blanc or a California Pinot Noir. However, when a dish is perfectly balanced among all five tastes, it will be an excellent companion to any wine.

Tannin, Alcohol, Oak and Fruit

There are a few elements in wine (usually not found in food) that add to the mix: tannin, alcohol, oakiness and fruit.

TANNIN: A bitter, astringent substance in wine, is balanced with fatty, grilled meats.

ALCOHOL: Not a friend of food; generally lower-alcohol wines are more flexible with food.

OAK: Some, like Myron Redford of Eola Hills Winery, say that "oak is the ketchup of the wine world." The oak taste found in some wines comes from the oak barrels in which some wines, such as Chardonnays, are stored. Oak can be tamed by creamy, earthy flavors like those found in a mushroom cream sauce.

FRUIT: The basis for all wine. Wines taste more "fruit forward" when they're young and they lose that fruit taste as they age. Fruitiness in wine can be oppressive to food, but in well-made young reds, the fruit is usually balanced by elements like tannin and earthiness, actually making the wine food friendly. When matching with food, enhance the other flavors in the wine to downplay the "bubble gum" fruit flavor.

Matching and Contrasting Points of View

There are two basic principles you can follow when pairing wine with food — the Matching Principle and the Contrasting Principle.

THE MATCHING PRINCIPLE: Matching the flavors in the wine with the flavors in the food can heighten and enhance those flavors much more than if either were consumed separately. An example of this would be if you eat a chicken breast with a delicate herb sauce, and you chose a wine that also had delicate herbal notes, such as a Sauvignon Blanc.

THE CONTRASTING PRINCIPLE: Contrasting the flavors in wines and foods is effective for keeping the palate awake and lively. If you're eating fatty foods, you may want an acidic or tannic wine to cut through the rich, palate-coating flavors. For example, pair salmon with a Chablis, and lamb with a Cabernet or a Syrah.

Remember to consider not just the central ingredients of the dish (e.g., beef, chicken, fish, pasta), but also the overall flavors and the various accompanying components. Often the marinade, glaze, sauce or accompanying vegetable or starch will have a more pronounced flavor than the main ingredient. For example, salmon with a dill sauce or citrus sauce suggests a crisp white wine while salmon with pesto pleads for a Pinot Noir.

Perfectly Balanced

Another easy rule you can follow is simply to match the boldness/body of the wine's flavor to the boldness/body of the food's flavor. Light wines go best with delicately flavored food, and very bold wines are the best matches for food with equally bold flavors. One general rule is to drink a wine that is at least as sweet as the dessert.

When is a Cork not a Cork?

Despite the historic and romantic allure of a cork in a wine bottle, wine producers are increasingly frustrated by the belief that the cork sometimes ruins their wine. Each year an estimated 3 to 10 percent of wines worldwide are spoiled by the chemical compound trichloroanisole (TCA), better known as cork taint. It is a vicious wine-killer that strikes at random, compromises the quality of the wine, and ultimately affects your enjoyment. A wine with TCA smells like a wet, shaggy dog lying on wet newspapers in a damp basement. You get the idea, it's sort of a dank, musty, cardboard-y smell. Needless to say, it does not enhance the fine dining experience.

Screw cap bottles prevent outside contamination. They provide consistency and allow the wine to develop naturally without outside influences, allowing the true characteristics of the wine to develop. The idea of screw caps on high-quality wines is heresy to some. When a customer of ours told us "They're taking the mystique out of wine," our answer was simply to ask him to taste the PlumpJack 1999 Limited Edition Reserve Cabernet Sauvignon. It costs a mere $145 per screw-capped bottle, and for those of you who like numbers, it was given 94 points out of 100 by *Wine Spectator* magazine.

Large numbers of Australian Riesling producers from the Clare Valley region decided in 2000 to bottle their products with screw caps — a move followed quickly by their neighbors in New Zealand. In America, Bonny Doon, PlumpJack, Sonoma-Cutrer Vineyards and Downing Family Vineyards, all in California, and Argyle Winery and WillaKenzie Estate in Oregon, use the new closures. Not exactly in the same league as Mad Dog 20/20.

The enjoyment of pulling the cork can be a great experience, but it can also be quickly ruined by the disappointment of an oxidized or tainted wine. Try replacing the gratification of the cork with the consistency of great wine. Save the cork for that new floor in your dining room. ❧

Metric Conversion Tables

Approximate Metric Equivalents

¼ teaspoon = 1.23 milliliters
½ teaspoon = 2.46 milliliters
¾ teaspoon = 3.7 milliliters
1 teaspoon = 4.93 milliliters
1 tablespoon = 14.79 milliliters
¼ cup = 59.15 milliliters
½ cup = 118.3 milliliters
1 cup = 236.59 milliliters
1 pint = 2 cups = 473.18 milliliters
1 quart = 4 cups = .946 liters
1 gallon = 4 quarts = 3.785 liters
1 ounce = 28.35 grams
1 pound = .454 kilograms
32°F = 0°C
212°F = 100°C
350°F = 177°C
400°F = 205°C
450°F = 233°C

Converting to Metric

teaspoons x 4.93 = milliliters
tablespoons x 14.79 = milliliters
fluid ounces x 29.57 = milliliters
cups x 236.59 = milliliters
pints x .473 = liters
quarts x .946 = liters
gallons x 3.785 = liters
ounces x 28.35 = grams
pounds x .454 = kilograms
inches x 2.54 = centimeters
Fahrenheit subtract 32 multiply
   by 5 divide by 9 = Celsius

Sources and Information

Cheese

Cowgirl Creamery
P.O. Box 594
80 Fourth Street
Point Reyes Station, California 94956
Phone: 415-663-9335
Fax: 415-663-5418
www.cowgirlcreamery.com

Project Truffle — Artisan Cheeses
Phone: 866-328-7325
www.projecttruffle.com

Rogue Creamery
311 North Front Street (Hwy 99)
P.O. Box 3606
Central Point, OR 97502
Phone: 866-665-1155
Fax: 541-665-1133
www.roguegoldcheese.com

Chocolate

Cocoa Barry & Callebaut
Barry Callebaut USA Inc.
400 Industrial Park Road
St. Albans, Vermont 05478-1875
Phone: 802-524- 9711
Fax: 802-524-5148
www.callebaut.be
www.cacaobarry.com

EMC Inc. / Valrhona
1901 Avenue of the Stars, Suite 1800
Los Angeles, California 90067

Phone: 310-277-0401
www.valrhona.com

Scharffen Berger Chocolate Maker, Inc.
914 Heinz Avenue
Berkeley, California 94710
Phone: 800-930-4528
Fax: 510-981-4051
www.scharffen-berger.com

Culinary Equipment

Allyson's of Ashland
115 East Main Street
Ashland, Oregon 97520
Phone: 541-482-2884
Fax: 541-482-2885
www.allysonsofashland.com

Bridge Kitchenware Corp.
214 East 52nd Street
New York, New York 10022
Phone: 212-688-4220
Fax: 212-758-5387
www.bridgekitchenware.com

Cameron's Stove Top Smoker
CM International Inc.
P.O. Box 60220
Colorado Springs, Colorado 80960.
Phone: 888-563-0227
Fax: 719-390-0946
www.cameronssmoker.com

City Kitchens
1527 Fourth Street
Seattle, WA 98101
Phone: 800-683-6950

J.B. Prince
36 East 31st Street, 11th Floor
New York, New York 10016
Phone: 212-683-3553
Fax: 212-683-4488
www.jbprince.com

Sur La Table
1765 Sixth Avenue South
Seattle, Washington 98134
Phone: 800-243-0852
www.surlatable.com

Williams-Sonoma
P.O. Box 7456
San Francisco, California 94120
Phone: 800-541-2233
www.williams-sonoma.com

Game and Specialty Meats

D'Artagnan
280 Wilson Avenue
Newark, New Jersey 07105
Phone: 800-327-8246
Fax: 201-792-0113
www.dartagnan.com

Game Sale International
P.O. Box 7719
Loveland, Colorado 80537
Phone: 800-729-2090
Fax: 970-669-9041
www.gamesalesintl.com

Grimaud Farms
1320-A South Aurora
Stockton, California 95206
Phone: 800-466-9955
Fax: 209-466-8910
www.grimaud.com

Nicky USA Inc.
223 SE Third Avenue
Portland, Oregon 97214
Phone: 800-469-4162
Fax: 503-234-8268
www.nickyusawildgame.com

Petaluma Poultry
P.O. Box 7368
Petaluma California 94955-7368
Phone: 707-763-1904
Fax: 707-763-3924
www.healthychickenchoices.com

Wild Game, Inc.
2315 West Huron
Chicago, Illinois 60612
Phone: 773-278-1661

Maple Sugar and Maple Syrup

Canadian Organic Maple Co. Ltd.
P.O. Box 524
Bath, New Brunswick, Canada E7J 2N3
Phone: 800-651-2284
Fax: 506-278-3966
www.canadianorganicmaple.com

Seafood and Shellfish

Browne Trading Company
Merrill's Wharf
260 Commercial St.

Portland, Maine 04101
Phone: 207-766-2402
Fax: 207-766-2404
www.browne-trading.com

Eco Fish Inc.
78 Market Street
Portsmith, NH 03801
Phone: 603-430-0101
www.ecofish.com

Fishermen Direct Seafood
Located in the Cannery Building at the
Port of Gold Beach
P.O. Box 547
Gold Beach, Oregon 97444
Phone: 888-523-9494
www.fishermendirect.com

Marinelli Shellfish
Pier 33, Space 1-17
The Embarcadero
San Francisco, California 94111
Phone: 415-391-0846

Sterling Caviar & Farm Raised
White Sturgeon
Stolt Sea Farm
Phone: 800-525-0333
Fax: 916-991-4334
www.stoltseafarm.com

Smoked Meats and Bacon

Applegate Farms
10 County Line Rd, #22
Branchburg, New Jersey 08876
Phone: 866-587-5858
Fax: 800-358-8289
www.applegatefarms.com

Hobbs' Applewood Smoked Meats
San Rafael, California 94901
Phone: 415-453-0577
Fax: 415-453-1653

Nueske's Hillcrest Farm
Rural Route #2, P.O. Box D
Wittenberg, Wisconsin 54499
Phone: 800-392-2266
www.nueskes.com

Smoked Seafood

Ducktrap River Fish Farm
57 Little River Drive
Belfast, Maine 04915
Phone: 800-828-3825
Fax: 207-338-6288
www.ducktrap.com

Gerard & Dominique
P.O. Box 1845
Bothell, Washington 98041
Phone: 800-858-0449
Fax: 425-488-9229
www.gourmetseafoods.com

Taku Smokeries
550 South Franklin Street
Juneau, Alaska 99801
Phone: 800-582-5122
www.takusmokeries.com

Specialty Food

Bob's Red Mill Natural Foods
5209 SE International Way
Milwaukee, Oregon 97222
Phone: 503-654-3215

Fax: 503-653-1339
www.bobsredmill.com

Dean & Deluca
560 Broadway
New York, New York 10012
Phone: 800-221-7714
www.deandeluca.com

The Epicentre
Telephone: 705-292-5247
Fax: 705-292-7378
www.theepicentre.com

Earthy Delights
1161 E. Clark Road, Suite 260
DeWitt, Michigan 48820
Phone: 800-367-4709
Fax: 517-668-1213
www.earthy.com

Fresh & Wild, Inc.
P.O. Box 2981
Vancouver, Washington 98668
Phone: 800-222-5578
Fax: 360-737-3657

Gourmand Inc.
2869 Towerview Road
Herndon, Virginia 20171
Phone: 703-708-0000
Fax: 703-708-9393
www.specialtygame.com

nSpired Natural Foods / Maranatha
Natural Foods
14855 Wicks Blvd.
San Leandro, California 94577
Phone: 510-686-0116

Fax: 510-686-0126
www.nspiredfoods.com

Roland Foods
71 West 23rd Street
New York, New York 10010
Phone: 800-221-4030
www.rolandfood.com

Soups, Stocks and Broths

Pacific Foods
19480 SW 97th Avenue
Tualatin, Oregon 97062
Phone: 503-692-9666
Fax: 503-692-9610
www.pacificfoods.com

Sustainable Organizations

The Audubon Guide to Seafood
550 South Bay Avenue
Islip, NY 11751
Phone: 888-397-6649
www.magazine.audubon.org/seafood/guide

Center for Marine Conservation
www.cmc-ocean.org

Chefs Collaborative
262 Beacon Street
Boston, MA 02116
Phone: 617-236-5200
Fax: 617-236-5272
www.chefscollaborative.org

CSA Resources
Fulton Center for Sustainable Living
Wilson College
Chambersberg, PA

Phone: 717-264-4141 ext. 3352
www.csacenter.org

Eat Wild — The clearinghouse for information about pasture-based farming
www.eatwild.com

Environmental Defense
257 Park Avenue South
New York, NY 10010
www.environmentaldefense.org

Farm To Table is run by Earth Pledge
(www.earthpledge.org) and connects you
to your local farmers and helps you build
an understanding of how your food was
grown or raised.
www.farmtotable.org
Fisheries Department of the United
Nations Food & Agriculture Department
www.fao.org/fi

Green Advisor
www.greenadviser.org

The Marine Stewardship Council
4005 — 20th West
Seattle, WA 98199
Phone: 206-691-0188
Monterey Bay Aquarium Seafood Watch
Chart
www.mbayaq.org

National Campaign for Sustainable
Agriculture
www.sustainableagriculture.net

Seafood Choices Alliance
1731 Connecticut Avenue SW
Suite 450
Washington, DC 20009
Phone: 866-SEA-MORE
Fax: 202-483-3518
www.seafoodchoices.com

Slow Food USA
www.slowfoodusa.org

Index

grilled vegetables and
rib-eye of beef, 133–34
in Jerusalem artichoke
pickles, 207
marmalade, 203
and potato tart tatin,
54–55

Oranges
and olive salsa, 200
and pistachio biscotti, 189

Ostrich ferns. *See* Fiddlehead
ferns

Oyster mushrooms, in three oyster stew, 52–53

Oysters
about, 45–47
cornmeal fried, with organic
greens and lemon-caper
aioli, 50–51
dipping sauces for, 48–49
three oyster stew, 52–53

P

Parsnips
in caramelized assorted root
vegetables, 56–57
in Pacific halibut a la Nage,
96–97
and potato rösti, 59

Pastry cream, Grand Marnier,
and berry coulis with honey
tangerine-meringue tartlet,
186–87

Pavé, root vegetable and onion
marmalade, 160

Peaches, upside-down polenta
cake with peach syrup, 179–80

Pears, compote, 205

Peas
English, chilled soup, 72–73
snap, and fiddlehead ferns,
green garlic and soft
polenta with pan-seared

sablefish, 99–100
snow, in arugula, fava beans,
fennel and citrus salad
with hot-smoked
salmon, 101–2
spring radish and butterhead
lettuce salad with white
balsamic dressing, 68–69

Peerless Restaurant, The
overview and philosophy, 1–3

Peppermint, and chocolate
brownie, 174–75

Peppers
red
in couscous and spicy
eggplant with white
sturgeon, 114–15
in poached halibut
cheeks, 24–25
sauce for heirloom toma-
to and squash torte,
158–59
in tomato-lavender
pipérade, 202
red and yellow
in grilled vegetables and
rib-eye of beef with
balsamic glazed
onions, 133–34
in summer vegetable slaw,
35–36
toasted barley and sweet,
filling with roasted
whole onions, 154–55
yellow
in yellow tomato gazpa-
cho with avocado-
tomato salsa, 80–81

Persimmons, and duck salad with
hazelnut-sherry vinaigrette,
84–85

Pesto vinaigrette, and grilled red
torpedo onions with heir-
loom tomato salad, 78–79

Piccata, marinated tofu, 161–62

Pickles
Jerusalem artichoke, 207
shiitake mushroom, 198

Pies, warm apple, with apple
brandy sauce, 184–85

Pigs, about, 130

Pipérade, tomato-lavender, 202

Pistachios, and orange biscotti,
189

Polenta, soft, and fiddlehead
ferns with pan-seared sablefish, 99–100

Polyculture, 6

Pomegranates, and walnut sauce
with seared venison medallions, 142–43

Porcini mushrooms, in crêpes
with red wine reduction,
167–68

Pork, sage rubbed, with apple-
fennel pan sauce, 128–29

Potatoes
in caramelized assorted root
vegetables, 56–57
and cauliflower purée with
lavender honey glazed
venison roast, 140–41
cream of, leek and Jerusalem
artichoke soup with
Jerusalem artichoke pick-
les, 91–92
in hot-smoked salmon salad
with horseradish-mustard
dressing, 89–90
and mushrooms and spinach
ragoût with slow roasted
salmon, 106–7
and onion tart tatin, 54–55
and parsnip rösti, 59
in roasted elephant garlic
soup with grilled eggplant

About the authors

AFTER TRAVELING AND WORKING all over the United States and France, executive chefs Stu Stein (University of Illinois and Culinary School of Kendall College graduate), Mary Hinds (Whitman College and Culinary Institute of America graduate) and their two dogs, Coriander and Shamrock (both obedience school drop-outs), landed in southern Oregon and took over The Peerless Restaurant. Under their leadership, The Peerless has earned countless praise and awards from the *Oregonian* newspaper, *Northwest Palate* magazine, *Wall Street Journal, Wine Spectator* magazine including receiving their Award of Excellence and Outstanding Oregon Wine List Award from *Wine Press Northwest* magazine.

Stu, once the executive chef at Washington DC's renowned Oval Room, is the winner of Champagne Mumm Award for Culinary Excellence, and is a featured chef on the nationally syndicated cooking series New American Cuisine. Mary's seafood expertise has made her a sought-after chef, and in 1999 and 2000 she was invited to Hong Kong as a guest chef at the exclusive Aberdeen Marina Club to promote American seafood and introduce an international audience to methods and techniques of preparing seafood dishes.

Stu and Mary are firm believers in slow food, an international movement that has a snail as its symbol and a manifesto calling for the defense of the right to pleasure at the table. When not spending ridiculously long hours at their restaurant, Mary can be found skiing down various mountains, while Stu can be heard on Jefferson Public Radio using the airwaves to inform, guide and advise the culinarily-challenged of America.

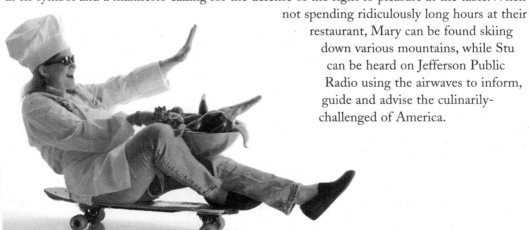

If you have enjoyed *The Sustainable Kitchen*, you might also enjoy other

BOOKS TO BUILD A NEW SOCIETY

Our books provide positive solutions for people who want to make a difference. We specialize in:

Sustainable Living • Ecological Design and Planning • Natural Building & Appropriate Technology
New Forestry • Environment and Justice • Conscientious Commerce • Progressive Leadership
Educational and Parenting Resources • Resistance and Community • Nonviolence

For a full list of NSP's titles, please call 1-800-567-6772 or check out our web site at:
www.newsociety.com

New Society Publishers

ENVIRONMENTAL BENEFITS STATEMENT

New Society Publishers has chosen to produce this book on recycled paper made with 100% post consumer waste, processed chlorine free, and old growth free.

For every 5,000 books printed, New Society saves the following resources:[1]

37	Trees
3,370	Pounds of Solid Waste
3,708	Gallons of Water
4,836	Kilowatt Hours of Electricity
6,126	Pounds of Greenhouse Gases
26	Pounds of HAPs, VOCs, and AOX Combined
9	Cubic Yards of Landfill Space

[1]Environmental benefits are calculated based on research done by the Environmental Defense Fund and other members of the Paper Task Force who study the environmental impacts of the paper industry.

NEW SOCIETY PUBLISHERS